Going Abroad

Going Abroad: Travel, Tourism, and Migration. Cross-Cultural Perspectives on Mobility

Edited by

Christine Geoffrey and Richard Sibley

Cambridge Scholars Publishing

Going Abroad: Travel, Tourism, and Migration. Cross-Cultural Perspectives on Mobility,
Edited by Christine Geoffrey and Richard Sibley

This book first published 2007 by

Cambridge Scholars Publishing

15 Angerton Gardens, Newcastle, NE5 2JA, UK

British Library Cataloguing in Publication Data
A catalogue record for this book is available from the British Library

ISBN (10): 1-84718-394-8, ISBN (13): 9781847183941

CONTENTS

EDITORS' NOTE

All foreign-language texts have been translated into English. Unless otherwise indicated, translations are by the authors or editors. The original has been included only in bibliographical references, and in cases where necessary for a proper understanding, e.g. plays on words that do not translate easily.

We decided at an early stage in preparing the typescript to dispense with footnotes and endnotes. All bibliographical references use the author/date system, with full details at the end of each chapter.

ACKNOWLEDGEMENTS

We would like to thank the following for their kind assistance with the early stages of preparing this book: Helen Chupin, Kerry-Jane Wallart, Deirdre Gilfedder, Jonathan Bloom, Anthony Fowler, and Tim Riley.

List of Illustrations

Foreword

Going Abroad is addressed to those readers who are inquisitive about the meaning of the different forms of mobility which concern almost all of us today, directly or indirectly, in our leisure time or in our professional lives. Most of us have been tourists or travellers, and there are increasing numbers of potential and actual migrants: in 2006 over a thousand Britons left the UK every day, of whom more than five hundred were going to live or work abroad for more than a year.

If you are tempted by emigration, enjoy being a tourist, or just love the adventure of travel, real or imaginary, we invite you to join us on a journey of discovery through time and across the continents, to explore and reflect on diverse experiences of mobility, past and present, and what it all means.

Several chapters analyse both the practical problems and the differing states of mind experienced by British emigrants to France and Spain today. But emigration, although on the increase, is not a new phenomenon—as shown by chapters on nineteenth-century Scottish emigrants to Canada and Australia, an early British presence in the French Alps, and the arrival of Brits and Americans in turn-of-the-century Paris. And if you have ever wondered about the impact of British immigrants on the host communities, there are clues in all those experiences, past and present, as well as a fuller analysis of the material and cultural consequences of immigration today on Marrakesh and Chamonix. We examine different kinds of emigration—the more or less voluntary search for economic improvement, the choice of a different lifestyle, and the imposed condition of political exile—and also visit Britain as a host country seen by French immigrants over a hundred years ago.

If crossing the Channel has become a mundane act apparently bereft of any significance today, next time you take the tunnel or a ferry you might pause to think about the multiple real and symbolic meanings that that crossing has had, as illustrated by travel literature and films. We visit turn-of-the-century Capri and Morocco today, in search of a carefree life of residence in the sun and exotic surroundings, with certain freedoms that often seem impossible at home. The life of a Filipino sailor, curiously neither at home nor really "abroad", is a singular example of mobility that few of us have ever considered. And we examine stranger forms of travel—old and new—in backpacking across four continents, the real and the fantasized exotic in nineteenth-century orientalist art, and the sanitized utopias of today's theme parks. In two 'afterwords', some personal reflections follow their own very different directions, from a common starting-point: memories of a grandfather.

The key to this collection of texts is our attempts to understand the different meanings of mobility, a phenomeon that, though not new, is central to today's—and no doubt tomorrow's—globalized world.

Going Abroad is also, of course, for academic specialists, for students, teachers and researchers who are interested in the different approaches to issues of mobility. The book is both *inter-disciplinary*—drawing on the methodologies and subject-areas of history, geography, sociology, literature, the media, tourism, painting and architecture... what we in foreign-language departments of French universities call "la civilisation", roughly translatable as "cultural studies"—and *cross-cultural*, the subjects and perspectives covering not only France and Britain (Scotland, Wales and England), but also Spain, Capri, the Middle East, North Africa, the Far East, and Latin America, as well as the waters between lands and continents (the Channel, the oceans of the world) and beyond (the imaginary worlds of painting, of theme parks...). Behind this multiplicity of places and approaches, the book explores both explicitly and implicitly the terminologies, "conceptuology" and methodology of a subject which features in the curricula of many different academic disciplines.

The authors of *Going Abroad* represent six different nationalities, live in or regularly move between a dozen different countries, and work or have worked in at least seven different academic systems. They incarnate the cross-national exchanges, migratory flows and—in some cases—the tranformation from tourist to migrant, that are central preoccupations in *Going Abroad.*

Christine Geoffroy & Richard Sibley
Paris, autumn 2007

PART I -

TRAVELLERS AND MIGRANTS OF YESTERYEAR

CHAPTER ONE

THE FRENCH IN ENGLAND (1880-1914): ANONYMOUS TRAVELLERS AND MIGRANTS

CONSTANCE BANTMAN,
ANGÈLE DAVID-GUILLOU
AND ADÈLE THOMAS

For many French people, leaving for London in the late nineteenth century no longer meant setting out on an adventure in unknown territory. For some it meant partaking in a long tradition of forced religious or political exile, whilst for others it was a matter of choosing economic migration or work-related travel. The Franco-British diplomatic exchanges of the period are well known, but the rivalries and the *entente* do not account for the wealth of relations woven in Britain by many anonymous French travellers and migrants. The interplay between travel, tourism and migration—between short voluntary stays, long exiles and permanent settlement—was at the heart of this French presence. We have chosen to illustrate it through three particular case studies:

– musicians who visited Britain by choice, either independently or on tour with others, and who instrumentalized their nationality in order to achieve success;

– anarchist refugees, forced to travel and often isolated, although some did form relations with their host nation;

– French people who settled in Britain and, reflecting about how to preserve their identity, began organizing themselves as a group.

French musicians in England: truly Gallic travellers

In both France and England, the end of the nineteenth century saw the strengthening of what might be called an "industry" of the performing arts. The first stage of musical industrialization was essentially marked by the unprecedented growth of public concerts for paying audiences. On both sides of the Channel, music was becoming increasingly professional and in order to train and make a living, many musicians began to perform at a national and international level. Helped by the expansion of transport, geographical mobility became an indispensable feature of a musical career. The French musical union's journal *Le Progrès Artistique* wrote in 1878:

> A female artist who has just graduated from the *Conservatoire* had better go abroad to sing, and then come back to France with honours, rather than vegetate here for five or six years attached to the *Opéra* or the *Opéra-Comique*, where [...] a career can never get started, where [...] all sorts of obstacles are encountered during the best years of one's voice. (*Le Progrès Artistique*, 15 August 1878)

Sometimes musicians would group together in order to buy train tickets in bulk and negotiate cheap rates. They even created associations for that purpose, like the British Music Hall Artistes' Railway Association, founded in 1897. By the late 1870s, the mobility of musicians between Paris and London, the European capitals of entertainment, was particularly intense. The reasons for and modalities of these professional trips were diverse, and reflected the heterogeneity of the musical scene in the period.

Some musicians crossed the Channel on their own, in search of higher earnings. An article published in *L'Europe Artiste* even mentioned "boatloads of starving musicians" disembarking every morning onto the streets of London (11 February 1894). At the time, the *Conservatoire National de Musique*, an extremely powerful and renowned institution in France, had no equivalent in England. There did exist a Royal Academy of Music, but its teaching remained very poor until the early twentieth century (Ehrlich 1985: 76-80). Qualified foreign "labour" was thus much sought by British musical directors. Germans in particular had a very good reputation, but so too to a lesser extent did the French. This demand declined by the end of the 1880s, as the level of training of English musicians improved with the development of a higher-quality musical teaching (Russel 1987: 52-53) and as musicians organized their first professional associations: the Society of Professional Musicians in 1882, the Music Hall Artistes' Association in 1886, the Amalgamated Musicians' Union and the Orchestral Association in 1893.

Other, more settled musicians travelled in a much less spontaneous and isolated manner, within organized musical tours. This was the case of musicians in the great French orchestras, such as the *Orchestre des concerts Lamoureux*, which performed all around Europe (see *Le Courrier de l'Orchestre*, 1 November 1904). It was also the case of music-hall artists, for whom the trip to England was a necessary step in an international career and, by 1900, for any success in the United States. Among the French music-hall stars who then travelled to England were Yvette Guilbert, Odette Dulac, Gaby Deslys, Harry Fragson, Alice Delysia, Anna Held, Méaly, Adrienne Augarde, Max Dearly, Réjane, Mlle Polaire, Louise Balthy, and Alice Aubrey. Their numerous autobiographies and memoirs recount their stay. Tours were organized by the great artistic producers, who were new actors in the industrialization of the stage and the professionalization of music. Two of them played an essential role in the export of French music hall and of its artists to England: Tom Barrasford, who produced cross-Channel tours as from 1905 (the year his Alhambra music hall opened in Paris) and thus facilitated the circulation of French artists in England and of English artists in France, and C.B. Cochran, who exported numerous French productions and launched in 1914 French-style *revues* (Jacques-Charles 1956: 80-92).

The success of French musicians in England undoubtedly rested on their nationality. For orchestral musicians, it represented proof of artistic quality. For music-hall singers as for actors, to whom they were very close, being French—and particularly being Parisian—conjured up a colourful image which attracted an audience keen on merry entertainment. In the end, the reality of those artists' "Frenchness" or "Parisianness" did not matter that much—what was important to the British public was that artists fitted what they imagined to be French culture and French character. In Marcel Lherbier's film *L'Entente Cordiale*, Edward VII says of a singer "This woman is really Paris." When someone says "I thought she was foreign," he replies "Perhaps, perhaps, but Parisian" (Lherbier 1939). The image of *Gay Paree*, circulated through the universal exhibitions and tourist guides of a new kind such as *Paris after Dark, containing a description of the fast women ..., of the night amusements and other resorts ... in the French metropolis*, and others like *Pleasure Guide to Paris for Bachelors* or *The Gentlemen's Night Guide. The Gay Women of Paris and Brussels* had a big impact on the English mind, with its puritan past. In fact the success of French artists, women in particular, was often given momentum by more or less calculated scandals in the media.

Thus the *risqué* singer Odette Dulac performed in 1900 at the London *Empire*, in a production by C.B. Cochran. Her reputation having preceded her, all but two of her songs had cuts made by the censors. To some journalists, eager to hear her impressions after her first show, she explained that she was very satisfied but surprised that the two songs free of censorship in England were the only ones censored in France (Jacques-Charles 1956: 84-5). The remark spread rapidly all around London and soon everyone came to hear her songs, hoping they were very daring. Similarly, Gaby Deslys created a sensation in 1913 when her performance at the Palace Theatre was targeted by the violent criticisms of some right-thinking moralizers, who were trying to have her censored. The *Daily Mail*, which covered the affair, talked about her "*French vivacity*" (13 November 1913). The show in which she was the lead performer became of course a great success. There were many other similar examples. Even when the British public adopted a French music-hall artist, as was the case with Alice Delysia who lived the rest of her life in London, exoticism remained the fundamental element of success.

The professional mobility of musicians from 1880 to 1914 played an essential role in the artistic exchanges between France and England. In the case of music hall, until the end of the 1880s the English influence dominated French popular entertainments, as the adoption in France of the term "music hall" shows. At the turn of the century the situation was reversed. Thus the *revue*, so typical of French music hall, settled in England and dethroned English *variety* after 1910. It was then that the ballet tradition, a speciality of English music hall (the *Alhambra* and the *Empire* even possessed their own ballet troupe, making music hall the only real English institution that, prior to 1910, taught dancing) was gradually abandoned in England but exported to France. At the beginning of the twentieth century, the majority of male and female dancers in French music halls were from England, though later they would come from the United States.

The mobility of musicians was also a vector for transferring militancy as musicians' organizations progressed in the 1890s. Every French association of orchestral instrumentalists had correspondents across the Channel. They met British union representatives, produced regular reports about the situation of musicians in England, the progress of their organizations, their methods of action and their achievements.

Anarchists, from indifference to exploration

Around five hundred French anarchists found shelter in Britain between 1880 and 1914, most of them fleeing prosecution in France. Their London exile was in many ways a rite of passage, since they had been preceded in Britain by several generations of continental political exiles. By this period, working-class tourism to Britain was not exceptional: the anarchist paper *Le Père Peinard* frequently featured adverts from seafaring companies offering trips across the Channel. Professional migration was becoming increasingly common too. Moreover, the anarchist ideal proclaimed that the comrades should be travellers at heart—*trimardeurs* was then the current expression (a cross between a tramp and a journeyman)—free from the bourgeois sin of patriotism. The fact that crossing over to London seemed so easy and natural to these individuals testifies to a high degree of working-class cosmopolitanism, at a time more usually associated with popular anglophobia (Guiffan 2004) as well as the rise of middle-class and lower-middle-class tourism (Gerbod 1995, Bruillon 2002, Porter 1995).

Despite such apparent internationalism, in many respects the anarchists' exile could be described as the very opposite of travelling—a voyage without any discovery, any adventure, characterized by national self-segregation and regrouping, and even by a relative degree of hostility towards Britain. As Switzerland and Belgium refused political refugees, Britain became a substitute land of asylum. The anarchists were thus more of a nomadic, wandering colony rather than a truly cosmopolitan colony of travellers. After the newly-elected President Faure declared an amnesty in 1895, most of them actually returned to France within a few months, two or three years at the most.

Like their predecessors, the exiles regrouped along national and linguistic lines, around Soho and Euston, often in the same streets and even the same houses. There they mainly rubbed shoulders with other anarchist refugees—Belgians, Swiss, Francophone Italians—and spoke little or poor English. Their survival largely depended on their fellow Frenchmen, since many set up businesses providing for the other exiles, or relied on intra-communal charity. Their political life was very much focused on France. Some of them took up the old anglophobic stereotypes against the foul English weather, English materialism, or the political reformism. The journalist Emile Pouget thus cursed "this goddam London sky—always almost as black as a judge's conscience," (*Le Père Peinard. Série Londonienne*, October 1894) and contrasted French hospitality and warmth with "this dull city where watering holes are nowhere to be found" (*Ibid.*, September 1894). The exiles' boredom was summarized by the anarchist sympathizer Zo d'Axa, who railed against "London, where I have spent three months vegetating in an exile's retreat" (d'Axa 1895: 103).

However, on the margins of this colony, there were some better integrated individual trajectories. Some comrades remained in exile even after being allowed to return to France, and so became voluntary travellers, and even tourists keen to experience life abroad. This was the case of the antimilitarist novelist Georges Darien, who stayed on after 1895, and of Louise Michel, who alternated between France and London, to avoid prison but also out of preference for British liberalism. In Britain she was very well integrated personally, professionally, socially and as an activist (Thomas 1971).

Some comrades practised what could be called "militant tourism", nobody more so than Charles Malato. This journalist was one of the most anglophile members of the French anarchist colony and experienced a good degree of personal and professional integration while in London. In 1897 he published *Les Joyeusetés de l'Exil*, a comic chronicle of the harshness of life as an exile. He was one of the few to look beyond the closed circles of the exiled: the book was full of observations and information on Britain, proving the anglicization of its author and setting it halfway between a militant's diary and a tourist guide. This dual nature culminates in the last chapter, which is entitled "the exile's practical guide to London" (1897: 206), in which Malato addresses potential refugees. The chapter ends with a ten-page French-English glossary, including a guide to pronunciation. It features very factual information: how to order a cup of tea or translate typically French phrases. These are mixed with typically anarchist comments, like "Is it true that in England, there have been honest politicians?" or "First of all, avoid X***. He's a mole who just pretends to be starving in order to get us into trouble" (1897: 314, 318).

Lastly, some comrades settled for good in Britain, and thus became immigrants. The first one was Gustave Brocher, who by the late 1870s was in the Camberwell district of London, working as a language tutor and active in the first local socialist groups (Brocher archive). Gustave Mollet was another example, one of the few exiles to settle outside the capital. A native of Lyon, he was in Norwich by 1892. At the end of the century, after inheriting some money he set up a sawmill in Liverpool, spreading some informal anarchist propaganda and helping comrades get to the United States. Finally, Victor Cails was the true embodiment of the anarchist *trimardeur*. Imprisoned in 1892 after being implicated in the manufacture of bombs near Birmingham, he was still in Britain in the early years of the twentieth century, working on the building site of the Victoria and Albert Museum (Louise Michel Archive: letter from Cails to Michel, n.d.).

So, despite the isolation of most of them, some anarchists did set about discovering the British Isles. Such trajectories testify to a surprising working-class mobility between the two countries, and triggered international contacts which played an important role in exchanges between activists. However, the anarchists' British sojourn was above all an exile, an involuntary journey, and in this respect Malato's conclusion is highly revealing: "Do go to London, dear readers, if fate takes you there, but stay there as little as possible. In the name of the President of the Republic, the Minister of the Interior, the Prefect of Police, Amen" (1897: 328).

When the London French get together and organize

Whatever their initial plans when they crossed the Channel, many French people eventually settled in England as a result of family or professional bonds they had formed there. Having excluded any idea of returning to France, their concerns and expectations differed greatly from those of temporary migrants. The number of French people living in England at the beginning of the twentieth century has been estimated at between twenty and thirty thousand (Gerbod 1995: 73, 134; Atkin 2003: 3, 188). Most of them opted for London and in 1883, after a long absence, the French Consul General was surprised to discover "a numerous and industrious colony, on its way to prosperity and tending to unite and gather together", instead of the isolated French, little inclined to frequent each other, that he had known twenty years earlier (SNPFA 1883: 30-31).

Within a few decades, a whole set of associations developed, meeting the needs of a population aware that it was putting down roots. From 1862 onwards, the French colony was "revealed" by a series of yearbooks aiming to identify its composition and structure (Hamonet 1862: 5-9). While the Hamonet yearbook found only two French societies in 1862, fifty years later the Barrère yearbook (1909-1910) mentioned many more. At the time, the creation of a new association was often accompanied by criticism of former practices, the idea being to break with a tradition of isolation and to free French initiatives from their habitual failures (SPLFA 1832: ix; Hamonet 1880: 118; SNPFA 1882: 4-8). Whether this dark picture of the past was accurate or not, it is clear that migrants of that period felt like pioneers in bringing together and organizing the colony. Claiming inspiration from John Stuart Mill, one of them even asserted that the French colony should be represented in the French National Assembly (Hamonet 1880: 119).

The presence in London of a new generation of French ambassadors—W. H. Waddington and then Paul Cambon—probably played an important part in the success of this structuring process. French diplomats in England had not always been on good terms with their exiled compatriots (*Le Courrier de l'Europe*, "Chronique de Londres", 12 January 1878; France

1900: 266) but these two took an active interest in the colony. In addition, their patronage and participation in various banquets, meetings and lectures gave credit and respectability to French institutions in Britain.

At the beginning of the twentieth century, the French colony was organized along the classic associative lines such as religion, education, charity, health, professional associations and culture (CADN 1919). The French had had Catholic and Protestant churches for a long time, together with denominational schools. During the nineteenth century they created a French Benevolent Society (1842), a French Hospital (1867) and a Convalescent Home in Brighton (1896). At the end of the century, the rise of an elite among the colony led to the formation of a Chamber of Commerce (1883) and a French National Society (*Société Nationale Française*). It was the more successful members of the colony who took a leading role in most of these French institutions. At the same time, professional associations were founded in activities most favoured by the French: teaching, cooking and hairdressing for instance. They offered services such as help in finding employment or English lessons. When it seemed that the influence of a nation also depended on the diffusion of its language and arts, many cultural clubs and circles developed, frequently with the help of francophile British people. Such collective organization was not peculiar to the French in London. The Germans in London and the Italians in Paris structured their colonies along similar lines (Couder 1986; Panayi 1995), and a spirit of emulation meant that what one of them did, the others did as well, or better.

French institutions also enabled members of the colony to assert and cultivate their specificity while fitting into a new society. But what was the common ground which united all these French people? Religion and politics, often suggested in the case of immigrant populations (Payani 1995: 148, 256-7), did not seem able to federate the various elements of a very mixed French colony (SNPFA, *Sixième Congrès (1887)*: 96; CADN 1897: 20). Fearing division, the National Society of French Teachers even made clear in its constitution that "no political or religious matters shall be discussed during the official meetings of the Society".

Language was perhaps the common denominator, since many of the French institutions already mentioned were intended for all French speakers, irrespective of their nationality. Indeed, tensions arose in others when the use of the French language appeared to be threatened by the growing power of members who, while being of French descent, could not speak French, witness the debates concerning the French Protestant Church in London (CADN, Londres—Ambassade, CH 280).

It must be admitted that the opening of these organizations to an entire speech community was probably not wholly disinterested: it obviously widened the spectrum of potential grants. Yet one should not underestimate the importance these exiles gave to their language, as illustrated in a question that both Franco-British and Franco-French couples had to tackle at some point: their children's identity. In 1899, a Frenchman wrote to the French ambassador in London about his concerns: children of the French colony were, according to him, becoming "more English than John Bull's sons" (CADN, Londres—Ambassade, CH 269). Of course military duties imposed on Frenchmen—at a time when uncertainty prevailed as to the nationality of children born in England of French parents—were often an important consideration when it came to opting for a nationality. Under these conditions, many parents thought of language as a means of checking this phenomenon, and thus wanted their children to acquire a good command of French. They thought this should take place in a non-denominational French school, "where at least French children, brought up among themselves, would lose neither the love nor the language of their motherland" (France 1900: 275.)

Different experiences of otherness

We have focused on three groups, and whilst there were links between them, these were only occasional. The musical artists on a short stay had no reason to make contact with the French institutions in London. The anarchists could not afford a bourgeois evening at the music hall and preferred their own celebrations. The elite of the French colony, keen to preserve its respectability, kept clear of the anarchist "dynamiters". Professional travellers, political refugees and migrants thus faced different experiences of otherness and different realities while abroad. Long before the era of mass migration, the French presence across the Channel was therefore rich and manifold. Each group, in its own way and in its own time, contributed to Franco-British cooperation, whether from abroad by taking part in friendship, professional or militant networks, or in France through correspondence and press reports. The International Musicians' Confederation was thus born on May 10th 1904, from the *Fédération des Artistes Musiciens de France* and the British Amalgamated Musicians' Union. The anarcho-syndicalism which gained ground in France after 1904 was partly inspired by trade unionism, which some anarchist exiles had observed while in Britain. Several members of the French colony wrote articles and books on England for French readers. Lastly, representations of the French were fashioned by this presence. While the music-hall artists reinforced the clichés attached to the French by playing with their image in order to conquer British audiences, and while the anarchists perpetuated the French revolutionary myth, the French who had settled in Britain long before endeavoured to rectify negative stereotypes.

Bibliography and References

ATKIN Nicholas (2003) *The Forgotten French: Exiles in the British Isles 1940-44*, Manchester: Manchester University Press.

BROCHER ARCHIVE. International Institute of Social History, Amsterdam, Gustave Brocher Archive.

BRUILLON Michel (2002) "Le séjour des Britanniques en France à l'époque victorienne, de la villégiature au tourisme," pp. 97-111 in Marielle Seichepine (ed.), *Le Départ à l'époque victorienne*, Metz: Centre d'Études de la Traduction.

CADN (1897) Centre des Archives Diplomatiques de Nantes. Unions Internationales, 1er versement, n°793, *Rapport du Comité de la SFB pour 1897.*

CADN (1919) Centre des Archives Diplomatiques de Nantes. Service des Œuvres Françaises à l'Étranger, n°141, Dossier Grande-Bretagne, rapport "Œuvres françaises et d'influence française de la circonscription du consulat général de France à Londres," Auteur: Marchat, 22/04/-06/05/1919.

COUDER Laurent (1986) "Les Italiens de la région parisienne dans les années 1920," 501-546 in Pierre Milza (ed.), *Les Italiens en France de 1914 à 1940*, Collection de l'École Française de Rome (94), 1986.

D'AXA Zo (1895) *De Mazas à Jérusalem*, Paris: Chamuel.

EHRLICH Cyril (1985) *The Music Profession in Britain since the Eighteenth Century: A Social History*, Oxford: Clarendon Press.

FRANCE Hector (1900) *Croquis d'Outre-Manche*, Paris: Fasquelle.

GERBOD Paul (1995) *Les Voyageurs français à la découverte des Iles Britanniques*, Paris: L'Harmattan.

GUIFFAN Jean (2004) *Histoire de l'anglophobie en France. De Jeanne d'Arc à la Vache Folle*, Rennes: Terre de Brume Éditions.

HAMONET A. (annual) *Annuaire commercial et industriel des Français en Angleterre*, London: W. Jeffs.

JACQUES-CHARLES (1956) *100 ans de Music-Hall*, Geneva & Paris: Éditions Jeheber.

—. *Le Courrier de l'Europe*, London: 1840-1886.

—. *Le Courrier de l'Orchestre*, Paris: 1902-1912.

—. *L'Europe Artiste*, Paris: 1853-1904.

—. *Le Père Peinard. Série londonienne*, London: November 1894-

February 1895.

—. *Le Progrès Artistique. Journal des artistes: musiciens, instrumentistes, choristes, etc.*, Paris: 1878-1908.

LHERBIER Marcel (1939) Film: *L'Entente Cordiale* (black and white, 110 min., with Gaby Morlay and Victor Francen).

LOUISE MICHEL ARCHIVE. International Institute of Social History, Amsterdam.

MALATO Charles (1897) *Les Joyeusetés de l'exil*, Paris: Stock.

PANAYI Panikos (1995) *German Immigrants in Britain during the 19th century, 1815-1914*, Oxford: Berg.

—. *Pleasure Guide to Paris for Bachelors. Paris by day, Paris by night, how to enjoy one's self, where to enjoy one's self.* (1903) London & Paris: Nilsson & Co.

—. *Paris after Dark, containing a description of the fast women, their haunts, habits, etc.; to which is added a description of the night amusements and other resorts; also particulars relative to the working of the social evil in the French metropolis. The only genuine and correct night guide published annually.* Paris: published annually from 1865.

PORTER Roy (1995) "Les Anglais et les loisirs," pp. 21-54 in Alain Corbin (ed.), *L'Avènement des loisirs*, Paris: Aubier.

RUSSEL Dave (1987) *Popular Music in England 1840-1914. A Social History*, Manchester: Manchester University Press.

SNPFA (Société Nationale des Professeurs de Français en Angleterre). *Congrès* (annual reports). London: Hachette.

SPLFA (1832) *Introduction aux Annuaires de la Société des Professeurs de Langue Française en Angleterre*, London: Dulau.

—. *The Gentlemen's Night Guide. The Gay Women of Paris and Brussels, commonly called Cocottes or Lorettes, etc.* (1865) Paris: publisher unknown.

THOMAS Edith (1971) *Louise Michel ou la Velléda de l'anarchie*, Paris: Gallimard.

CHAPTER TWO

BRITS AND AMERICANS IN PARIS: FROM TRAVELLING ELITE TO FOREIGN COLONIES (1855-1937)

JOANNE VAJDA

Travel first emerged as an activity reserved for the idle rich, and has today become a mass tourist industry. There was, however, an intermediary phase in which travel/tourism was an elegant distraction, enjoyed primarily by those members of the aristocracy and the wealthy middle classes who had enough time for leisure activities (see Corbin 1995). Furthermore, many of those who had been to Paris as "tourists" decided to stay there for a longer period of time. This group, that we have labelled "the travelling elite", then became "foreign colonies" in Paris, and in this chapter we analyse the impact they had on certain districts of the city. We will show that the patterns of movement initiated by the travelling elite, and the underlying logic of their arrival and settling in Paris, not only had an effect on the construction of an image of the city, but also influenced the development of its urban space and the social manners of its fashionable upper classes.

Studies of this subject, whatever the discipline—sociology, social or literary history, anthropology—are usually based on the tourist–traveller dichotomy. However, Harvey Levenstein noted in 1998 that the systematic opposition of these two terms was hampering the development of research in this area (Levenstein 1998: ix). Our notion of a "travelling elite" corresponds to no existing historical category and is used here, in the absence of any other adequate term, to designate a missing link which will enable us to follow the slow transformation from eighteenth-century traveller into twentieth-century tourist, and from cultural travel into leisure tourism. Furthermore, this categorization may stimulate reflection about the links between tourism and migration, since the movements of the travelling elite involved a temporary or a permanent settling of fashionable foreigners, and the creation of foreign colonies.

The travelling elite was never a homogenous group, but consisted of travellers who were all apparently rich and had in common, in the eyes of their contemporaries, a taste for luxury, frivolity and fashionable society. In reality, it encompassed a very varied population who all shared similar attitudes and customs: diplomats and dignitaries, millionaires, ruined or exiled monarchs and lords (some genuine, others less so), nabobs and maharajas, financiers, industrialists and wealthy merchants, not forgetting "swindlers": impostors who were not really aristocrats or not really wealthy, and all sorts of tricksters, thieves and procurers.

This diversity of sociological characteristics makes it impossible to classify the travelling elite in accepted social categories. The term aims simply to describe this new form of migration, which implies a process of evolution from individual travel towards mass movement. The notion of travelling *elite* does not imply any judgement on our part about its members. The concept is derived from their own ambition to be so considered, occupying the highest rank among travellers, generally thanks to their striking personalities, and sometimes to the financial power or social rank which they really had, or pretended they had, or to which they aspired. The travelling elite, far from representing a coherent whole, was composed of extremely diverse individualities. It is therefore not possible to draw a portrait of a typical traveller, although a distinction can be made between two basic types: those who were just visiting, and those who formed more settled foreign colonies. After the First World War, the first category was warmly welcomed as a substantial source of income, whereas the second was considered undesirable because of fears over its influence on the French economy, which shows just how actively present it was.

La rue de Castiglione – an English and American street

The history of members of this elite who eventually settled in Paris often followed the same pattern: first a few trips to the city, then a request to set up in residence there, and finally perhaps naturalization. In other words, they first lived in a hotel (preferably a grand hotel), then a rented furnished flat, and finally a private mansion which they rented or bought or even had built. This elite contributed to the construction of the urban identity of Paris by stimulating, among other things, the development of trade in luxury items and of the hotel industry. This phenomenon can be observed by analysing the development of the districts they frequented.

Before 1850, most of the buildings in the rue de Castiglione were either furnished houses for rent or had rooms to let—only numbers 1-3, occupied by the Ministry of Finance, and numbers 8 and 14 were not let out for rent (Archives de Paris: D1P4-192). From that date onwards, they began to be turned into residential hotels, and soon other kinds of establishment began to appear. By 1855, there were already numerous buildings offering accommodation for foreigners. There were three hotels—the Hôtel Clarendon at No. 4, particularly recommended to Americans, the Grand Hôtel de Londres at No. 5 [see Fig. 2-1], and the Hôtel Castiglione at No. 12—as well as two furnished rented houses (Nos. 6 and 9). To satisfy the demands of the foreign travellers, building and extension work took place from the mid-1870s, which altered the appearance and the comfort not only of these buildings but of the whole district, and pushed up the rentable value of the buildings and the price of rented rooms. The opening in 1878 of the Hôtel Continental (at No. 1) simply confirmed the appeal of this district to foreigners.

Fig. 2-1. The Grand Hotel de Londres, as shown in *The American Travellers guide to Paris prepared for the Correspondents of Messrs. J. Munroe & Co., American bankers, 7, rue Scribe, Paris*, London, W.H. & L. Collingridge, Aldersgatest, E.C., 1869, p. LX.

The small trades that occupied the ground-floor shops in 1855—fancy goods, second-hand clothes, draperies—were gradually taken over by watchmakers, jewellers and curiosity shops in the 1870s, and then in the

1890s by various kinds of service agencies, exchange agents, transport companies and different businesses. In 1855 the even-numbered side of the street was already favoured by English-speakers, with two English chemists, Hogg's at No. 2 and Swann's at No.12 on the ground floor of the Hôtel Castiglione, and at Nos. 10 and 14 business agencies and wine and tea merchants (Arthur & Sons and Johnston's). This is how Edmond Deschaumes described the street in 1889:

> Incidentally, very English, that little area between the Place Vendôme and the Tuileries Gardens: agents offering rented accommodation, bars, wine-merchants, Guerre's shop with its 'pastry cook' sign, English bookshops, and shop-windows displaying photographs, cloth-bound guidebooks and maps of Paris. (Deschaumes 1889: 239)

These businesses had appeared primarily to meet the requirements of the foreign clients of the luxury hotels, thus contributing to the international reputation of the rue de Castiglione and helping to create the image of Paris as a cosmopolitan city.

Of the various businesses and agencies, John Arthur's deserves particular attention, not only because he claimed to have founded the first rented accommodation agency in Paris (*Manuel Officiel* ... 1899: 100-101), but also because he was the English-speaking elite's favourite—indeed for a long period, their exclusive—estate agent. Other nationalities had recourse to his services, as we can read in the tales of travellers who recommend him to their compatriots (Ochoa 1861: 30-33). According to a card and a 1913 bill in the Debuisson Collection (Paris, private collection), the agency was first known as A. Arthur & Sons and had been founded by John's father in 1818, although an advertisement in *The Paris Way Book* (Jerrold 1867) suggested the agency had existed only since 1830. The agency moved to the rue de Castiglione in 1853, John Arthur describing himself as the official agent for the British Embassy, a wine- liquor- and tea-merchant, broker, furnished accommodation agent, and exchange agent (Archives de Paris: D1P4-192). He also undertook to ship goods to England, America and India, rent out and sell property, and provide insurance, and he even had an agency to patent inventions in Britain. By 1867 he was the co-publisher of guide-books, such as Blanchard Jerrold's *The Paris Way Book*, in exchange for detailed advertisements for the activities of his firm. At that time, John Arthur & C° also described himself as the official agent for the American Embassy, with a banking and exchange office, an estate agency for buying and selling property as well as renting out houses and furnished or unfurnished apartments, a forwarding agent for all kinds of goods including *objets d'art*, and a merchant selling French and foreign wines. It was to John Arthur's that Jerrold's character, the Englishman Timothy Cockayne, went the day after his arrival in Paris (Jerrold 1871: 95). Tom Lévis, the foreigners' agent described by Alphonse Daudet in *Les Rois en exil,* was very probably inspired by John Arthur, a hypothesis confirmed by the fact that Daudet's original plan situated Tom Lévis's agency at the same address as that of John Arthur: 10, rue de Castiglione (Daudet 1990: 1463, note). In 1878, George Augustus Sala described him as the most helpful of bankers and estate agents, constantly assisting English-speakers in Paris (Sala 1879 vol. 2: 325). Little by little, property transactions and letting rented accommodation became his principal activities, indicating that more and more foreigners were settling in Paris. By the 1880s the number of this type of agency was growing.

Foreign colonies

By settling in Paris, the travelling elite helped form the city's cosmopolitan society. They became part of Parisian high society ("le tout-Paris"), for whom by the 1850s, coming from a particular place or belonging to a particular nation was less important than segregation by social class. The travelling elite, accused by its critics of being superficial and indifferent, had little time for the universalist ideas of the eighteenth century (considered to be the century of cosmopolitanism). Nevertheless, through its habits and its demands, it gave a concrete form to this universalism, transforming intellectual cosmopolitanism into what one might call "material" or "economic" cosmopolitanism. Anne-Marie Thiesse has already shown how national identities, which since the eighteenth century have structured the concept of "community", are related to intellectual cosmopolitanism (Thiesse 1999). From the middle of the nineteenth century onwards, a new cosmopolitan ideal can be seen to emerge, based on fashionable social practices connected to travel, and quite distinct from the cosmopolitanism of the Enlightenment. This ideal helped to construct another form of collective identity, an identity marked by cosmopolitan sociability.

The colony can be defined as a group of people coming from one place, living in another, and conserving their own traditions. The notion of a foreign colony in Paris implies neither a desire to dominate a territory nor any ambition for economic exploitation, but simply designates a fashionable elite settled, for a while or permanently, in the French capital. Foreign colonies were not recognized as such until there existed some form first of social, then of cultural representation. Even if they underwent important transformations due to political or economic changes in their country of origin, the foreign colonies were in fact often represented by the idle rich, and by businessmen, artists and writers. Intermediary activities then brought in a large number of foreigners, for travelling elites were the starting point for a new type of immigration, which played an important part in the economic development of France and fostered relations between France and the countries of origin of the travellers. The *American Register* was one of the American colony's most popular papers.

Nationality was not a criterion for membership of the colony, many continuing to be part of it even after obtaining French nationality. Others were accepted into the colony through marriage with a member. As for national customs, the particularity of these foreign colonies was that they tried to develop a dialectical relationship with each other and with the indigenous population. Without abandoning their own traditions, they thus accepted French influence at the same time as they were spreading their own habits in Parisian society, without being obliged to merge with it.

The directories which list the members of the colonies are often incomplete but they allow us nevertheless to analyse the image that such publications projected of these groups, taking into account the criteria for selection of names to be included. They also enable us to study the establishment of the fashionable elite in the city and to observe the consequences of its arrival in terms of how open the city was to the practice of certain professions by foreigners. The *Anglo-American Annual, a Directory & Handbook for Residents in Paris*, which appeared in 1890, published for the first time a list of names which recorded 1,087 British and American people resident in Paris. The list of occupations and the list of English- or American-owned businesses, also included in this directory, show that the colonies resulted in various tradesmen setting up businesses to help the colonies maintain certain cultural traditions, and also to turn to their compatriots to defend their interests or obtain health care. The directory included fourteen British or American lawyers, nine interpreters, forty-five dentists and twenty-one dental surgeons. Incidentally, the advice given in this publication encouraged the British and American elite to settle in districts already frequented by their compatriots.

The American colony

Of all the foreign colonies, the American colony is one of the most visible in the source material, and had a strong impact on the city and its customs. It was established in Paris at almost the same time as the British colony, from 1830 onwards, but was smaller. By the time of the Second

Empire (1852-70), Americans were flocking to Paris since, despite their republican ideas, the Imperial Court was for them a true ideal. Napoleon III and Empress Eugénie particularly appreciated them, which is why they were often invited to receptions through the intermediary of the U.S. Legation or of certain Americans who were close to the Emperor, such as his dentist, Thomas Evans (Evans 1910: 96-99).

In 1867, the American colony was centred around the Champs Elysées. It was estimated at five thousand but its numbers declined between the end of the Second Empire and the turn of the century because the arrival of the Third Republic in 1870 swept away the entertainments of a court. Furthermore, Americans no longer had to turn to Europe for amusement as the United States was in transformation, its big cities also offering numerous forms of leisure. Political relations between the two countries were also an influential factor. General Grant's publicly expressed delight at the Prussian victory in 1870 hardly went down well with the French, who gave a less warm welcome to Americans as a result.

In 1882, there remained about one and a half thousand Americans. Transatlantic millionaires had long supplanted the English lord in terms of personal fortune, but Parisian society looked at them with a certain disdain, considering them to be products of speculation, mere upstarts, as the following lines by "Old Nick Jr." demonstrate:

> They have formed their own society where they lead a separate existence with exotic, original behaviour, acting with as much liberty and independence as if they owned the place. They are the ones with the smartest clothes, the finest carriages, the jauntiest horses, the best seats at our theatres, the most popular *ricevimenti*. They play the tune, and now we listen. They have their own aristocrats, clans, and gossip (which can be quite cruel). They have their favourite entertainments, their special dances—the *boston,* the *racket*, and even the *saratoga*—[…], their own national club (the *Stanley*), their newspaper (the *American Register*), their own exclusive bankers (Mr. Munroe and Drexel Hartjes and Co.), their own doctors, lawyers, pharmacists, etc. To sum up, within our old Paris they have built a new little Paris just for themselves. […] In Paris today, they are the ones with the largest fortunes. With his two hundred million, Mr. Mackay, the lucky miner who got rich thanks to his pickaxe, can afford to pity our ruined princes of the Union Génerale, our distraught stock traders and our poor businessmen. The Vanderbilts, and the Jay Goulds […] are certainly entitled to enjoy themselves. […] The problem is that just being with these princes of finance is terrible since next to them, everyone appears poor. [...] Another worry is that all that gold is not as pure as it may seem. ("Old Nick Jr." 1882)

Despite these criticisms, guests were lavishly entertained in the American colony. Thanks to the hostesses, their *salons* were very hospitable, there was frank discussion, codes of conduct were not as strict, young ladies were very independent [see Fig. 2-2], and there was a lot of dancing, which attracted the French.

Fig. 2-2. *La Vie parisienne*, 9 March 1878, p. 132: one of a series of images of "foreign girls" is this American, described as "wildly independent but very decent, goes out alone, travels alone, but does so with a friend when it is more convenient for her..."

In 1887, the American colony was mostly made up of the rich, of diplomats, bankers, artists and journalists. There were not many tradesmen (those that there were, were all prosperous) or employees. *The Americans in Paris* mentions about six hundred and fifty names but its author specifies that the list is not exhaustive (1887: 55-59). Among the names are those of James Gordon Bennett and Ferdinand Bischoffsheim (Avenue des Champs-Elysées), J.F. Loubat (rue Dumont d'Urville) and Edward Lee Child (rue François 1er). Some resided at hotels, like Mrs. Lowery who rented rooms every year at the Bristol, as did the Vanderbilts and the Lorillards (the Bristol, situated in the Place Vendôme, was also frequented by the Prince of Wales).

In the eyes of their compatriots, towards the end of the nineteenth century the American colony in Paris was a separate entity, its members being no longer American and yet not considered as French (Davis 1895: 188). The British and American colonies had close links at this time, and English-language accounts invariably mention both colonies. About twelve thousand British subjects were living in Paris at the beginning of the twentieth century, compared with approximately five thousand Americans, but the American colony was considered more important, because its members were wealthier. The distance between America and France and the cost of the journey explain why fewer Americans of modest means settled in Paris (Noyes 1910: 139).

After the First World War, twenty-five thousand Americans were estimated to be living in Paris permanently (BHVP). Several reasons can be put forward to explain this substantial increase. Some arrived during the hostilities and, finding the way of life and the atmosphere pleasant, decided to stay. Also, the exchange rate was favourable, and American business activity was developing in France. 1,766 American names appeared in the 1923 *Tout étranger*, a directory listing foreign "personalities" resident in France and the French colonies. As well as those with their own Paris address, the place of residence of sixty-seven Americans was given as a first-class hotel, that of thirteen as a hotel of a lower category, while others (continuing to shuttle between France and the United States) gave a bank as their address, particularly the American Exchange (11, rue Scribe) and Morgan Harjes (14, place Vendôme)—this was a common practice, for the banks undertook to forward all mail thus received. The American Chamber of Commerce directory listed five thousand Americans living in Paris in 1928 (Fouché 1994: 7-10). The index of their professions showed the American colony was active in all areas of French life—social, political, cultural and economic—a point seldom underlined in cultural history, which tends to dwell more on the presence of artists, painters, writers and musicians.

The Americanization of Paris

From 1890 onwards, the American conquest of France was a recurrent theme in French literature and the French press. Baudelaire was the first to coin the term "to Americanize" (*américaniser*) in 1851; the Goncourt brothers wrote of the "Americanization" of France (*l'américanisation*), manifest, in their opinion, in the supremacy given to industry over art at the 1867 Universal Exhibition (Goncourt 1935: vol. III, 77, 16 January 1867). This Americanization of Paris developed on several different levels and in various different ways. As early as the beginning of the nineteenth century, shop signs had begun to include references to the New World, thus targeting both foreigners and French customers attracted by "exotic" products. Up until the First World War, anything strange or lavish was described as *américain*, and advertisements adopted this adjective for all types of innovation (on Franco-American relations see Roger 2002 and Mathy 1993). Americanization was later associated with the development of industry, a trend that seemed to fascinate so many people (Bonin 1988: 63). France was importing methods of organization, patents and industrial material, all of which contributed to a more prosperous economy.

French upper-class society changed as it, too, adopted English or American customs. This is perhaps one of the most significant contributions of the travelling elite. The importance of a foreign colony was measured by the *salons* held by its members. However, since the French upper classes looked down on any *salon* where not enough French was spoken (Claretie 1892: 21), its legitimacy depended on its ability to attract the French aristocracy. "Getting *un comte* to come to their salon is a supreme delight for American hostesses; if they can get *un marquis* they are in seventh heaven" (Wilmant 1896). This is why an invitation to the salon of Kate Moore, a friend of the Duchess of Luynes, was so sought after by the travelling elite, as the memoirs of Boni de Castellane showed (Castellane 1986: 60-61 and 303). The salons held by the American colony, such as those of Mrs. Harris-Phelps, Mrs. Ridgway and Mrs. Munroe, were among the most fashionable in the capital (Wilmant 1896). The ladies of the foreign colony thus became a very important factor in the sociability of Parisian high society.

Paris had become more cosmopolitan since the middle of the nineteenth century, a process that continued and accelerated in the 1890s, particularly in the smartest residential districts where the international elite were settling. At this time the rue Galilée was described as "the official American street" in *The Anglo-American Annual* (1890: 125-127), but the Americans' favourite area was still, as it had been since the middle of the century, around the Place de l'Étoile. In 1906 an article in *Le Magazine Illustré* described it in the following terms:

> Whole avenues in this luxurious area belong to them and they have organized their lives according to their own national customs and traditions. Even the shops there are American and aim to satisfy only American tastes. The district is in truth a little American town, spilling over with riches and the most brilliant luxury. A Parisian actually feels out of place in certain parts of the Avenue Kléber or the Avenue Mac-Mahon: it is all too big and too rich. The very air smells of the cosmopolitanism that the native independence of the Americans brings with it. The Parisian feels he is in a strange land where the avenues are too wide, too straight, too cold. (R.V. 1906)

The Trocadéro district was also to become one of the favourite spots of the richest and most famous Americans. Several statues donated by Americans are present-day reminders of their presence. The bust of Benjamin Franklin, for example, in the square above the Trocadéro, was given to the city of Paris in 1906 by a member of the American colony, the Philadelphian banker and philanthropist John H. Harjes (whose bust, by John J. Beyle, was a reproduction of the statue in Philadelphia). The Place des États-Unis is one example among several of how the members of the foreign colonies contributed to the urban landscaping of Paris.

La Place des États-Unis – the square of the two Americas

Until 1881 this square was called the Place de la Bitche. The American Legation was then at No. 16. After Norton MacLane, the U.S. ambassador plenipotentiary, complained to the authorities that the name was a source of embarrassment and ridicule to his compatriots, it was changed to the Place des États-Unis.

The development of this square is an example of the contribution of foreigners to the city's westward expansion. All the buildings were constructed after 1880 with the exception of No. 7, which was built in 1877 and was owned by Charles Morgan before being purchased in 1887 by the American painter Julian Russell Story, who then modified and extended it. No. 5, built in 1883, was bought by Marie Georgina Stafford Jermingham (Archives de Paris: D1P4-388). In the same year, No. 10 was built and was the property of Viarma Martius da Silva, who sold it in 1889 (Archives de Paris: VO11-1138). No. 18, also built in 1883, was bought three years later by the New York banker Jean Otto Plock, who in 1887 added, as his personal touch, the belvedere looking onto the rue Galilée.

The U.S. ambassador was practically the first tenant at No. 16. He was followed by the Duke of Padua in 1885, then by Francisco de Yturbe of the Mexican colony, who lived there from 1889 to 1900. Another member of the Mexican colony, Manuel de Villamil, was the owner of a new building at No. 6, which by 1894 was the property of one of his compatriots, Idaroff de Yturbe. The No. 3 plot was developed in 1890 by its owner, Albert Eugène Van den Bosch. The following year, on the neighbouring plot (No. 3b) Count Arevedo de Silva had a small building constructed, which between 1896 and 1898 belonged to Théobald Chartran, a painter specializing in portraits of foreign personalities.

In 1886, the banker Jules Ephrussi, born in Odessa in Russia and married in 1876 in Vienna to the Austrian Françoise (Fanny) von Pfeiffer, had a house built at No. 2 by the architect Paul-Ernest Sanson. The style was full of references to the French eighteenth century, but this neoclassical building accommodated modern comfort in the form of a lift, installed by the American Elevator Company (Archives nationales: 143AP–7/8-9). The mansion was later bought by Fouad I, son of Khedive Ismael Pasha and king of Egypt between 1922 and 1936, and is today the Egyptian ambassador's residence.

Sanson was probably the architect who designed the most buildings for cosmopolitan society in Paris. Gérard Rousset-Charny has traced the relations he and some of his fellow architects had with the travelling elite (Rousset-Charny 1990). His greatest achievement was certainly the *Palais Rose* (the Pink Palace), built for Boni de Castellane and his wealthy American wife, Anna Gould, at No. 40 Avenue du Bois de Boulogne (today the Avenue Foch). The building, opened in 1902, was inspired by the Grand Trianon at the Château de Versailles (Archives nationales: 143AP–5/1-181; Rousset-Charny 1990: 76-91). Although the *Palais Rose* was presented as a manifestation of the count's personal taste, as Boni himself confirms, it was his wife's financial contribution that made it possible (Castellane 1986: 232). The building was demolished in 1969.

Ferdinand Bischoffsheim bought the house located at No. 11 in 1894. It had been built eight years earlier for Mariano Santiago Arcos del Carmen, but Bischoffsheim, who also owned two buildings at Nos. 138 and 140, Avenue des Champs-Elysées, had it demolished immediately and called on Sanson to design a new house which was completed in 1898. This all goes to show just how fast the city was changing at this time. Bischoffsheim must have been a very demanding customer if we are to judge from the number of versions of the plans presented to him by the architect (Archives nationales: 143AP–2/1-276 and Archives de Paris: D1P4-388). The building, which dominated the square due to its extra 1.66-metre elevation, showed the influence of French styles of the seventeenth and eighteenth centuries, but the interior decoration showed Italian influences. To decorate the ballroom, Bischoffsheim even had a ceiling brought from Palermo. The magnificence of the building was underlined by its far from traditional lay-out, with a huge central staircase leading to reception rooms on the first floor, leaving the ground floor to the couple's private apartments (Archives de Paris: VO11-1138). It was in this mansion that Ferdinand Bischoffsheim displayed his art collection, comparable, according to specialists, to the Rothschild, Jacquemart-André and Camondo collections. His grand-daughter, Marie-Laure de Noailles, later added a modern art collection (Rousset-Charny 1990: 68-69). After being taken over by the international elite, at the beginning of the twentieth century the Place des États-Unis was adopted by the younger generation of French aristocrats (Archives de Paris: VO11-1138).

This example of the Place des États-Unis leads us to a new interpretation of the development of western Paris, different from that which is commonly accepted. It shows the role of the international elite in urban transformations. Wealthy foreigners contributed to the opulent appearance of the areas in which they resided, although the private homes they had built showed few signs of their foreign origins, for their expatriation and their desire to be accepted into Parisian society resulted in their spiritual and material integration, and the loss of their American culture. Since architecture can confer nobility, the travelling elite, when settling in Paris, was forced to adopt more traditional values. From the end of the nineteenth century, a return to French classicism characterized the houses of this foreign colony. Most of the foreigners living in Paris eventually defended this style, even resuscitating it in the form of pastiche. Thus these buildings, which could not be considered original or modern, nevertheless helped to form the image of the city. Through them, the story of the rich foreigners passing through Paris is associated not only with frivolity and travel, but also with finance, art and architecture.

Mobile *and* sedentary

From the middle of the nineteenth century onwards, the travelling elite was a driving force in the development of tourism, hotels, travel and estate agencies, in the diversification of retail establishments and places of entertainment, and also in the construction of private mansions. Moreover, as the foreign travellers took up a sedentary lifestyle, they contributed to the transformation of the customs and manners of Parisian society. As we have seen, this subject links the history of the city, social and cultural history, and the history of tourism, without necessarily opposing the concepts of "mobile" and "sedentary".

The author wishes to put on record her special thanks to Roxana Debuisson, Florence Quignard Debuisson and Goulven Guilcher, who generously put their collections at her disposal, assisted her in her research, and gave permission to reproduce a number of documents.

Bibliography and References

—. Archives de Paris: 18, Bd Sérurier, 75019 Paris.

—. Archives Nationales: 60, rue des Francs-Bourgeois, 75003 Paris.

CORBIN Alain (ed.) (1995) *L'Avènement des loisirs, 1850-1960*, Paris: Aubier.

BHVP: Bibliothèque Historique de la Ville de Paris, Actualités–Série 82–Etrangers à Paris (the library is located at the Hôtel de Lamoignon, 24, rue Pavée, 75004 PARIS).

BONIN Hubert (1988) *Histoire économique de la France depuis 1880*, Paris: Masson.

CASTELLANE Boniface de (1986) *Mémoires, 1867-1932*, Paris: Perrin.

CLARETIE Jules (1892) *L'Américaine. Roman contemporain*, Paris: Dentu.

DAUDET Alphonse (1990) *Œuvres, t. II. Les Rois en exil*, Paris: Gallimard.

DAVIS Richard Harding (1895) *About Paris*, New York: Harper & Brothers.

DESCHAUMES Edmond (1889) *Pour bien voir Paris. Guide parisien pittoresque et pratique. Ouvrage contenant tous les renseignements nécessaires aux Touristes*, Paris: F. Pigeon.

—. *Les Echos de Paris,* 22 April 1906.

—. *L'Eclair*, 27 April 1906.

EVANS Thomas W. (1910) *Le Second Empire. Mémoires du Dr. Thomas W. Evans*, Paris: Plon.

FOUCHÉ Nicole (1994) "La présence américaine en France (XIXe-XXe siècles): à la recherche d'une problématique," *Revue française d'études américaines*, n° 59, February 1994, pp. 7-10.

GONCOURT E. et J. de (1935) *Journal. Mémoires de la vie littéraire, 1867-1870*, Paris: Flammarion/Fasquelle.

JERROLD Blanchard (1867) *The Paris Way Book*, Paris & London: J. Arthur & C°/Smart & Allen.

JERROLD Blanchard. (1871) *The Cockaynes in Paris or "Gone Abroad"*, London: J.C. Hotten.

LEVENSTEIN Harvey (1998) *Seductive Journey: American Tourists in France from Jefferson to the Jazz Age*, Chicago & London: University of Chicago Press.

—. *Manuel officiel des affaires immobilières et foncières. Annuaire spécial des architectes et des affaires.* (1899) Paris.

MATHY Jean-Philippe (1993) *Extrême-Occident: French Intellectuals and America*, Chicago & London: University of Chicago Press.

NOYES H.E. (1910) *Seventeen Years in Paris: a Chaplain's Story*, London: Baines & Scarsbrook.

OCHOA Eugenio de (1861) *Paris, Londres y Madrid*, Paris: Baudry.

OLD NICK Jr. [pseudonym of E. Daurand Forgues] "La colonie américaine à Paris," *La Vie élégante,* 15 April 1882, 247-254.

R.V. "À propos du voyage de M. et Mme Longworth. Les Américains à

Paris," *Le Magazine Illustré. Madame et Monsieur,* n°59, 22 July 1906, pp. 545-546.

ROGER Philippe (2002) *L'Ennemi américain. Généalogie de l'anti-américanisme français*, Paris: Seuil.

ROUSSET-CHARNY Gérard (1990) *Les Palais parisiens de la Belle Epoque*, Paris: DAAVP.

SALA George A. (1879) *Paris Herself Again in 1878-9*, London: Remington & C°.

—. *The Americans in Paris with names and addresses, sketch of American art, lists of artists and pictures, and miscellaneous matters of interest to Americans abroad.* (1887) Paris: T. Symonds.

—. *The Anglo-American Annual, a Directory & Handbook for Residents in Paris.* (1890) Paris: Neal's Library and Brentano's.

THIESSE Anne-Marie (1999) *La Création des identités nationales: Europe XVIIIe-XXe siècle*, Paris: Seuil.

—. *Le tout étranger de France. Annuaire de la société mondaine, diplomatique, financière et commerciale étrangère en résidence fixe en France et dans les colonies.* (1923) [3rd year] Paris: M. de Toledo.

WILMANT G. (1896) "Notes parisiennes. La colonie américaine à Paris," press cutting in BHVP, dated 7 June 1896.

CHAPTER THREE

TRAVEL, TOURISM AND MIGRATION SEEN THROUGH EXILE

SYLVIE APRILE

This chapter explores the relationship between the three different but complementary forms of mobility—travel, tourism, and migration—through a fourth form: exile, or forced mobility. The French political exiles of the Second Empire (1852-1870) were of course travellers, their exclusion beginning with a journey which was a more or less rapid flight from France after the *coup d'état* of December 1851. They crossed the frontier in conditions that were often unusual or dangerous, and mostly settled in Belgium or Britain. Their residence abroad was envisaged as temporary since, for them, long-term settlement was unthinkable. Nevertheless, the refusal on the part of the more committed of them to accept a pardon or even an amnesty during the Second Empire was to prolong their exile and to lead to further travel which resembled migration or tourism. With their status of intellectuals some, like Hugo and Quinet, became part of a wandering elite, and continued to travel and go on "pilgrimages" as in the past. Others, finding that exile gave rise to new habits, were to turn travel into a profession.

Publishing in exile was often their only honourable means of subsistence and so, in their particular way, they participated in the development of travel literature as authors of guidebooks, photograph albums, or of more scientific works. Their vision of the host countries was marked by a complicity with the French public. Hence, their descriptions often resembled timeless stereotypes and comparisons were more or less explicitly favourable to France. It was principally outside Europe that the exiles were able to report on new realities and to put some of their ideas into practice. This was the case of Amédée Jacques, for example, who planned his exile in South America around the possibilities for developing his educational projects there. Even more famous was the arrival in the New World of Elisée Reclus: he not only discovered his vocation for geography, but also defined the role of the geographer in the words "to know it, you have to see it" (1911: 109).

Banishment under the Second Empire resembled the forms of travel initiated at the time of the French Revolution and perpetuated by the Romanticism of the first half of the century, for exile can be situated within a framework of elite mobility and the art of travelling, which characterized the great names of literature such as Mme de Staël, Chateaubriand and Byron (Guyot & Massol 2003).

A wandering elite

Victor Hugo, in exile in Belgium and later in the Channel Islands, undertook once again the annual trips he had ritually made with Juliette Drouet. He resumed the wandering he had begun before the Second Republic (1848-51), covering similar territory, principally in north-west Europe, in countries neighbouring France. He resided in Holland, Belgium, Germany and Switzerland. Although he was forced to make a halt in Great Britain, he never resided there and never expressed the desire to do so, detesting London in particular. He returned tirelessly to the regions he had discovered, mainly in the 1830s. These journeys gave rise to few publications. Hugo drew on them principally for his images, forms, memories and ideas, and for his sketches. This type of travel does not imply a lack of curiosity: although leaving home means escaping everyday life, it also implies beginning a journey of self-discovery. What we might call "romantic travel"—admittedly a slight caricature—is a process of self-construction and a meditation on the past. Such journeys have a narcissistic element to them, as is suggested by images such as the poet or writer striking a pose before the stormy ocean. The journey is also a leap into the past. Hugo—but this analysis would also apply to Quinet or less well-known writers—travelled as a Romantic poet but also as a man of the Enlightenment, meditating on History and on the future of humanity. As Nicole Savy points out, the world according to Victor Hugo is characterized by its temporal density, and through his travels what he was resuscitating was the past of Christian Europe (1997). This does not contradict the idea of the construction of the new Europe, the United States of Europe, the first stage on the road to the universal Republic which Hugo and many other exiles ardently defended. It also explains why such journeys entailed little contact, other than the necessary minimum, with the native population. Furthermore, social and economic conditions were of little interest. In fact, Hugo did not speak the languages of the countries he visited and had hardly any desire to meet people with whom he could talk, or to find interpreters.

This nomadic lifestyle was strongly marked by the specific context of government repression and by the asylum conditions offered in the countries neighbouring France. The volume of poetry published by Etienne Arago reveals the precarity of exile, which makes travel inevitable. His poems relate his journey from London to Belgium, then to Switzerland and finally to Italy. A comparison with the Wandering Jew comes easily to mind as with Mme de Staël—an earlier travelling exile—who, in her novel *Corinne*, has her heroine declare that "travelling is life's saddest form of pleasure" (1999: 1-I, chapter II; first edition 1807).

Arago too echoed Mme de Staël's "the geography of Napoleon's Europe can be learnt only too well through unhappiness" (1996: 243, first edition 1821), although he tried to find some satisfaction and self-improvement in his travels, writing that "exile has given me an immense homeland" (1860 edition: 15; see also Toulotte 1993).

Travel was an activity reserved for an elite, an activity they chose although often seeing it as an internal rather than an external quest. This is also shown in the famous words about Gustave Flaubert's hero Frédéric Moreau—"He travelled"—following the *coup d'état* of December 1851 (Neefs 2004). The words following this quotation merit attention: "He travelled. He knew the melancholy of ships, the cold of tents in the morning, the dullness of landscapes and ruins, the bitterness of interrupted friendships. He returned home" (Flaubert 1999: 542). Maurice Agulhon has drawn attention to the emblematic value of this abrupt change: "In order to communicate the sense of change that a large part of French society experienced when Bonaparte's dictatorship evinced the Republic, these simple but prodigiously elliptic words ["He travelled."] in *L'Éducation sentimentale* are worth more than all the trumpets of *Les Châtiments*" (1981: 41).

At the same time, Ernest Coeurderoy, a young Republican in 1848, glorifying his condition as an exile, repeats obsessively over many pages of his autobiography the same sentence, conjugated here in the future tense: "I will travel," he writes, "My travels will be profitable because I undertake them not to fill up empty leisure time, but to observe men and the road to the Revolution" (1991: 267). Here he expresses his refusal to undertake a sort of shortened Grand Tour, motivated by boredom or excessive leisure, preferring a passionate quest in search of humanity itself: "Let us make of all the corners of the earth our homeland!" he concludes. We may note, however, that in another part of his autobiography he declares just as passionately "I will commit suicide", which he actually did a few years later.

Does this mean a great distance separated these exiles from the new travelling habits which developed throughout the century, particularly after 1850? No, for they too expressed a new taste for nature and the pleasures of tourism. Hermione Quinet describes enthusiastically in her memoirs her discovery of the Swiss mountains or of the bucolic scenery of the woods surrounding Brussels. The real transition to tourism occurred while they themselves were not in France. Their political situation meant that their path crossed that of these new cultural habits and gave them a role of intermediary between foreigners and the French.

Travelling becomes a profession

In order to survive, many exiles cashed in on their knowledge, of their host countries in particular. They published many articles in French journals and magazines, especially the *Revue des Deux Mondes* and, more surprising and new at the time, they contributed to travellers' guidebooks. They invited their readers to travel, whilst insisting on their own attachment to France. A profusion of guidebooks and travel routes had already appeared during the Revolution, from Reichard's *Guide des Voyageurs en Europe* in 1793, to *Itinéraire complet de l'Empire français*, published in 1806 and in 1811. According to Gilles Bertrand, almost seven hundred works on travel and the geography of France appeared between 1789 and 1812 (2002). But generally speaking, the political exiles distinguished their work from travel literature, deliberately and out of a sense of conviction. Did this "forced" immersion in the foreign culture really bring deeper knowledge with it? That at least was what Alphonse Esquiros claimed, to justify his publications:

> "Hasn't everything already been said about England?" I asked an Englishman three years ago. "Yes," he replied, "and yet everything still remains to be said." What reinforces this opinion is that the writers who have written about Great Britain—and there are a number of eminent ones—have all viewed it as travellers. My advantage over them, which many of them may not envy me, is that I have set down roots in this civilization which they have only passed through. [...] I have kept enough foreign elements—as the Duc de Saint-Simon used to say—in both my language and my tastes to be able to judge impartially the people among whom I reside." (Esquiros 1867: introduction)

The same desire to distinguish the vision of the exile from that of the traveller is also present in the prologue of Louis Blanc's *Dix ans de l'histoire de l'Angleterre,* which appeared in 1879 (see Blanc 2001).

The exiles relate "their" England, whether their approach is that of the historian or the columnist. Ledru-Rollin, Louis Blanc, Martin Nadaud and Talandier all published a history of England or of the British working class. In what one might call their "potboilers", which are usually articles or books on the life and customs of the host country, they barely touch on contemporary reality but instead use a series of clichés and stereotypes that create a feeling of connivance and complicity between the French reader and the author in exile. By describing what the reader already knows, the author remains fixed in the past, as Corinne Samindayer Perrin underlined in the context of a series of articles written by Jules Vallès:

> Thus *La Rue à Londres* presents an England which is both resolutely contemporary (its modernity is that of industrialization and colonial imperialism) and curiously timeless. *La Rue à Londres* is clearly anchored in the fixed temporality of exile, with constant references to its founding event: the Commune. Nothing is clearly marked in real time, the author significantly employing the present tense of eternal truths. The attention paid to the typical explains the dissolving of temporality marked and dated by history into the cyclical repetition which characterizes the everyday. (Samindayar-Perrin 2000: 39)

This observation can be applied to more or less all the exiles who published many studies of English life and customs. Alphonse Esquiros or Louis Blanc rarely referred during the Second Empire to any precise events or news items, preferring to describe recurrent events which appear typically English, such as the Derby. Their timeless descriptions also show a more or less explicit and somewhat nostalgic bias towards France, whether comparing boxing or feminine charm.

There were, however, a few efforts to depict local geography with greater precision. Alphonse Esquiros uses geology to describe both the landscape and the customs of the inhabitants. In his work entitled *La Néerlande et la vie hollandaise*, he professes: "So far travellers and moralists have not paid enough attention to the physical theatre upon which the different European civilizations have come to be established" (1859: 72). He then goes on in a long chapter to associate peat with the legendary patience of the Batavians. He also published two articles on Belgium in the *Revue des Deux Mondes,* choosing an original angle: zoological gardens and life down the mines. He explained in a letter to Noël Parfait that he wished to study a village of lunatics in Flanders: "Much has been said about art in Belgium but it seems to me that there remain some local institutions that have yet to be introduced to the public."

To earn a living, however, the exiles also had to become guides to future travellers. The travel document *par excellence*—the *Guide Joanne de l'Angleterre*—was the work of the exile Esquiros who published it in 1867, under the title *Itinéraire descriptif de la Grande-Bretagne et de l'Irlande*. His first biographer, Van der Linden, keen to present Esquiros's convictions, describes it in emotional terms: "Leafing through this book, one is astounded to discover the amount of material collected, the objective and precise use of language. How can our 'Montagnard' remain so cold, so realistic, for more than 700 pages?" (1948: 85). Employed to write guidebooks, the exiles had—it should be noted—little leeway to express out-of-the-ordinary opinions. They thus played a major role in the writing of guidebooks, whose numbers increased as more and more tourists crossed the Channel or the Atlantic. Specific publications were particularly required for the universal exhibitions. Better known for his geographical works than as a London guide, Elisée Reclus was rather surprisingly the author of a guidebook for the 1862 Universal Exhibition. The link between exhibition and expulsion was made in 1851 by J-M Loewe: "You know that the Great Exhibition in London is no more than a sort of complement to the universal expulsion, which sent political specimens to England from all over Europe" (Loewe 1851: 141, cited by Hancock 2005).

Many famous exiles also contributed to the *Paris-Guide* published for the 1867 Universal Exhibition. Prefaced by Hugo, their articles show their nostalgia for a pre-Haussmanian Paris and stigmatize the recent urban development as a sign of the Emperor's authoritarianism, the very source of their own exile. Louis Blanc wrote:

> Paris is full of memories cast in marble, wood or stone. Are they destined to disappear? Among the children of France who have been away for a long time, I know some who turn pale with fright when told, "If you came back to Paris tomorrow, you wouldn't recognize it." Already? Alas, it was so good to recognize Paris! ("Le vieux Paris", *Paris-Guide* 1983 reprint: 18)

The exiles often remarked that a Frenchman never takes refuge in London unless forced to do so: "One has to admit," wrote Hector Malot, "that broadly speaking France is not represented in England by the real cream of its population, for the very simple reason that no Frenchman goes to England for pleasure or resides there by choice, and thinks of nothing but leaving that country as soon as possible." Once again, we find here the clichés and stereotypes which circulated between the two countries, and that inevitable comparison between Paris and London (on this subject see

Hancock 2003). Greater originality is certainly to be found in their photography. Uprooted, some took up the occupation of those who have none—photography—publishing the first travel albums. Victor Frond, a former Parisian fireman, learnt this trade in Portugal and illustrated Charles Ribeyrolles's *Le Brésil pittoresque*. It was also for financial reasons that Hugo's sons considered taking up photography and planned to publish books on the Channel Islands.

They often adopted a moralizing tone towards tourism. Many of them stayed at Spa, believing, perhaps erroneously, that they were thus escaping the attention of the Belgian police. The numerous descriptions they left of this resort, famous for its waters and particularly for its gambling establishments, are strongly disapproving. One exile, Emile Deschanel, wrote:

> Its cemetery contains examples of all European nationalities, which makes it different from other cemeteries, sadder, and, one might say, at times painfully ironic. There they lie, those tireless tourists, immobile forever. [...] Rushing across Europe in pursuit of pleasure, they found death. In one instant, they passed from agitation to immortality. Who knows but that they may have found something better than that which they sought after? They have found the great, supreme repose, the end of all struggle and hatred; they lie in the long grass, forgotten, sheltered by fir trees, on the slope of a mountain, bathed in the scent of resin [...] Let us not pity them! ("Le cimetière de Spa" 1856: 20)

Etienne Arago, who spent seven months in Spa in 1850, wrote an enormous epic poem in seven cantos criticizing gambling in Spa (*Spa et ses jeux*), which he presented as a symbol of the *mores* of the time.

From adventurer to migrant

The image of emigration that exiles gave through the places they had been to or through their writing revealed a great spirit of adventure, or at least a close identification of the migrant with the adventurer in the broadest sense. The commonest figure in the mid-nineteenth century was that of the bankrupt, arriving in England to escape justice in France or to set up some shady business. This appears clearly in the travel guides which advise readers to avoid the French districts or their compatriots if the latter seem too enterprising. Travellers must remain on their guard against those who claim to offer assistance.

Other examples of travel literature, dealing with more distant areas, show on the contrary a certain fascination with both the adventure of travelling and settling in places seen as still being off the beaten track (see Cordillot 2001 & Foucrier 1999). Patrick Vermeren's biography of Amédée Jacques, who fled to Argentina, shows that his destination was chosen partly by chance, but also because of an intellectual and political project that interested him before he left France (2001). He chose Argentina because he had met members of the literary elite of the New World who spoke highly to the French of the opportunities to put their ideas into practice in South America. In 1847, he received a visit from Sarmiento, the Governor of San Juan who was passing through Paris. Jacques published in *La Liberté de Penser*, a magazine he edited with Jules Simon, two reviews of works by Sarmiento, written by his friend Champgobert. Sarmiento was the author of *Argyropolis*, a text which describes the banks of the River Plata as a veritable paradise on earth, a promised land. In his work he addressed a vibrant invitation to the French.

Amédée Jacques' curiosity about the New World coincided with the absence of any professional or intellectual perspective for him in France, since the government had removed him from his post at the Lycée Louis le Grand in Paris in 1850. He arrived in Montevideo on June 30th 1852, with a little money and above all a letter of recommendation from Alexandre Humboldt, an acknowledged expert on Latin America, who acted as guarantor for Jacques and his ambitions in education. Forced to remain in Uruguay, he opened a chemistry and mechanics class, though with little success. He then set up a meat preservation company. This may appear surprising but there are all kinds of twists and turns in the paths of exile. This project was also a failure. Next, he turned to daguerreotypes with Alfred Cosson, another exiled Frenchman. Jacques finally reached his original destination, Argentina, where he continued to have varied activities. First he became a surveyor, then he set up a sugar-cane business, but still without success. From Rosario in 1850, he wrote to General Urquiza, the director of the Argentine Federation, who awarded him a mission of scientific observation in the Chaco and geographical and economic research in the province of Tucuman. The mission never took place. He took part in expeditions to explore the Rio Salado and Chico areas, and wrote accounts of them under the title *Excursion dans l'intérieur de la confédération argentine: le Rio Salado et le Chaco*. This was published in two March 1857 issues of the *Revue de Paris*, a magazine edited at the time by Maxime Ducamp (Belloni 1999: 195-205). He described the geography of the region, trying to convince his readers that this country could welcome those oppressed by poverty in Europe. Initially this invitation corresponded to Jacques' militant social project, but he seems to have adopted, without much hesitation, the objectives of the Argentine authorities linking immigration with the eviction and extermination of the Indians. Was he aware that he was taking part in this crusade against the Indians of the Chaco, by pushing back the frontiers of the province? It is difficult to decide, without making an anachronistic judgement. Ribeyrolles and Frond were faced with the same realities when preparing *Le Brésil pittoresque*, and their album illustrated with lithographs made from Victor Frond's photographs also ended with an appeal to Europeans to colonize the country.

Amédée Jacques seems to have abandoned his educational projects and to have become integrated. With his family, he bought land along the Rio Salado. His job as a scientific assistant, his work and his publications soon won him a certain local notoriety and he was welcomed into the best families. He settled down in Tucuman where the new governor of the province entrusted him with the task of setting up the *Cursus Studiorum* of the San Miguel College in April 1858. Jacques announced the curriculum, giving pride of place to natural science and to languages, which he considered indispensable to teaching in a new country. Jacques undertook numerous initiatives in this town of eight thousand inhabitants: he set up a public library, and planned a provincial museum.

The governor, having meanwhile been promoted to Vice-President of the Confederation, was able to get Jacques transferred to Buenos Aires. In 1862, he was appointed director of studies in the capital's national college, realizing his dream too late in his life, since he died soon afterwards. As his biographer Patrick Vermeren shows, Amédée Jacques is now a legendary figure in the history of promotion through education in Argentina. His action linked a European political and educational project with the South American elite's desire to "push back the frontiers of barbarity" by populating their country with Europeans. Apart from the particular case of Amédée Jacques, French exiles settled in the French "colonies" in Montevideo and Mexico. In 1900, the French colony in Montevideo had twelve thousand members, out of a total population of two hundred and fifty thousand inhabitants.

Elisée Reclus's discovery of the New World is better known. He observed American society, particularly in the South. His judgement of the United States was severe, as in a passage written to his brother in 1855: "It's a big auction room where everything is for sale—slaves, and even their owners, votes and honour, the Bible and men's consciences. Everything goes to the highest bidder" (1911: 91-92). His interest in geography in particular grew, and a good knowledge of the field seemed indispensable to him:

> Seeing the land is to study it, as far as I'm concerned. My only serious

> research work has been on geography and I believe that it is much better to observe nature in the raw rather than to imagine it when sitting at home. No description however fine can be true, for it cannot reproduce the life of the landscape, the water running through it, the rustling leaves, the singing birds, the perfume of the flowers and the changing shapes of the clouds; to know it, you have to see it. (1911: 109)

Geography is an adventure, in this case involving the conquest not of a territory but of the land. Elisée Reclus's accounts mix reflections on the landscapes with the expression of his hope of settling there permanently:

> Tired of waiting for old Chassaigne, I've gone ahead with his son to explore the Sierra and to decide where we will plant our first banana trees. I've found a charming spot whose beauty will contribute considerably to our happiness. There is everything you could imagine: vast grassy hilltops, blocks of rock scattered along the riverbeds, untouched forests climbing up to the top of high mountains, green scenery sloping down an avenue of peaks to the sea, and so many charming little corners hidden beneath leaves on the banks of cool streams! Who needs the Batignolles or even the pré des Catalans? All that is missing is you and I and the first blow struck with the pick announcing man's domination. (1911: 134. Riobacha, October 1855)

Like so many other projects, that particular adventure failed. Elisée Reclus gave up for good his agricultural projects, writing to his mother:

> I have tried several times to go into farming seriously, and nothing would be more pleasing to me than to realize my lifelong ambition. But (for there is a but) would I be perfectly free to cultivate the land as I wish, and who would lend me the capital to undertake experiments that my own uncle and grandmother would no doubt esteem to be acts of folly? [...] I prefer to postpone the realization of my dream." (1911: 164)

The great adventure of mobility

Agricultural adventure in America did not always end in failure, but success depended on rejecting such wild areas and on better integrating into American agriculture. Although the experiences of these two intellectuals are not necessarily representative of the diversity of the experiences of migrants, they do reveal ideas constantly associated with the New World and with the great adventure of mobility. In conclusion, there are multiple interpretations of different forms of mobility, during this pivotal period of the mid-nineteenth century, marked by legacies—both older and more recent—of the travels of the elite, and by new forms made possible by the development of new modes of transport. Outside France French exiles, involuntary yet curious mediators, participated to a greater or lesser extent in all these new adventures, by observing and by taking up their pens.

Bibliography and References

AGULHON Maurice (1981) "Peut-on lire en historien *L'Éducation sentimentale*?" pp. 35-41 in *Histoire et langage dans "L'Éducation sentimentale"*, Paris: SEDES-CDU.

ARAGO Etienne (1960) *Une Voix de l'exil*, Geneva: Blanchard et Rive (first edition 1860).

BELLONI Estella (1999) "Excursion dans l'intérieur, Amédée Jacques," pp. 195-205 in *Le Voyage dans le monde ibérique et ibéro-americain*, Saint Etienne: Presses Universitaires de Saint Etienne.

BERTRAND Gilles (2002) "Le cosmopolitisme à l'épreuve de la Révolution française. Pratiques aristocratiques et bouleversements des idéaux chez les voyageurs émigrés français en Italie," pp. 101-114 in R. Chagny (ed.), *La Révolution française: idéaux, singularités, influences*, Grenoble: Presses Universitaires de Grenoble.

BLANC Louis (2001) *Lettres d'Angleterre (1861-1865). Choisies, commentées et annotées par Gilbert Bonifas et Martine Faraut*, Paris: L'Harmattan.

COEURDEROY E. (1991) *Jours d'exil*, Paris: Canevas éditeur (first edition 1854).

CORDILLOT M. (2001) "L'utopie en Amérique, Réunion (Texas)," pp. 225-242 in Michele Riot-Sarcey (ed.), *L'Utopie en questions*, Paris: Presses Universitaires de Vincennes.

FOUCRIER Annick (1999) *Le Rêve californien. Migrants français sur la côte Pacifique, XVIIIe-XXe siècles*, Paris: Belin.

DESCHANEL Emile (1856) "Le cimetière de Spa," first published 1st October 1856 in *L'Indépendance belge*; republished pp. 251-259 in *A pied et en wagon*, Paris: Hachette, 1862.

ESQUIROS Alphonse (1859) *La Néerlande et la vie hollandaise*, Paris: Lévy frères.

ESQUIROS Alphonse (1864) *L'Angleterre avant les hommes, le quinzième déluge ou 40.000 squelettes humains antédiluviens...*, Paris: Passard.

ESQUIROS Alphonse (1867) *Itinéraire descriptif et historique de la Grande-Bretagne et de l'Irlande*, Paris: Hachette (les guides Joanne).

FLAUBERT Gustave (1999) *L'Éducation sentimentale*, Paris: GF

Flammarion (first edition 1869).
GUYOT Alain & MASSOL Chantal (2003) *Voyager en France au temps du romantisme. Poétique, esthétique, idéologie*, Grenoble: ELLUG (Éditions Littéraires et Linguistiques de l'Université de Grenoble).
LOEWE J-M. (1851) *Lettres d'Angleterre*, Paris: Kugelmann.
HANCOCK Claire (2005) *Paris et Londres au XIXe siècle*, Paris: CNRS Éditions.
NEEFS Jacques (2004) "Flaubert, sous Napoléon III," pp. 259-267 in S. Aprile *et al.* (eds.), *Comment meurt une république, autour du 2 décembre 1851*, Actes du colloque de Lyon (Société d'histoire de la révolution de 1848 et des révolutions du XIXe siècle), Paris: Créaphis.
—. *Paris-Guide* (1983 reprint) Paris: La Découverte.
RECLUS Elisée (1911) *Correspondance*, Paris: Schleicher Frères/A. Costes, volume I (décembre 1850-mai 1870).
SAMINDAYAR-PERRIN Corinne (2000) "Romanesque et reportage dans *La rue à Londres*," pp. 30-45 in *Les Amis de Jules Vallès*, December 2000.
SAVY Nicole (1997) *Victor Hugo, voyageur de l'Europe, essai sur les textes de voyage et leurs enjeux*, Brussels: Éditions Labor ("Archives du futur").
STAËL Mme de (1999) *Corinne, ou l'Italie*, Paris: Folio (first edition 1807).
STAËL Mme de (1996) *Dix ans d'exil*, Paris: Fayard (first edition 1821).
TOULOTTE Muriel (1993) *Etienne Arago 1802-1892: une vie, un siècle. Préface de Jean Tulard. Suivi de la biographie de la famille Arago par Lucie Laugier*, Perpignan: Les Publications de l'Olivier.
VAN DER LINDEN Jacques (1948) *Alphonse Esquiros: de la bohême romantique à la république sociale*, Paris: Nizet.
VERMEREN Patrice (2001) *"Le rêve démocratique de la philosophie d'une rive à l'autre de l'Atlantique," suivi de "Essai de philosophie populaire par Amédée Jacques"*, Paris: L'Harmattan.
ZIELONKA A. (1990) *Alphonse Esquiros, Choix de lettres*, Paris & Geneva: Champion-Slatkine.

CHAPTER FOUR

EMIGRANT LETTERS IN THE SCOTTISH HIGHLANDS PRESS (1846-1854)

CHRISTIAN AUER

On February 28th 1850 the *Inverness Courier*, the newspaper that recorded the economic and social changes which marked the history of the Highlands of Scotland in the nineteenth century, published a letter describing the arrival in Montreal of a group of Scottish emigrants:

> They arrived in Montreal in perfect health, after a quick and pleasant passage; the greater number having remained among their relatives in that neighbourhood, who received them with the greatest kindness, and whose circumstances they represent as highly prosperous. ("Letters from Emigrants", 28 February 1850)

In May of the same year, the paper published a letter written by a Highlander who had also chosen to emigrate to Canada:

> I have seen nothing yet which I do not like. […] We frequently heard in the old country that the people here were destitute of clothing: this is not the case; they live comfortably in every respect. They have, in particular, a great advantage over those in Scotland in the large, clean and comfortable houses they possess. I hear that some of those who came out last summer are discontented, but I believe the fault lies with themselves. I am fully satisfied with my lot, and glad that I undertook the voyage. ("Letters from Emigrants", 16 May 1850)

In the 1850s, the *Courier* published a large number of letters of a similar content, which all explained the countless advantages of emigration and the satisfaction of the emigrants. Can we therefore conclude that conditions on the transatlantic crossings were perfect, that emigrants met with a warm welcome and that emigration was entirely without problems? This chapter will attempt to answer these questions by examining the dozens of emigrant letters that were published in the pages of the *Inverness Courier* from the second half of the 1840s onwards, considering both their content and their function, and will situate these letters in the context of a more comprehensive strategy.

By the middle of the nineteenth century, emigration was not a new phenomenon in Scotland. It has been estimated that around one hundred thousand Scots left their country in the seventeenth century, and that eighty thousand people emigrated in the course of the decades that followed the battle of Culloden in 1746 (Duchein 1998: 319, 381). However, at the end of the eighteenth century the flow of emigrants was checked: most landlords vehemently opposed emigration since they feared that it would cut off the supply of cheap labour and thus slow down the movement of modernization that had begun to spread in the Highlands. Landlords tried to persuade potential emigrants that the voyage to America or to Australia was fraught with danger, and that when they arrived in what they imagined to be the promised land they would face countless difficulties. This strategy of deterrence proved unsuccessful and Highland landlords became more and more convinced that only government measures could curb the exodus that they saw as detrimental to the economic growth of the region. Their efforts were eventually successful when, in June 1803, Parliament passed the Passenger Vessels Act, which dramatically increased the price of transatlantic crossings.

A change in strategy

Only in the 1820s, when the economic situation deteriorated, mainly because of the spectacular fall in the price of kelp and cattle that coincided with the return of the thousands of Highlanders who had fought in the Napoleonic wars, did the ruling classes of the Highlands begin to consider that emigration could solve the problem of overpopulation. Landlords then put increasing pressure on the government to set up an emigration scheme, and this led to the rescinding, in 1827, of the restrictions on emigration that had existed since the 1803 Act. The Highlander, whose presence had been essential twenty years before to cater for the needs of a growing economy, had become an outcast or, in the words of those who favoured economic rationalization, "redundant".

In the following two decades, the economic situation of the Highlands continued to deteriorate. At the end of 1846, the potato blight came to the Highlands and the government was obliged to intervene in favour of the thousands of peasants who were threatened by an unprecedented famine. In 1851, when the *Central Board of Management of the Fund for the*

Relief of the Destitute Inhabitants of the Highlands—created four years earlier—was wound up, landlords were left to support their peasants, further impoverished by several consecutive years of disastrous harvests. Parliament reacted rapidly by passing, on July 22nd 1851, the *Emigration Advances Act* that enabled landlords to obtain loans at reduced rates to help them finance emigrants' expenses. Under the pressure of Highland landlords who considered that largescale emigration had become inevitable because of the state of utter destitution of a large part of the population, the *Highland and Island Emigration Society* was created in 1852, its remit being to provide financial help to those of the landlords who promised to pay one third of the travel costs of potential emigrants. One landlord went as far as to say that "it would be absolute insanity not to take advantage of the present opportunity of getting rid of our surplus population" (quoted in Devine 1988: 250). It is thus not surprising that, from the end of the 1840s onwards, the national and regional press devoted more and more articles to emigration, an issue that had become of prime importance to the whole of the British population.

By the middle of the nineteenth century the press, both national and regional, had established itself as an essential component of British democracy. According to Robert McNair Wilson Cowan, the author of a study of the Scottish press in the first half of the nineteenth century, "the newspaper in Scotland rose to real power in the half-century after Waterloo" (1986: preface). The following comment of the *Inverness Courier*, faithful spokesman of the Scottish landowners, amply demonstrates that the press itself was aware of its power and responsibility: "We have come to a time when the power of the press in public opinion is felt, and its position as one of the necessary social institutions recognized" (25 May 1847).

From the end of the 1840s onwards the Inverness press, and more particularly the *Inverness Courier*, gave more and more space to emigrant letters. The *Courier*'s edition of June 2, 1853, for example, devoted three full columns to six different letters, all written by Highlanders that had emigrated to Canada. The following week, realizing that its readers might lose interest in the question, the *Courier* wrote that "we have received some more of the Highland emigrants letters from Australia, but too large a supply may surfeit our readers. We shall, however, look over them and select facts that may be useful for intending emigrants" ("Hard work at the diggings", 9 June 1853). The last sentence shows that the paper was fully aware of the part it could play in informing potential emigrants.

In the middle of the nineteenth century, letter-writing was a fundamental aspect of human life, be it in the professional, social or domestic spheres, letters being the only means to establish a form of communication with distant correspondents. In the context of emigration, letters abolished time and distance and transformed absence into presence, albeit a fictitious or symbolic one. Apart from providing vital sources of knowledge for prospective emigrants, letters also served to link two worlds, the new and the old. Letters as featured in newspapers had gone through an initial filtering process: they obviously did not appear in their original manuscript form, and would be edited to make them more readable. So it is legitimate to question the authenticity of these documents. Did the editorial staff of the paper make merely formal changes, or did they decide to undertake major changes as regards content, thus presenting a modified version of the original documents? As the passage quoted above explicitly indicates, the *Inverness Courier* assumed the right to publish only letters or extracts of letters that were deemed to be of use to prospective emigrants.

Emigrant letters were generally written in a very basic style, with short paratactic sentences, as in the following example: "I went to work next morning, but could not eat breakfast. I was fairly beat, every inch of my body was suffering. I could hardly touch it without giving pain. I thought I was in for a fever" ("The ship *Countess of Cawdor*", 6 April 1854). Some letters were written in a more elaborate style, as was the case of one published by a resident of Hamilton (Ontario): "I should be delighted to hear that your commissioners or agents for the Highland poor were exerting their influence and means to send out a large number of emigrants to this country. […] The average wages will be about 3s. sterling per day—a better prospect than living by public subscriptions and relief fund" ("Letter from Canada", 27 March 1851).

Recurrent themes

The same themes tend to recur from one letter to another. Letters generally started by mentioning that the crossing had been uneventful: "After a pleasant passage of three and a half months, we arrived in safety. […] Let intending emigrants not be frightened for the long voyage; for I have experienced worse weather on the north coast of Scotland than after leaving the English Channel" ("Emigration to Australia", 11 November 1846). Emigrants would often mention the relatives or friends that had left with them: "I met three countrymen from the Highlands. […] They have all done well at the diggings and I expect you will see some of them home shortly with their pockets well lined with gold" ("Letter from Australia", 2 September 1852). They often drew comparisons between their native land

and the countries or regions that had welcomed them: "What a difference between this country and Scotland! Here we have plenty of everything, […] and at home you can scarcely get a living" (*ibid.*). The country was magnificent, the climate much better than in the Highlands, the grass of better quality, the firewood plentiful, the cattle well fed and well looked after, and there was land as far as the eye could see: "In Canada there is room and employment for your redundant population. There are millions upon millions of acres of rich, uncultivated land extending to the very outskirts of creation" ("Letters from Emigrants", 16 May 1850). All in all there was no reason why the Highlander should insist on staying in his homeland. Indeed emigrants could not understand their fellow countrymen's reluctance to leave, witness the following letter in the *Inverness Journal* (created in 1807, upholding ideas similar to those of its rival the *Courier*): "It is no less a wonder than a pity, that you and some of your acquaintances would not emigrate to this part of the world" ("South Australia", 31 March 1848). Some emigrants added a spiritual dimension, suggesting a divine inspiration was showing Highlanders the path to follow: "Dear friends, you do really make me angry and vexed against you, because of your slothfulness of leaving a country where you see the hand of the Almighty turned against it, especially as He has opened a door to a better country" (*The Inverness Courier*, "Letter from an emigrant", 7 November 1850). Some of the letters were tinged with irony: "But I see it is complete nonsense for me to be advising you to come here. You would rather starve on the rocks there" ("Letter from Australia", 9 January 1851).

Although the foundations of the ancient clan structure had all but disappeared by the middle of the nineteenth century, Highland peasants were still at the mercy of those who owned the land and who exercised an almost absolute power over them. Thus it is hardly surprising that emigrants seemed almost obsessed by the possibility of attaining independence within a few years. The *Inverness Courier* again:

> The correspondent of the *Daily Mail* writes as follows: By a recent account of Australia, we learn that among those who have been highly successful at the digging are several young men natives of the Isle of Skye. […] On the theme, the richness and fertility of the country, they dwell with strong emphasis, describing it as a paradise in comparison to the unfruitful moors of their native Island; while the craving claims of the factor, and the espionage of the scion ground officer, are matters unheard of. ("Skye emigrants to Australia," 13 July 1854)

Emigrants also seemed to be fascinated by the wages in the colonies:

"Tradesmen will do remarkably here – carpenters are getting 20s. per day; blacksmiths charge 30s. for putting a new set of shoes on a horse; shoemakers charge 40s. for a pair of Blucher boots; cartwrights ask £40 for a cart" (*Ibid.*). For destitute peasants, heavily in debt and at the mercy of a climate that could wipe out the fruits of their labour, letters such as these must have been a big incentive to emigrate. Some emigrants prided themselves on easily being able to find jobs for their fellow countrymen. A Highlander who had emigrated to Australia indicated that the two hundred people that had left with him had all managed to find a job in less than three days. But only those who were ready to work hard were likely to succeed, this reservation appearing as a leitmotif in most of the letters: "It [Canada] is a good country for industrious well-working men and women" ("Letters from Emigrants", 28 February 1850). Another emigrant to Australia remarked that "it is hardworking emigrants that succeed best" ("Hard work at the diggings", 9 June 1853). Victorian society venerated work, loathed indolence and laziness and scathingly condemned the pariahs of the Highlands who took advantage of the generosity of the British population. It was only thanks to the generous support of their southern neighbours, whether Lowlanders or English, that the Highlanders could rid themselves of their congenital laziness and progress towards civilization. The *Inverness Courier* adhered to this postulate of the Highlander's laziness, although it did explain that the lack of attention and neglect on the part of landlords was one of its causes. Yet for the *Courier*, as soon as the emigrant boarded the boat that was to take him to his new destination, he underwent a spectacular metamorphosis from indolent, lazy and apathetic peasant to hardworking emigrant. The *Courier* was not in the least perturbed by this blatant contradiction. For example a correspondent presented as a "gentleman" praised the Highlanders' aptitude for hard work: "The Highlanders in every settled part of this vast continent turn out very successful colonists. For industry, perseverance, and prudence they rank second to none, and for powers of endurance have few equals" ("Letter from Australia", 16 October 1851).

The role of the landlords

How did these letters reach the newspaper, and what was the identity of those who wrote to the paper? Some of the letters were sent by the correspondents themselves, whereas others were forwarded by the landowners or their factors. It is therefore no surprise to find in most of these texts the prevailing views of landed elites. At the end of 1847, the *Inverness Journal* published a letter that had been forwarded by James

Matheson, the owner of Lewis, an island in the Outer Hebrides. The author of the letter, an emigrant to Australia who was of "irreproachable morality" and was particularly sensitive to the Highlanders' welfare, detailed all the advantages of emigration and did not forget to congratulate Highland landlords for their generosity: "Doubtless the great exertions made by Highland proprietors, to afford temporary relief, will be followed by extensive emigration" ("Emigration", 24 December 1847). The author of the letter invited Highlanders to emigrate to Australia, a continent that was short of workers: "Thousands of our Highland population, men, women and children, would find immediate and respectable employment here, and in the neighbouring colonies". The modern reader, however, cannot fail to notice the qualification "they [the Highlanders] must, of course, be of good working age—say, from 10 to 40 years." At the beginning of 1850, the *Inverness Courier* published a letter that had been forwarded by the factor of Lord Macdonald, one of the biggest landlords in the Highlands. The author of the letter, a person "intimately acquainted with the facts", told Lord Macdonald about a group of peasants that had left his estate. He then went on to justify emigration and denounced those who dared criticize a policy whose sole aim was to set the Highlander on the road to progress:

> These accounts, the truth of which cannot be questioned, are very satisfactory, and fully bear out the views of those who regard emigration not only as a necessary adjunct to any measures that may be adopted for permanently improving the condition of the Highlander at home, but also as a direct means of ameliorating the position of the emigrants themselves; and ought to put an end to the clamour which has been raised against the removal of our surplus population. ("Letters from Emigrants", 28 February 1850)

Such letters provided the *Courier* with the opportunity to remind its readers that Highland landlords, far from being the greedy oppressors depicted by the radical press, were generous and benevolent. For example:

> Two interesting letters from an emigrant, who left Glengarry for Australia early in 1848, have been sent to us by Mr Lathan, factor on the estate of Glengarry, who in communicating them, makes the following remark: "Sir, I enclose two letters from Australia, written by a young man who left Glengarry 18 months ago. I may remind your readers that Lord Ward's liberality and kindliness are well known." ("Glengarry letters from an emigrant", 8 November 1849)

The paper regularly published letters corroborating its strategy, but emigrant letters were just one aspect of the *Courier*'s propaganda. It would also reproduce articles originally published in newspapers in the colonies that supported its views. The paper would sometimes publish extracts from the numerous lectures on emigration that were organized all over Scotland at that time. There were also many advertisements for the ships that crossed the Atlantic. Ship-owners vied with one another to persuade emigrants: "This noble Ship (Africa), now on her first voyage, is the largest single-deck Vessel in the Merchant Service, presenting to the eye of the spectator a splendid piece of naval architecture" (*The Inverness Courier*, 21 October 1852). Advertisements would always insist on the following points: the speed of the ship, the comfort of passengers, the skill of the captain and of his crew and abiding by safety rules. The advertisements usually added that the ship had obtained the approval of the emigration services and of its inspectors: "the whole arrangements for dietary and sanitary purposes will be under the inspection of Captain C. Keele, Her Majesty's Emigration Officer" (*Ibid.*).

The positive message

At the core of the *Inverness Courier*'s strategy lay the leaders that were the main medium for the positive message about emigration. Week after week the same themes were taken up: the overpopulation of the Highlands, the voluntary emigration of the peasants or the promise of a better quality of life. When the *Courier* reported the departure of a group of emigrants, it usually stressed the fact that they had taken the decision themselves, as for example in the following article relating the departure of a group from the island of Lewis: "The people go away quietly, and are most anxious to leave, offering to sell their clothes, or to do anything to get away" ("Emigration", 22 August 1849). The *Courier* never missed an opportunity to assert that emigrants could rapidly provide for their families, a convincing argument for a people traditionally attached to family values:

> We advocate family emigration, because in Canada there are fertile lands by noble lakes and rivers—lands without a labourer of which the emigrant, by his own exertions may become not tenant only but owner—where he may sit under the shadow of his own trees, and see a race rise around him, comfortable, happy, and independent. If this is not a change for the better, from miserable cabins more wretched than an Indian wigwam—from valleys subject to recurring famine—from patches of high ground held at high rent and under perpetual fear from ejection for long accumulating arrears—if that freedom is not preferable to this slavery, we

> want altogether the perception of that nobler feeling which dignifies man—the spirit of independence. ("The threatened destitution", 28 November 1850)

The debate focused not only on the desirability of emigration, but also on the form it should take. As early as 1847 the *Courier* had stressed the necessity of encouraging emigrants to leave with their families. The paper even thought that the displacement of entire villages should be favoured above any other form of emigration: "Such villages should be placed in the vicinity of some of the great public works that are going on, or of some of the projected railroads, upon which the emigrants might find work. Each village should consist of from 100 to 200 cottages or log-houses. [...] There should be a church, and a house for the clergyman." ("Emigration—The Highlands", 27 April 1847).

A strategy of persuasion?

The strategy of the landed elites, which the *Inverness Courier* supported, apparently bore fruit since between 1846 and 1857 at least sixteen thousand Highlanders emigrated, with assistance from landowners and the Highland and Island Emigration Society, two thousand six hundred people emigrating to Australia in 1852 alone (Devine 1988: 201). As we have already remarked, since the letters went through the filter of publication, they may have lost something of their authenticity. Whilst they were written by real and authentic emigrants, of course the *Inverness Courier* selected the letters whose content corresponded to its ideas and reinforced its message. The proselytizing emigrant fitted perfectly into the paper's scheme of persuasion.

There is however ample evidence contradicting the *Courier*'s positive and optimistic view on emigration. One example illustrates this point, an extract of an article published in *The Times* which stressed the inhuman conditions emigrants were subjected to:

> The emigrant is shewn a berth, a shelf [...] in a noisome dungeon [...] airless and lightless, in which several hundreds of both sexes and all ages are stowed away, on shelves [...] still reeking from the ineradicable stench left by the emigrants on the last voyage... He finds that cleanliness is impossible, that no attempt is made to purify the reeking den in which he has been thrust... After a few days have been spent in the pestilential atmosphere created by the festering mass of squalid humanity imprisoned between the damp and steaming decks, the scourge bursts out and to the miseries of filth, foul air and darkness is added the Cholera. (Cited in Prebble 1963: 197)

Another element to be considered is language: only those who could express themselves in English could write letters likely to be published in a newspaper written in English only, but in the middle of the nineteenth century the Highlanders of Scotland were predominantly Gaelic speakers and the level of literacy was much lower than in other parts of Scotland (Withers 1988: 146). According to several reports dating from the beginning of the nineteenth century, a significant number of Highlanders could neither read nor write ("Moral Statistics..." 1826; "Second Educational Statistics..." 1834). The institution created in 1847 to help the destitute inhabitants of the Highlands and Islands gave precise figures for literacy on the Isle of Skye: "In Skye out of a population supposed to be now 27,000, there are only 3,166 who can read and 1,254 who can write" (*The Inverness Courier* "The last report of the Highland Destitution Board ", 27 March 1851). In January 1852 the Education Committee of the Church of Scotland carried out a survey in the twelve parishes of Lochcarron, a district in the north-west of Scotland. According to the results three quarters of the pupils went to school for only half the year. The same survey indicated that in one of the parishes half of the young people aged between thirteen and eighteen could read Gaelic but none of them could read English: "Beyond the signing of their names, all writing of English is hardly worth mentioning" (*The Inverness Courier*, "State of Education in the West Highlands", 11 November 1852). We can conclude that only a small fraction of the Highland population could write in English. Thus the letters published by the press came from the most literate part of the community, those who had had access to some form of education, those who were most likely to share the Highland elites' ideas even if, as we have noted, the basic style of the texts showed that members of the peasantry also wrote. Letters written in Gaelic would be of little interest for the *Inverness Courier*, since the paper thought that Gaelic represented a serious impediment to the economic development of the Highlands.

Thus it appears that the numerous emigrant letters published in the *Inverness Courier* around the 1850s supported or illustrated the ideas of the Highland landlords. Many of these texts seem to have been diverted from their primary function—the communication of news originally meant to be read within the private sphere—to be included in a more comprehensive strategy whose aims were to present emigration as a voluntary choice and to describe it very positively, without any mention at all of the difficulties and hardships the emigrants faced.

Bibliography and References

COWAN R.M.W. (1946) *The Newspaper in Scotland, a Study of its First Expansion, 1815-1860*, Glasgow: G. Outram & C°.

DEVINE T. M. (1988) *The Great Highland Famine*, Edinburgh: John Donald.

DEVINE, T.M. (1993) *Scottish Emigration and Scottish Society*, Edinburgh: John Donald.

DUCHEIN M. (1998) *Histoire de l'Ecosse*, Paris: Fayard.

HUNTER, J. (1976) *The Making of the Crofting Community*, Edinburgh: John Donald.

HUNTER, J. (1995) *A Dance Called America*, Edinburgh: Mainstream Publishing Company.

—. *Moral Statistics of the Highlands and Islands of Scotland, compiled from returns received by the Inverness Society for the Education of the Poor in the Highlands*. (1826) Inverness.

PREBBLE J. (1969) *The Highland Clearances*, Harmondsworth: Penguin.

—. *Second Educational Statistics of the Highlands and Islands of Scotland, 1833*. (1834) Edinburgh.

RICHARDS, E. (1982-1985) *A History of the Highland Clearances*, 2 vols., London: Croom Helm.

WITHERS C.W.J. (1988) *Gaelic Scotland: The Transformation of a Culture Region*, London: Routledge.

CHAPTER FIVE

THE EMERGENCE OF CAPRI AS A TOURIST CENTRE AT THE TURN OF THE CENTURY

PATRICIA MARCOZ

At the beginning of the nineteenth century, Capri was not very prominent in French travel literature. It seemed to have a three-fold stereotyped identity: stories of Tiberius the "Capri goat", with his cave and his debaucheries, memories of the invasion of Capri by the French army in 1808, and the hackneyed vision of a paradise island beginning with the *Grotta Azzurra*, rediscovered in 1826 by a German (Kopisch 1838). In the *Dictionnaire géographique et descriptif de l'Italie* by Jacques Barzilay, the island was described as a "place of pleasures [...] covered with delightful gardens" (1823: 60). Capri was to evolve from this three-fold identity towards a paradoxical Hell-Paradise duality. The lack of visibility of Capri in French travel literature stemmed from three main causes: difficult access (regular Naples-Capri connections were not established before the mid-nineteenth century), sudden climatic variations which frightened travellers (many stories underlined the storms which made it impossible to get back to the mainland), and the fact that this fortified island in the gulf of Naples did not seem to encourage approaches. This chapter focuses on a period beginning in the 1860s, when the first foreign residents arrived, and ending in the early years of the twentieth century.

An island paradise

Capri entered the age of tourism mainly due to the elaboration, diffusion and exploitation of an image as an island utopia, based on the above-mentioned *Grotta Azzurra* and Tiberius. These stereotypes were partly founded on objective realities. Within the overall vision of an island paradise, the *Grotta Azzurra* was one of the catalysts of mass tourism on Capri. Mentioned in French travel literature since the 1830s, it became prominent in French travel books in the 1860s, a decade which corresponded to an increase in the volume of visitors to Capri:

> Whoever goes to Capri absolutely must visit the *Grotto Azzurra*; for it is included in the programme, and the boat takes you directly there. This Cave, which all the Guidebooks call *the fairytale cave of the kingdom of Naples* (I do not know why), stands in the steep cliff facing the gulf. (Cordier 1866: 198)

By 1899, a bibliography with commentary dedicated thirty pages to Capri, and recorded many books published in Italian, French, English and German at the end of the nineteenth century (Furchheim 1899). This paradise was painted by the many artists who came to Capri in the 1880s for the "hundreds of views to be found [...] in this limited space" (Des Houx 1887: 258). These artists chose the Pagano Hotel as their head-quarters, and it became a place where there was not "a door panel that wasn't covered with a sketch by a famous painter, or a painter soon to become famous" (Puaux 1872: 68). The sunny climate also attracted the inhabitants of northern countries recovering from illness. Around 1860, Dr. Clark built a sanatorium, the Quisisana, for people suffering from rheumatism and pulmonary infections. It became a hotel, changed ownership, was extended and attracted wealthy guests. This corroborates the image of an island congenial to rest and oblivion.

Some travellers, disappointed by Capri and the *Grotta Azzurra,* criticized the paradise *cliché*, for example Eugène Facieu, who "rushed through the town of Capri, which offers nothing remarkable" (1880: 10), or Alphonse Cordier who wrote, of the *Grotta Azzurra*:

> The waters of this sea cave are a little more azure than those which wash the rocks around the island; but the light which penetrates them, a single beam coming through a narrow opening under the ground, produces an optical effect similar to that of a *camera obscura*, and then reflects in celestial hues on the walls of the cave which are more prominent than others. That is all there is to this marvel, the famous fairyland *Grotta Azzurra*; and if you add to it the spectacle of the urchin who will swim there for 50 centimes and show a *white* body and a *black* head, you will have beheld everything extraordinary which can be seen in the said cave. (Cordier 1866: 199)

In this lost paradise the Capriote was a figure of otherness, part of the myth of Capri, the archetype of the young beggar or primitive man. The local fishermen, leading a quiet life before the age of tourism, were a motif of local colour appreciated by French sculptors and writers, who noted their poverty. Whilst some complained of being harassed by beggars, others saw this as a picturesque feature:

> On the deck, a cosmopolitan crowd is milling about and boats are constantly bringing new travellers. On other boats, the famous Neapolitan divers, wearing bathing suits, call out loudly to catch the foreigners' attention: "Soldi, Signori!". [...] The Germans and the British greatly enjoy this little game, but it is the French who generally throw their coins. (Gochet 1914: 198-9)

Beggars appear to have been a recent phenomenon, unknown to the traveller of the 1830s who thought that in Capri, contrary to what happened in Naples, "he can look and enjoy the view without being saddened, disgusted, or harassed by the infinite poverty, infirmities and cries of beggars" (Le Mercher de Longpré 1835: 219). The image of the beggar followed that of the "noble savage" of the eighteenth century, as in *Le Voyageur françois*, which described the islanders as "frank and generous, ready to render their services in every possible way, and even to anticipate one's desires. Such were men at the beginning of times" (*Le Voyageur...* 1781: 361).

The isle of debauchery

Capri's reputation for sexual permissiveness had several causes. Firstly, travellers would arrive carrying Suetonius's chapter on the Roman Emperor Tiberius:

> Bevies of girls and young men, whom [Tiberius] had collected from all over the Empire as adepts in unnatural practices, and known as *spintriae*, would perform before him in groups of three [...]. He furthermore devised little nooks of lechery in the woods and glades of the island, and had boys and girls dressed up as Pans and nymphs posted in front of caverns or grottoes; so that the island was now openly and generally called 'Caprinium', because of his goatish antics. (Suetonius: 131)

French decadent literature enthused over the debauched emperor: in 1886, Capri was one of the "love islands" with which Catulle Mendès regaled his female readers in an illustrated volume (1886: 37-40). A visit to the ruins of the Villa Jovis became a must for tourists on Capri, and the Tiberius "brand name" was commercially exploited: "ruins, hotels, taverns, all bear the name of the tyrant" (Des Houx 1887: 245). Robert de Flers relates the conversation of an innkeeper: "Mind you, our Tiberius is a blessing; thanks to him we can pay our taxes, and God knows they are steep!" (1896: 63). If the reality of Tiberius's debaucheries as relayed by Suetonius were questioned by some travellers in the eighteenth century, their impact remained crucial and could not be ignored.

Secondly, we can note the impact of Neapolitan homosexual prostitution, which is mentioned for example in the novels by Achille Essebac, who describes Naples as a place of easy encounters with young *ragazzi*, with Capri as a kind of annex (1898: 116). Photographs also began to circulate for European customers, for example Plüschow and Gloeden's pictures of naked adolescent boys. Thirdly, Capri attracted many homosexuals who found escape from more repressive penal codes (like the English and German ones), for the new penal code for unified Italy—the Zanardelli Code, 1887—did not consider homosexuality as an offence. The French writer Jacques d'Adelswärd-Fersen, sentenced for enticing under-age persons into debauchery in 1903 in Paris, settled on Capri two years later, looking for a "pagan" land to "restore" Greek pederasty. Three decades later, Willy described the island as the "home of the future homosexual international" (Willy 1927: 67-68).

All these elements contributed to the encoding of Capri as a place of sexual tourism, and by the beginning of the twentieth century its reputation was made in the French imagination.

The impact of tourism on Capri

At the beginning of the twentieth century, each visitor to Capri paid a tax which was shared between the municipality and the poor. Part of it was used for the creation of the Pro Capri Society, which gave information to tourists about visits, tariffs, transport, etc. (Money 1986: 94). The part granted to the poor helped to improve the locals' living standards. However, this improvement consisted essentially in the creation of employment. On the one hand, there were jobs catering for tourists, such as donkey-drivers, shops, inn-keepers, guides: "All the islanders know the history of Tiberius after Suetonius by heart and tell it to the uneducated foreigners" (Bellanger 1882: 246). On the other hand, there were jobs catering for residents: builders, models for painters, servants, shops.

The infrastructures created for foreign residents sometimes improved conditions for the locals (the paving of roads, for example). Transport to and from the island also improved: James Money mentions a Naples-Capri ferry "on Sundays and holidays in summer, sometimes on other days" by 1860 (1986: 32). By the 1880s, there was a daily service which took two hours, with musicians and pedlars soliciting tourists (Bellanger 1882: 244;

Money 1986: 44). Adequate harbour facilities were built at Marina Grande, which still is the major port of Capri. Such improvements helped the hotel industry: Antoine-Claude Valery mentioned two inns in the 1840s (nd: 173), in 1896 Baedeker counted five inns plus twelve hotels, including the above-mentioned Quisisana. The tourist season gradually extended: the first tourists came mainly in spring and autumn (Baedeker 1896); by the 1900s, the tourist season lasted almost the entire year, with a slight fall in summer (Money 1986: 62). By 1905, there were more than thirty thousand visitors per year and the circulation of so many tourists was putting pressure on this restricted and insular environment. But the municipality created facilities so that tourists could enjoy the scenery: "in the heart of the mountains, I find every hundred yards a small bench where tired tourists can sit and rest" (Lécolle 1908: 99).

The cosmopolitan colony of Capri

In the middle of the 19th century, *Le Magasin pittoresque* noted that "Capri is perhaps the one island in the Gulf where foreigners most extend their stay" (*Le Magasin pittoresque* volume 22: 93). Some travellers even settled permanently:

> Several lords, princes and marquesses, all with genuine titles, have sought to forget the world in Capri. They spend their days there far away from worries, business and politics. They have made themselves at home there for ever, under the most delicious climate in the world. They are quite content to relish no earthly pleasure other than that of the sight of faraway Vesuvius, the spectacle of the incomparable Gulf, the happiness of breathing clear and pure air which entices one into *far niente*. They bathe forever in the azure sky and sea. To enchant the loneliness of their retirement, they have chosen their partner from the beautiful, sun-tanned girls with blonde hair, black eyes, a Greek nose and shining teeth which the island produces in abundance, just as it produces the golden grape, the honey-tasting fig, the fragrant orange tree. They live, they love and they die on this God-blessed rock, big enough to shelter all the enchantments of a sensual life, and small enough for there to be no room for the troubles and miseries of social life. (Des Houx 1887: 246-247)

This was indeed the ideal of the French composer Jules Massenet (1912: 57): "To live in Capri, to work there, is existence in its ideal form, everything you could dream of." Putting this ideal into practice, many tourists settled for various periods of time, living isolated or, more usually, in linguistically homogeneous colonies, a kind of cosmopolitan macro-structure divided into several microstructures, British, German, French and

American colonies living apart yet interacting. Illustrating his social utopia, Henri Des Houx declared: "There is no concern for social distinctions on the island of Capri. There are neither peers, nor bourgeois, nor proletarians. Some own less than others, some more; but no-one is excluded as undeserving of the banquet of life" (1887: 248). In what Dieter Richter called "Capri-mondo" (1996: 111), rich migrants were joined by exiles seeking asylum. Yet each group had its own circles, like the *salon* of the Wolcott-Perrys at the Villa Torricella, where members of the American and British colonies would gather every Sunday afternoon (Money 1986: 78).

Interactions between the islanders and foreigners

The islanders were favourable to foreigners as long as they brought improved living standards by spending their money on the island and providing work for the locals. But even if the Capriotes felt that they were the "real natives who own property on the island, whose ancestors were born there, and who ask for nothing save to be allowed to go on with their work in peace" (Douglas 1934, cited by Money 1986: 59), they could not prevent the arrival of a number of labour migrants—Italian "adventurers" from the continent—who came to Capri attracted by the opportunities of the tourist industry. At the same time the islanders themselves participated in a counterflow of labour migration: "Most of the men were absent from the island for much of the year 'at sea, either coral-fishing, or employed in the coasting trade or on long voyages'" (Money 1986: 39). Interestingly enough the low number of local adult males was no obstacle to the development of the tourist industry by the natives and "their skill in exploiting the foreigner" (Money 1986: 39). As underlined by Robert de Flers, competition was already firmly established in 1896 between the two cities of the island, "Capri-Capulet" and "Anacapri-Montaigu", especially competition for "the exploitation of foreigners, [who were] easy game" (1896: 67).

The French poet Jacques d'Adelswärd-Fersen provides an interesting illustration of relations between the locals and the foreign colony. In the early years of the twentieth century, he was "the hero of all the residents" (Compton Mackenzie 1965: 184), living in "the finest villa on Capri" (Respighi 1977: 74). His first receptions were a great success and the Villa Lysis became an important social centre on the island. According to James Money, the inhabitants "welcomed the fact that he was building a sumptuous villa with local labour and spending money on the island" (1986: 92). But the good relations soon came to an end, firstly because some members of the colony wanted to disclose his past brushes with the law in France. On Capri he lived with a fifteen year old "private secretary", Nino Cesarini, along with an adolescent domestic servant, and rumours began to spread (Compton Mackenzie 1965: 184), the foreign residents siding with or against him: "A new class of foreign residents, having more money than was good for them and nothing whatever to do, broke into cantankerous little cliques [...] and made the place almost uninhabitable for those who refused to take sides with one or the other of them" (Douglas 1952: 6). While the colony was tearing itself apart over this scandal, the Villa Lysis was forbidden to young locals. Secondly, in 1909 a novel by d'Adelswärd aroused the fury of the foreign colony and the islanders. In *Et le feu s'éteignit sur la mer...*, the "Capri people" were presented as a heteroclite social cocktail: "Bankrupt bankers, corrupt lawyers, former Riviera croupiers, needy peers or newly rich bottle-washers mixed with virtuous old geese, unmarriageable girls or over-fervent admirers of Lesbos" (d'Adelswärd 1909: 107). Furthermore, d'Adelswärd-Fersen called for the purification of the island, "a land of murder, a land of vice and of lechery" (*Ibid.*: 231). According to Compton Mackenzie, every inhabitant and member of the colony was affronted by something in the novel (1998: 274), which contradicted the myth that residents tacitly agreed to respect when they settled. The Municipal Council protested officially on September 9th 1909, and condemned the writer for his offence against the host country (Archivio municipale di Capri 1909). Thirdly, Jacques d'Adelswärd-Fersen was responsible for a scantily clad pagan procession in a grotto, which caused a scandal on August 25th 1910 (Fiorani 2005: 83). After these episodes the French poet was forced to leave Italy, but he was back on Capri in March 1913 (Compton Mackenzie 1998: 298), staying there until his death in 1923. Having escaped from French justice, Jacques d'Adelswärd-Fersen lived his homosexuality openly on Capri, although on the island he found new judges in the shape of those he called the "gossips of Paradise" ("les concierges du paradis", d'Adelswärd 1909: 88). Marcella Leone de Andreis suggested that "his suicide [...] was welcomed on the island with a general sigh of relief" (2002: 208).

The heritage

Today the municipality of Capri stresses the heritage of the island's identity as a tourist centre from the 1860s to the 1900s, its fame promoted by all the visitors who have written about it and created it in the imagination, and also the residents to whom the Tourist Information

Centre of Capri now gives prominence. This period created a rich artistic corpus—visual and written—in which *romans à clé* respond to each other, especially novels by Norman Douglas, Compton Mackenzie, Jacques d'Adelswärd-Fersen or Axel Munthe. The corpus of the myth of Capri in French literature is even greater, and as yet unstudied. There is also an important architectural heritage, composed of the numerous villas built by foreigners, like d'Adelswärd's Villa Lysis and the Villa San Michele of Axel Munthe, the physician of the royal family of Sweden, which has been turned into a museum. There is also a cemetery where several residents are buried. Capri is currently restoring these places where the cosmopolitan presence is remembered: the restored villa of Jacques d'Adelswärd-Fersen was acquired in 2001 and is part of a planned circuit including the most beautiful villas of residents from the beginning of the twentieth century. Now there are plans to turn the Villa Lysis, where concerts and conferences are already given, into a museum.

Bibliography and References

—. Archivio municipale di Capri (1909) Decision n° 8232, September 9.

BAEDEKER Karl (1896) *Italie méridionale. Sicile, Sardaigne et excursions à Malte, Tunis et Corfou. Manuel du voyageur,* 11th edition, Leipzig: Karl Baedeker; Paris: Paul Olendorff.

BARZILAY Jacques (1823) *Dictionnaire géographique et descriptif de l'Italie, servant d'itinéraire et de guide aux étrangers*, Paris: Truchy.

BELLENGER Alfred (1882) *A travers l'Italie, Souvenirs de voyage*, Paris: A. Roger & F. Chernoviz.

COMPTON MACKENZIE Edward (1965) *My Life and Times*, London: Chatto and Windus.

COMPTON MACKENZIE Edward (1998) *Le Feu des vestales*, Paris: Payot (originally *Vestal Fire*, 1927).

CORDIER Alphonse (1866) *A travers la France, l'Italie, la Suisse et l'Espagne, 1865 et 1866*. Paris: J. Vermot.

D'ADELSWÄRD Jacques (1909) *Et le feu s'éteignit sur la mer...*, Paris: Albert Messein.

DE FLERS Robert (1896) *Vers l'Orient*, Paris: Flammarion.

DES HOUX Henri (1887) *Ma prison*, Paris: Ollendorff.

DOUGLAS Norman (1934) *Looking Back: An Autobiographical Excursion*, London: Chatto & Windus.

DOUGLAS Norman (1952) *Footnote on Capri*, London: Sidgwick & Jackson.

ESSEBAC Achille (1898) *"Partenza"... Vers la beauté!* Paris: Imprimerie

de Chamerot & Renouard.
FACIEU Eugène (1880) *A travers l'Italie. La rose de Capri ou La grotte d'Azur*, Toulouse: Douladourre.
FIORANI Tito (2005) *Vita ed opere di Jacques Fersen in A la jeunesse d'amour. Villa Lysis a Capri: 1905-2005,* Capri: Edizioni La Conchiglia.
FURCHHEIM Federigo (1899) *Bibliografia della isola di Capri e della penisola Sorrentina, aggiuntavi la bibliografia di Amalfi, Salerno e Pesto, anticamente Posidonia o Paestum in Lucania, compilata e corredata di note critiche da Federigo Furchheim*, Naples: F. Furchheim.
KOPISCH August (1838) *Entdeckung der Blauen Grotte auf der Insel Capri*, Berlin: Wagenbach, 1997 (first edition 1838).
—. *Le Magasin pittoresque* (1833-1899) Paris: Lachevardière.
LE MERCHER DE LONGPRÉ Charles (Baron d'Haussez) (1835) *Voyage d'un exilé de Londres à Naples et en Sicile, en passant par la Hollande, la Confédération germanique, le Tyrol et l'Italie*, Paris: Allardin.
—. *Le Voyageur françois, ou La connoissance de l'ancien et du nouveau monde*, tome XXVII, Paris: L. Cellot (1781).
LÉCOLLE Gabriel (1908) *L'Italie et la Sicile: Récits de voyage*, Guise: Minon-Bourdanchon.
LEONE DE ANDREIS Marcella (2002) *Capri 1939*, Rome: In-Edit-A.
MASSENET Jules (1912) *Mes souvenirs (1848-1912)*, Paris: L. Lafitte.
MENDÈS Catulle (1886) *Les Iles d'amour*, Paris: Frinzine.
MERLINI Madeline (1987) "Capri, island of Gossip," *Bollettino del C.I.R.V.I* n° 15-16, Jan-Dec. 1987, pp. 153-156.
MONEY James (1986) *Capri: Island of Pleasure*, London: Hamish Hamilton, 1986.
PUAUX Frank (1872) *Notes de voyage. Deux mois en Italie*, Nîmes: Clavel-Ballivet.
RESPIGHI Elsa (1977) *Cinquant'anni di vita nella musica 1905-1955*, Rome: Trevi.
RICHTER Dieter (1996) *Il giardino della memoria. Il cimitero acattolico di Capri. Storia di un luogo*, Capri: Edizioni La Conchiglia.
SUETONIUS. *The Twelve Caesars*, Book III, "Tiberius". Translated by Robert Graves. Harmondsworth: Penguin, 1957.
VALERY Antoine-Claude (n.d.) *L'Italie confortable: manuel du touriste, appendice aux voyages historiques, littéraires et artistiques en Italie*, Paris: J. Renouard.
WILLY (1927) *Le Troisième sexe*, Paris: Paris-Édition.

CHAPTER SIX

ORIENTALIST PAINTERS: "THE TRAVELS OF AESTHETICS"

RICHARD SIBLEY

In the visual arts orientalism is unusual in that it is not a school or movement in terms of style or technique, but is defined solely by its perspective on the notion of place: orientalist paintings are defined as *western* representations of *the Orient*. This latter term is usually taken to mean the predominantly Muslim cultures that have surrounded the Mediterranean, in other words the Ottoman Empire at its greatest extent (the Balkans, the lands bordering the Black Sea, Anatolia, the Levant, Persia, Mesapotamia, Arabia, Egypt, Tunisia, Libya and Algeria) plus Morocco and southern Spain. The Indian sub-continent and the Far East are excluded from most definitions of orientalist painting, since representations of these areas comprise quite different artistic traditions. Western artists include not only Europeans (mainly French, British, Italian, Spanish and German), but also several Americans and some Australians. So *East* and *West*, *Orient* and *Occident* are terms that reflect cultural preconceptions and imagination rather than strictly geographic precision, a configuration not without paradox: for example the Maghreb is part of the Orient, yet "Maghreb" means "the setting (sun)" or the west, whereas the word "Orient" comes from the Latin word for the *rising* sun or the east. Morocco and parts of Algeria in fact lie west of most of western Europe, including Paris and London.

In chronological terms, the narrow definition of orientalist painting covers the nineteenth and early twentieth centuries. Some art historians would include the eighteenth century—notably Auguste Boppe's "Bosphorus" painters (Boppe 1911)—and others might include the whole of the twentieth century. It can even be argued that many earlier European painters belong to orientalism, going as far back as the Turkish conquest of Constantinople in 1453, which would allow the inclusion of Venetian and Florentine schools and paintings such as Bellini's famous *Sultan*

Mehmet II, housed in the National Gallery, London, and recently on show in Paris at the *Venise et l'Orient* exhibition at the Institut du Monde Arabe.

The geography and the chronology of orientalist painting are relevant to questions of mobility and to definitions of its terms. For example, parts of the Orient once closed to all but the most *intrepid explorers* struggling against a hostile natural and human environment, advancing slowly under hazardous conditions which were often a threat to their health and sometimes to their lives, may later have become playgrounds for *package tourists* flying in and staying for a few days in relative comfort and luxury. One interesting facet of orientalist art, particularly nineteenth-century orientalist art, is that much of the Orient as defined above had been more or less closed to christian westerners for centuries, but for a variety of reasons it progressively opened—or was opened—to western penetration from about 1800 onwards: orientalist painters both recorded this process and were part of it.

The "who, where and when" of orientalist painting suggests a wide range of mobility profiles. Taking a corpus of several hundred painters, extending beyond the one hundred and fifty or so included in the French edition of Lynne Thornton's *The Orientalists: Painter-Travellers, 1828-1908*, we have roamed through biographical details on the one hand, reflected about concepts on the other, and attempted somewhat empirically to discover what the life-stories of painter-travellers can contribute to the construction of a typology. We have provisionally ignored classic contributions to the conceptuology of mobility, thus stepping outside existing travel theory, on the grounds that perhaps painters have both seen and done travelling and mobility differently.

Orientalist fantasies, or, the imaginary traveller

Gerald Ackerman opened *Les Orientalistes de l'École britannique* with the following statement: "What the artists included in this book have in common is that all, at one time or another, went to the Middle East or North Africa and then all painted on the basis of the experiences drawn from these travels" (1991: 6). If that sounds like a good starting point for a discussion of painter-travellers, how do we categorize those famous paintings by Ingres (1780-1867) that are reproduced in most books on orientalist art: the so-called *Great Odalisk* (1814), *The Little Bather in the Harem* (1829), the two versions of the *Odalisk and Slave* (1839 and 1842) and above all *The Turkish Bath* (1862) [see Fig. 6-1]? These are always cited as classic French orientalist paintings of harems and hammams, yet Ingres had never travelled further east than Rome! For more than half a century he painted naked women in "oriental" settings, from his early bathers wearing nothing but turbans (*Half-figure of a Bather* 1807, *The Bather of Valpinçon* 1808), through the paintings we have cited where the women are surrounded by various oriental trappings (narghiles, pipes, slippers, stools, incense-burners, peacock feathers, mandolins), with black female slaves and eunuchs situated in "Islamic" interiors, finally culminating in *The Turkish Bath*, which he seemed to have been working towards ever since 1807.

Fig. 6-1. Jean A-D INGRES, *The Turkish Bath*, 1862, musée du Louvre, Paris.

However, not only had Ingres never been to Turkey, but—firstly—like all those male artists who painted harem women or naked women in baths, these were purely imaginary visions since no western man could ever have entered such places, and—secondly—Ingres apparently based his *Turkish Bath* on the description he found in a letter dated 1st April 1717 by Lady Mary Wortley Montagu, wife of the British ambassador to the Sublime Port. Yet the Ingres painting—with its lasciviously posed female nudes and explicit depiction of erotic lesbianism (the round form of the painting has been attributed to the censor's scissors cutting an over-explicit pose in what had been the bottom right-hand corner, Lemaire 2001: 202)—contrasts with Lady Montagu's description of women in the hammam at Adrianopolis (Edirne):

> The first sofas were covered with cushions and rich carpets on which sat the ladies; and on the second, their slaves behind them, but without any distinction of rank by their dress, all being in the state of nature, that is, in plain English, stark naked, without any beauty or defect concealed. Yet there was not the least wanton smile or immodest gesture among them. (cited in Thornton 1994b: 68)

Another example of this rather special combination of fantasy and plagiarism was the eunuch depicted in both the 1839 and the 1842 versions of the *Odalisk and Slave*: the figure was copied directly from a 1714 collection of engravings by the Flemish orientalist Jean-Baptiste Van Mour (Hitzel 2002: 76).

So Ingres' orientalist paintings were the product of an imagination that, feeding on travel books and earlier illustrations, distorted and misrepresented the oriental subject it was depicting. He was eighty-two when he finally produced *The Turkish Bath*, and proudly inscribed his age in Latin on the back of the painting. If Ingres is the most celebrated example of the "studio orientalist", the fantasy or imaginary traveller, of what might be called "mobility in the mind", there were others whose depictions of the Orient likewise owed nothing to any direct experience of real mobility. The detailed scenes of Napoleon's Middle-Eastern and Egyptian campaigns, such as *Bonaparte Visiting the Plague-Stricken of Jaffa 11th March 1799*, which can today be viewed in the Louvre, were faithfully recorded by the artist Antoine-Jean Gros on the basis of... the reports he received in his Paris studio!

However, in the visual arts at least, there is not a simple contrast between "imagined" and "real" travel, and the total fantasy of Ingres' orientalism is a useful reminder of the complexity of the relations between imagination, travel, and representations of the Other, whether in orientalist painting, art more generally, or representation of otherness and mobility in general. We might suppose that those artists who travelled very little—just one brief journey to the Orient, for example—and who for many years thereafter painted dozens or hundreds of orientalist pictures back home in a London, Edinburgh or Paris studio, would have had greater recourse to imagination or fantasy than those who lived for years in Constantinople, Cairo, Bou Saâda or Tangiers. Yet all orientalist artists introduced imaginary elements into their paintings, and thereby "misrepresented" the Orient. Artefacts, buildings, costumes, rituals, stereotypes and symbols were added or removed or indiscriminately mixed together in a more or less consciously subjective and distorted vision of the East. We might say that there is by definition no such thing as a realistic (i.e. true-to-place) orientalist painting. Imagination or fantasy are always present in the works of the much-travelled orientalist painters as well as the stay-at-homes.

Our evocation of the fantastic and imaginary component in the work of painter-travellers suggests three conclusions relevant to other travellers. Firstly, a vision of the foreign Other is inevitably distorted, by both personal and cultural factors. If in art this is regarded as "normal", there is little to be gained from a persistently pejorative or negative critique (dismissing artists as "colonialist" etc.): as Forsdick argues in defence of travellers and "exoticism" (2005), so with orientalism and travellers' views of the Other in general. Secondly, it is interesting to note that in the art world at least, the work of the imagination may be more highly regarded than a faithful representation. Roger Benjamin quotes the French art critic Arsène Alexandre writing in 1896: "The important thing is that the painting be good. The Orient as imagined and painted by a great artist who may never have left his Montmartre studio will be much more satisfactory than a true Orient brought home by a landscapist who is literal and dry" (Benjamin 2003: 86). Thirdly, we might ask not just how but also *why* the artist travels and imagines, or travels in fantasy: there may be many answers, but one of the functions of both art and travel—whether in the imagination or in reality—is to visualize, live and do what cannot be visualized, lived and done at home...

Painter-travellers: profiles of mobility

Having rather perversely begun our exploration of orientalist painter-travellers with one who never travelled to the Orient—the justification being the importance of imagination and fantasy for *all* travellers—how can we classify the many forms of real mobility experienced by orientalist artists? A few carefully selected examples of different mobility profiles, and glimpses of some others, will provide a basis for constructing a list of variables and types.

The early orientalist paintings of Ingres' great rival Eugène Delacroix

(1798-1863) were also the product of the latter's imagination, feeding on travel books, romantic poetry (notably Byron), discussions with Greek refugees and with friends who had travelled east, as well as borrowed artefacts which appeared in his paintings. Such celebrated orientalist works as *Massacre at Chios* (1824) and *Death of Sardanapalus* (1827), and also several lesser-known paintings of Turks and "oriental" women, were all painted before Delacroix visited the Orient: by 1832 his only travel abroad had been three and a half months in England in 1825.

Fig. 6-2. Eugène DELACROIX, *Women of Algiers in their Apartment*, 1834, musée du Louvre, Paris.

Although he continued to paint purely imagined orientalist subjects, in the sense that he depicted historical and literary scenes and places he had never visited, in 1832 Delacroix visited Morocco (Tangiers and Meknès), southern Spain and then Algiers. He spent only three or four days in the latter city, but this visit gave rise to one of the most famous of all orientalist paintings, his *Women of Algiers in their Apartment* (1834) [see Fig. 6-2]. Some sources suggest that Delacroix did manage the impossible, a visit inside a harem, but the painting is more likely—once again—a product of imagination or fantasy. Last year an Algerian student of mine, standing spellbound in front of this painting, remarked "Parts of it are true, parts of it are false" ("il y a du vrai, il y a du faux"). When pressed for an explanation she detailed the true (the furnishings and artefacts) and the false (the attitudes of the women, which were "western" and could not possibly be Algerian). "Parts are true, parts are false" is not a bad definition of orientalist painting, underlining the combination of realism and fantasy.

Before his brief stay in Algiers, Delacroix, who had managed to attach himself to a French diplomatic mission to the court of the Sultan of Morocco, spent a few weeks in Tangiers (January to March 1832), followed by a one-month expedition to Meknès and a two-week excursion into Spain. He filled seven books with sketches and watercolours, rapidly recording his impressions and adding notes, and these were the basis for the many orientalist paintings that he was to accomplish back in his Paris studio over the following decades until his death in 1863. He never returned to the Orient, and in fact thereafter only ventured abroad for brief stays in Germany, Belgium and Holland.

This is typical of many orientalist painters: a few weeks or months of travel, followed by a lifetime of reconstructions back home in the studio. But studio reconstruction of travel is a feature shared by artists who spent many years in the Orient. Eugène Fromentin, who produced not only many splendid paintings but also two books full of perceptive and sensitive observations on the Sahara and cultural relations between East and West, noted that "processed by memory, [...] landscapes become pictures" (Thornton 1994a: 94). At once perhaps the most famous and infamous of orientalist painters, Jean-Léon Gérôme was much travelled, but his paintings were almost all painted back home in Paris, with Parisian models and props.

At the other end of the scale from those who spent only a few weeks in the Orient, Etienne Dinet (1861-1929) first visited Algeria in 1884, accompanying friends to the Sahara in search of beetle specimens. He immediately fell in love with the country, and returned every summer to the oasis towns of Biskra, Bou-Saâda and Laghouat. In 1904 he took up residence in Bou-Saâda, where he lived every summer, returning to Paris in the winter to complete—and sell—his paintings. He converted to Islam in 1913, and took on the name of Hadj Nasr Ed Dine Dini. He bought a villa in Algiers in 1924. After a pilgrimage to Mecca in 1929, he died whilst on a visit to Paris, but was buried at Bou-Saâda (where the Nasr Eddine Dinet museum was opened in 1993). Like many orientalists, he has been in and out of fashion, with his brightly coloured canvasses illustrating children and young people at love and at play in southern Algeria [see Fig. 6-3], along with some townscapes and landscapes and a few more sombre images of prayer and daily life. Such a profile is not infrequent among painters: a chance visit to the Orient, instant enchantment, further visits, seasonal migration, permanent residence, various forms of cultural integration (in Dinet's case, linguistic and religious), and in a few cases, like Dinet, "migration for eternity" in the grave!

Fig. 6-3. Etienne DINET, *Girls Dancing*, 1906, private collection.

Somewhere between the fantasy travellers and the permanent migrants, we find a wide range of visitors, travellers, explorers, wanderers, and tourists. Jules Laurens (1825-1901) lived for many years from his paintings, engravings and writings illustrating and describing an extraordinary two-year expedition to Turkey and Persia. He is best known for his depictions of mosques, fountains, cemeteries and streets in Constantinople and Smyrna, and his eerily atmospheric landscapes of eastern Anatolia and Persia [see Fig. 6-4]. In 1846 Laurens left Paris with the famous geographer Xavier Hommaire de Hell on a scientific mission, going via Malta to Constantinople, with excursions to Bulgaria, Moldavia, Smyrna and Bursa. They set off to Persia in July 1847, on a journey which might euphemistically be described as "arduous":

> The route to Persia, through Trebizond, Erzeroum and Tabriz to Teheran, had rarely been attempted by Westerners. Twelve or fourteen hours a day on horseback, often with little or no food or drink, the menace of cholera, terrible weariness, miserable nights spent in caravanserais with minimal comfort, and practically impassable tracks made their journey a nightmare. Hommaire de Hell was temporarily blinded from the sun's reflection on the snow, while Laurens, delirious with fever, was tied to his mule. Unbelievably, he went on sketching at each stop, filling sheet after sheet with drawings of people and landscapes. (Thornton 1994a: 120)

They reached Teheran in February 1848, where they lived a paradisiac existence of "sumptuous feasts and lavish hospitality" for a few months. There followed an expedition to the Caspian Sea, including "the province of Manzanderan, with its rice fields, orange groves, cascades and luxurious vegetation [which] delighted them", whilst "in Ashraf, which they found enchanting, a handful of ruined palaces were nearly swallowed up in a chaos of overgrown, mossy, humid greenery." After more trying journeys and expeditions, through a great salt desert and later to Isphahan under the August sun, Laurens had to bury his companion, who had succumbed to fever, then himself had "a narrow escape from the pillaging hordes of tribesmen during the disturbances following the death of Mohammad Shah" (Thornton 1994a: 121-123). Laurens returned to the safety of Paris in February 1849, refusing later invitations to retum to Persia and contenting himself with organizing a literary and artistic circle of orientalists in Paris. So he too spent many years living on the memories of an expedition abroad. The French painter Eugène Flandin (1809-1876) had similarly difficult experiences in the same regions.

A list of British orientalist painters would comprise several hundred names, though perhaps none of an artistic stature comparable with those French artists of international repute whose *oeuvre* included orientalist works: Ingres, Delacroix, Renoir, Marquet and Matisse, for example. Among the deservedly more illustrious British artists, several lived in Cairo for many years and integrated into local society, not just the expatriate community. This was the case for John Frederick Lewis (1805-1876), Frederic Leighton (1830-1896)—who had travelled very widely and spoke many languages including Arabic—and, much later, Robert Talbot-Kelly (1861-1934), who also spoke fluent Arabic. On the other hand David Roberts (1796-1864), probably the best-known of all British artists to depict Egyptian scenes, which he did endlessly, in fact spent only eleven months there.

Fig. 6-4. Jules LAURENS, *The Lake and Fortress of Vann in Armenia*, private collection.

The Scottish artist Arthur Melville (1855-1904), whose repertoire as an orientalist painter was technically varied and brilliant, travelled very extensively: India, Arabia, Persia, Anatolia, the Black Sea, Constantinople, Algeria, Morocco and Spain, where he caught the typhoid from which he died. He was constantly on the move, unlike his friend Joseph Crawhall (1861-1913), who lived a somewhat isolated and marginal existence for more than ten years in Tangiers, where he painted mostly animals rather than people or places. Crawhall did not seem to be interested in the locals, but in painting camels and snakes as well as his beloved horses. A similar case was the Irish painter John Lavery (1856-1941), whose work is in many ways reminiscent of his French contemporary Maurice Utrillo's depictions of streets and houses in and around Paris, and who was spellbound by Tangiers, where he went every year from 1890 to 1920. He bought a house there and painted hundreds of views of the city, yet he prided himself on never learning Arabic, and on spending his time with the European expatriate community. He was in fact more interested in his painting, his art, than in Morocco and the Moroccans. Lavery was interested in light, shade and the surfaces of the urban scene. He felt challenged by the intensity of the Moroccan light and colours, but his painting reveals not the slightest interest in the Arab people, who are impersonal blurred shapes, just parts of the scenery. In many of his paintings he literally looks down on the crowd, none of whom is observed closely [see Fig. 6-5]. Lavery was interesting as an artist yet, though he loved Tangiers, he remained aloof.

Fig. 6-5. John LAVERY, *A Street in Tangiers*, private collection.

Edward Lear (1812-1888)—well-known as an author of children's poems and nonsense verse ("The owl and the pussy-cat went to sea, In a beautiful pea-green boat...")—was also an accomplished orientalist artist. His life seems to have touched peaks of ecstasy and troughs of tragedy. Twentieth of twenty-one children, whose family was broken up when he was a child due to paternal bankruptcy, Lear had asthma, epilepsy, poor eyesight (not helped by the meticulous drawings and paintings of birds he undertook in his teens) and lungs that suffered from the cold and damp of English winters. He left England in 1837 and spent most of the rest of his life wandering abroad, except for brief returns to London each summer. Lear was what we might label an "eternal vagabond": he lived in Rome for ten years in all, and travelled in often hazardous circumstances through unexplored parts of Greece and the Greek islands, Turkey, Albania, Sicily, Malta, Egypt, the Sinai desert, Palestine, then latterly India and Ceylon. He eventually settled in Italy, and is buried in his own garden in San Remo. He left over seven thousand sketches and watercolours drawn or painted on the spot, over two thousand done at home in the studio, and over three hundred oil paintings (not to mention engravings and book illustrations as well as his writings).

Our last example of an orientalist painter-traveller profile is Richard Dadd (1819-1876), an equally tragic figure in that he became mentally unbalanced (apparently on account of sunstroke suffered during his oriental travels) and was interned for life at the age of twenty-four, after murdering his father. Dadd travelled through Greece, Anatolia, and the Middle East to Egypt with his patron, Sir Thomas Phillips, a journey executed "at an impossible pace [...] a lightning tour through Asia Minor to Beirut and Jerusalem, only to set out the following day for Jordan and the Dead Sea. The stages were long, the pace unrelenting and the conditions exhausting" (Thornton 1994a: 9). An example, perhaps, of the "whistle-stop painter-tourist"?

Painter-travellers: towards a typology of mobility

The above profiles were selected rather subjectively, according to their potential interest in the context of mobility. Consideration of these individual trajectories, and a more cursory glance at the movements of dozens of other painter-travellers, suggest the following typology.

Firstly, the nature, frequency, and duration of mobility each include a number of variables that can be crossed in many possible combinations. Apart from those whose mobility is in the realm of imagination or fantasy, we might distinguish between the visitor (one place), the traveller (moving from place to place) and the migrant (settling in one place). Each of these categories will have sub-divisions: visitors may be *tourists*, *pilgrims*, *refugees* or *fugitives*, for example; travellers can be each of these plus *explorers*, *wanderers* (or nomads or vagabonds: the French painter Georges Clairin described himself as a "vagabond by nature"), *adventurers*, etc.; migrants can be *seasonal*, *temporary*, or *permanent,* and may *integrate* relatively successfully with the host community (Dinet) or not (Lavery, Crawhall). There are also sub-sub-categories: the *lightning* or whistle-stop tourist, the *day*-tripper, the *package* tourist, and so on.

Secondly, and bearing in mind that all terms are relative, frequency of mobility can be classed as single (one visit or journey), occasional, frequent, and regular, whilst the duration of mobility may be short-term (days to weeks?), medium-term (weeks to months?) and long-term (months to years?): these words are relative in the sense that outside a particular context it does not seem reasonable to attach precise figures to them.

Thirdly, although theoretically the reasons behind different forms of mobility may be almost unlimited, there are common motives for the movements of painters. Many were sent on missions or expeditions that were *official* (state or publicly funded), *semi-official* (the press, royal patronage) or *unofficial* (private sponsorship) and included such categories as the *military* (Napoleon in Egypt, the Crimean War), *diplomatic* (Delacroix in Morocco), *colonial* (several French artists in Algeria), *scientific* (geographic, archaeological), *technological* (engineering projects such as railways or the Suez Canal), *religious*, etc. Many artists travelled for a variety of professional reasons (illustrating magazines and books, especially guide-books; collecting material to sell their paintings back home; selling paintings abroad, particularly to expatriate communities), to which may be added health as a relatively common motive (after his "studio orientalism" of the 1870s, some examples of which are close to parody, Renoir painted a few rare jewels of impressionist orientalism during a short period of convalescence in Algiers), and personal or artistic curiosity (the light, colours and atmosphere of the "Orient" were a stimulant and a challenge to almost every artist: Fabius Brest spent four years in Anatolia just experimenting on his technique, whilst almost every orientalist painter who set foot in North Africa was attracted by distinctive lights and shades). Inevitably, we have recourse to the catch-all category of miscellaneous, with its fascinating diversity: the orphaned Gustave Boulanger was sent to Algeria by the uncle who had adopted him, in what looks suspiciously like an attempt to get rid of him; the Welsh artist Frank Brangwyn, whose corpus includes several orientalist paintings, worked on board cargo ships for many years; Théodore Chassériau was invited to Algeria by the Caliph of Constantine, after a chance meeting in Paris. For artists, as for all other kinds of orientalist, different forms of escapism and especially sexual adventures which could not have been envisaged at home, were also often motives for travel.

Fourthly, the material conditions under which artists travelled and visited reflect both differing personal circumstances and changing times. A detailed study of the latter would be fascinating, as steamships, railways, guidebooks and hotels, not to mention expatriate communities and the infrastructures introduced by empires, transformed conditions of mobility and sojourn during the nineteenth century. Painters seemed to attract—or be attracted by?—extremes of luxury and discomfort, as our example of Laurens illustrates. In 1800, Cairo, Tangiers, Algiers and to a lesser extent Constantinople were almost off the beaten track, but a few decades later steamships and railways had transformed them into cities where European comforts could readily be found and expatriates could congregate. The same is true of many apparently more out-of-the-way places: Lynne Thornton explains that Biskra and Old Biskra in the Algerian desert, for example, were by the 1890s no longer "the untouched spots enjoyed by earlier generations of Orientalist painters. They had become a favourite wintering place for Europeans, complete with hotels and a casino, with a railway linking Biskra to Sétif" (1994a: 32).

The travels of aesthetics

This chapter has focused not on orientalism as art—what Roger Benjamin termed "the aesthetics of travel" (1997: 7)—but rather on orientalist art as an illustration of mobility, or "the travels of aesthetics". One of the attractions of orientalist art is that it is part of cultural and social history in the widest senses, and not just the history of art. So many perspectives are there to be explored: the importance of the new art public of the nineteenth century, buying and viewing orientalist paintings because they were excited by its exoticism (they too were "fantasy travellers"); the contribution of orientalism to painting technique (for example, such were the hazards of painting on the spot—the heat, the overpowering sunlight, the melting oil-paints, the insects and the sand, physical aggression from disapproving or marauding locals, diverse diseases and discomforts—that painting in watercolour was, especially prior to the development of photography, one of the few ways of quickly recording a scene before retiring to the studio to work on it in oils; hence, what had been a mode of painting regarded as just one of the social graces of the well brought-up English girl became an internationally recognized artistic medium); notions of art as illusion (one fascinating albeit anecdotal aspect of which is the recourse to all kinds of artefacts and props: artist's homes and studios were full of rugs, cushions, helmets, swords, tiles, furniture, not to mention Parisian "odalisks"... which all appear in the paintings, giving a completely false but reassuring sense of reality—though few artists went quite as far as Frederick Goodall, who brought sheep and goats back to England from the Levant to ensure the authenticity of his oriental scenes); the contrasting cultural perspectives of various categories of orientalists: artists of different nationalities, periods, movements, and of course the largely unexplored differences between male and female orientalist painters (whilst most if not all male artists at some time depicted their fantasized images of "oriental" women—a foretaste of sex tourism?—some female artists did enter harems and baths; Henriette Browne's painting is an extraordinarily different and unfortunately very rare illustration of life inside the harem [see Fig. 6-6]).

Fig. 6-6. Henriette BROWNE, *A Visit (harem interior, Constantinople)*, 1860, private collection.

The perspectives that painter-travellers projected in their paintings of oriental people and places are a central preoccupation of much post-colonial and post-modern criticism of orientalist art. Implicit rather than explicit in this chapter is our view that this criticism has on the whole been too severe (Nochlin 1989, Cherry 2002). As Lynne Thornton wrote, orientalist paintings...

> [are] marvellous invitations, visually, and through the imagination, to journeys to other lands and other times. Colourful, sunlit, strange, sanguinary, tender or instructive, they enchant and fascinate us as they did former generations. Each has its story to tell, of travel and adventure, sights and customs now changed forever, of the gradual lifting of the veils of myth and mystery in which the Orient had been shrouded and of the

heady discoveries of exoticism by Westerners accustomed to the greyness of the northern industrialized cities. (Thornton 1994a: 5)

The emotional and aesthetic pleasures that are the primary function of art did indeed motivate most European painters, with the excitement of new colours, lights and shades, peoples and places. Experiencing and portraying the strange, the exotic and the foreign, seeing all this as a thrill and not a threat, was one way of fulfilling that other function of all art, to stretch out beyond the limits of one's own identity and be fascinated by glimpses of the Orient, a welcome contrast to the numbingly tedious industrialized north. The travels of aesthetics are indeed an invitation to all who dream of escaping a narrowly restrictive existence at home.

Bibliography and References

ACKERMAN Gerald M. (1991) *Les Orientalistes de l'école britannique*, Courbevoie: ACR Édition.

ATIL Esin, NEWTON Charles & SEARIGHT Sarah (1995) *Voyages and Visions: Nineteenth-Century European Images of the Middle East from the Victoria and Albert Museum*, Seattle & London: University of Washington Press.

BEAULIEU J. & ROBERTS M. (eds.) (2002) *Orientalism's Interlocutors: Painting, Architecture, Photography*, Durham NC: Duke University Press.

BENCHÉRIF Osman (1997) *The Image of Algeria in Anglo-American Writings 1785-1962*, Oxford: University Press of America.

BENJAMIN Roger (2003) *Orientalist Aesthetics: Art, Colonialism and French North Africa, 1880-1930*, Berkeley: University of California Press.

BENJAMIN Roger & KHEMIR Mounira (1997) *Orientalism: Delacroix to Klee*, Sydney: Art Gallery of New South Wales.

BENJAMIN Roger (2003) *Renoir and Algeria*, New Haven & London: Yale University Press.

BOPPE Auguste (1911) *Les Peintres du Bosphore au XVIIIe siècle*, Paris: Hachette (republished 1989, Courbevoie: ACR Édition).

BRAHIMI Denise & BENCHIKOU Koudir (1984) *La Vie et l'oeuvre d'Etienne Dinet*, Courbevoie: ACR Éditions.

CAZENAVE Elisabeth (2001) *Les Artistes de l'Algérie: Dictionnaire des peintres, sculpteurs, graveurs (1830-1962)*, Paris: Bernard Giovanangeli.

CHERRY Deborah (2002) "The worlding of Algeria", pp. 103-130 in

Beaulieu & Roberts.

FORSDICK Charles (2005) *Travel in Twentieth-Century French and Francophone Cultures: The Persistence of Diversity*, Oxford: Oxford University Press.

HACKFORTH-JONES Jocelyn & ROBERTS Mary (eds.) (2005) *Edges of Empire: Orientalism and Visual Culture*, Oxford: Blackwell.

HITZEL Frédéric (2002) *Couleurs de la Corne d'Or, Peintres voyageurs à la Sublime Porte*, Courbevoie: ACR Édition.

LEMAIRE Gérard-Georges (2001) *L'Univers des orientalistes*, Paris: Éditions Place de la Victoire.

MACFIE A. L. (2002) *Orientalism*, London: Longman.

MACKENZIE John M. (1995) *Orientalism: History, Theory, and the Arts*, Manchester: Manchester University Press.

NOCHLIN Linda (1989) *The Politics of Vision: Essays on Nineteenth-Century Art and Society*, New York: Westview.

PELTRE Christine (1995) *L'atelier du voyage: les peintres en Orient au dix-neuvième siècle*, Paris: Gallimard.

PELTRE Christine (1997) *Les Orientalistes*, Paris: Hazan.

SIBLEY Richard (2006a) "Visual representations and cultural identity in theory and practice: British and French paintings of the Ottoman Empire," International IDEA Conference *Studies in English*, Boğaziçi University, Istanbul, April 2006.

SIBLEY Richard (2006b) "Travelling artists discover the Orient: theories of visual representation, orientalism and cultural imperialism put to the test", *Voyage, tourisme et migration*, Université Paris-Dauphine & Université Paris-Nord, June 2006.

SIBLEY Richard (2007) "Artistic visions of the Other and Otherness: British 'orientalist' painters and the Maghreb," *Middle Ground, Journal of Literary and Cultural Encounters* (Beni Mellal, Morocco), n° 1, 2007, pp. 101-126.

THOMPSON James & WRIGHT Barbara (1987) *La Vie et l'oeuvre d'Eugène Fromentin*, Courbevoie: ACR Editions.

THORNTON Lynne (1983/1994a) *Les Orientalistes: peintres voyageurs, 1828-1908*, Courbevoie: ACR Édition, 1983 (published in pocket edition as *The Orientalists: Painter-Travellers, 1828-1908*, 1994).

THORNTON Lynne (1998) *Du Maroc aux Indes: Voyages en Orient*, Courbevoie: ACR Édition.

THORNTON Lynne (1985/1994b) *La Femme dans la peinture orientaliste*, Courbevoie: ACR Édition, 1985 (published in pocket edition as *Women as Portrayed in Orientalist Painting*, 1994).

Paintings mentioned but not illustrated in this chapter can be viewed on various websites: simply insert the title of the painting and/or the artist's name into a well-known search engine.

PART II -

THE BRITISH AND FRANCE

CHAPTER SEVEN

BETWEEN THE ENGLISH CHANNEL AND *LA MANCHE*

CHARLES FORSDICK

Edouard Glissant, indicting French attitudes towards overseas departments in the 1960s and reflecting on the ambiguities of the epithet *francophone*, retorted: "Vous dites: outre-mer (nous l'avons dit avec vous), mais vous aussi êtes bientôt outre-mer." (1969: 21, "You say 'overseas' (and we said it with you), but soon you too will be overseas.") Written from the perspective of a scholar active in UK French studies, this chapter is inspired by a similarly troubling awareness of an adverbial phrase's relativity. To adapt Glissant: "Vous dites: 'outre-Manche', mais vous aussi êtes bientôt outre-Manche." ("You say 'across the Channel', but soon you too will be across the Channel"). What follows represents the beginnings of a reflection on the narrow seas that divide and connect France and Britain, on their status as a site of competing modes of mobility, and on their constant re-construction and re-consolidation in the British and French imaginaries, most particularly in travel writing.

In a comment that is illustrated by many of the contributions to this volume, Chris Rojek and John Urry claim (1997: 11): "All cultures get remade as a result of the flows of peoples, objects and images across national borders, whether these involve colonialism, work-based migration, individual travel or mass tourism." The centrality suggested here of questions of mobility to processes of cultural analysis is well established, as the recent work of a range of critics—both anglophone and francophone—has made abundantly clear. In a further development of this observation, the centrality of comparatism to the study of travel and its literary manifestations is becoming increasingly apparent. James Clifford's 1992 essay "Traveling Cultures" concludes with a call for "comparative cultural studies" (Clifford 1997: 17-46), and there is growing evidence of a sustained response to his suggestion.

As an intersubjective, intercultural activity (i.e. dependent on border-crossing, encounter and exchange), travel lends itself to such a critical approach, which may take various forms of which only three will be outlined here: (i) contrasting collective or individual accounts of a single place, the experience of which may be conditioned according to the traveller's class, gender, ethnicity, relative velocity or some other variable; (ii) exploring the contrapuntal relationship of the traveller and the travellee, brought together in what Mary Louise Pratt has dubbed the "contact zone" in which may be recognized the "spatial and temporal co-presence of subjects previously separated by geographic and historical disjunctures, and whose trajectories now intersect" (1992: 7); and (iii) comparing different modes of displacement—those of travellers, tourists and migrants, for instance, between whom the boundaries are often shifting or porous, and whose co-existence within a shared location (regularly even within a shared means of transport) often goes unremarked. In a number of recent interventions regarding comparative approaches to the experience and textualization of space, critics have privileged key zones or nodal points where, to quote Lucia Boldrini, "different cultures come into contact, and from where different historical, artistic, cultural forces irradiate" (2006: 16). Emily Apter speaks of the emergence of a "literary Chunnel" as part of "the charting of postcolonial cartography according to linguistic configurations" (2006: 56; see also Apter 2002). The identification of such sites contributes to a reconceptualization of space, to a shift away from the notions of nations and nationalism that travel itself—with its departures and arrivals, and the potentially transgressive activity that comes in between—both consolidates and destabilizes. In identifying such sites, Boldrini perhaps inevitably focuses on cities and islands, but extends the range to include various bodies of waters (oceans, seas, rivers, straits), whose literal fluidity brings with it a powerful metaphorical force. As such, she alludes implicitly to recent research on Atlantic and Pacific cultures (Gilroy 1992, Matsuda 2005, Marshall 2005, Foucrier 2005), as well as on various mediterranean seas, dividing and uniting cultures which, as Olivier Sevin reminds us, are "not so much given by nature, moulds into which man, societies and activities have flowed, as human constructions" (1999: 8-9).

An apparently insignificant stretch of water

Mediterranean seas are described by Jacques Lacarrière in terms of a self-sufficient "*vivier*, in the literal and figurative sense of the term, a place where live together, in relative and constant proximity, very different cultures which have in turn accepted and rejected each other"

(1998: 34; the French term *vivier* has two meanings which cannot be rendered by a single word in English—a pool, pond or tank in which fish are bred, and a "pool of talent"). However, of more interest than these complex yet at times self-contained systems, are more open-ended, less easily defined channels or straits: not only the English Channel but also the Bosphorus and the Strait of Gibraltar, for example: narrow, tight spaces which, seemingly forfeiting a concrete identity of their own, serve as connections or as means of connection between two land masses and two larger bodies of water. Here we intend to reflect on the Channel—only twenty-one miles wide at its narrowest—an apparently insignificant stretch of water when compared to the North Sea and to the Atlantic that it joins, yet one which remains, in Cohen and Denver's terms, "a liminal formation at the confluence of independent formations, both belong[ing] to these formations and constitut[ing] a distinct whole of its own" (2002: 2). A geographical reality and place of historical significance, the Channel thus both divides and links; continuing to freight an often dangerous concentration of people and goods, it is also a space with considerable symbolic status. The aim here is to explore the role of the English Channel/*la Manche* as what we might call a "tropological zone" in French and British travel writing, and so to supplement a number of recent studies exploring the history of this deceptively domestic space, or its more general literary representation (see Unwin 2003, Rainsford 2002, Falvey & Brooks 1991, Smith 1994, and, on the Channel Tunnel, Wilson 1994). Here we develop the idea that the different designations of this narrow stretch of water—the proprietorial English Channel, or the diminutive *la Manche* (echoed by the German *Ärmelkanal*)—reveal the culturally determined relationships to it of the inhabitants of the two countries it divides. "English Channel" seems to have been in existence since the later sixteenth century: "English Channel" and "British Channel" appear both to have existed until into the nineteenth century, but by the twentieth the former was almost exclusively employed. According to Alain Rey's *Dictionnaire historique de la langue française*, the understanding of *manche* ("sleeve") as *un bras de mer* (a "sound" or "stretch of water") emerged in the early seventeenth century (*la Manche d'Angleterre*, 1611), a meaning that persisted only in the proper noun *la Manche* (first attested 1771).

In geological terms, the Channel is a relatively recent phenomenon, seen by Rainsford as a "water-filled incision in the surface of the globe", slowly eroded in the rock that once attached Britain to continental Europe (2002: 1). Compared to other straits and seas, it appears insignificant, a barrier between France and England, a connection between Atlantic and

North Sea. Whereas geographers define the Channel according to strict limits, travellers tend to contract it even further to fixed trajectories in the middle Channel, often the shorter the better, between Dover and Calais, Folkestone and Boulogne (absent from the present study are those for whom trips to France permit the purchase of lower-duty alcohol and tobacco, for whom the Channel is little more than an unfortunate hindrance in this activity, and who are neither travellers, tourists, nor migrants in any conventional understandings of those terms). Historians, however, often allow it to expand beyond Brittany into the western approaches of the Atlantic (on differing disciplinary approaches to the Channel, see Unwin 2003: 3). This definitional instability, this expansion and contraction, are related to the Channel's significance beyond geology or conventional geography, and there is a growing awareness among scholars of the need to study its wider status: historical, political, commercial, cultural and (particularly in relation to identity formation) symbolic. As Peter Unwin makes clear, the Channel may be seen historically as one of the key sites at which "the Atlantic world [...] met the European", and as a space that now symbolizes strategic and cultural choices facing France and the United Kingdom, especially at a time when the distinctiveness of the nation state and the frontiers whereby it is traditionally defined are eroded (2003: 308). As Britain renegotiates its role in relation to an increasingly solipsistic US and an ever-expanding Europe, the Channel and the Atlantic will, respectively, become narrower or wider according to strategic choices made.

Progressive domestication of the Channel

It is thus both a barrier and bridge, serving before the Hundred Years War and the Reformation almost as interior sea, connecting elements of a small European empire, but becoming subsequently an essential, self-definitional dividing line (on the fifteenth-century collapse of any "Anglo-French family unity", see Gibson 1995), as two self-consciously different and often hostile nations sought to maintain tangible distinctions. Yet this shifting political significance is to be situated in relation to a history of progressive domestication of the Channel, as improvement in transport technology, the democratization of tourism and, ultimately, the digging of a tunnel have increasingly facilitated its crossing. By the 1850s even, the Channel had already become a thoroughfare, after a long tradition of often chauvinistic rivalry in new technologies. Not least with hot air balloons, the first crossing in which was achieved by Blanchard and Jeffries in 1784, although the tradition—and especially consideration of its military potential—continued well into the nineteenth century. Joseph Mangot's *Traversée de la Manche de Cherbourg à Londres* underlines the continued nineteenth-century geopolitical and diplomatic signification of Channel crossing: "Considering with a thoroughly French nonchalance the ocean depths waiting to swallow them up, [they] managed to fly our glorious tricolour flag in the very midst of the Thames fog" (1888: 4). Mangot, who would die the following month attempting a further crossing, gave this account of leaving Cherbourg at the end of July 1886: " 'Where are you going?' they shouted to us. 'To London!' Enthusiastic cheers were the reply, but the balloon quickly sped away" (1888: 12). On crossing the Thames, he states: "We had now reached our goal and after launching articifial torpedoes on the docks and arsenals of London, we started looking for a place to land" (1888: 16; see also Fonvielle 1882).

By 1925, Channel crossing had become a mass activity, with one million visitors travelling that year to exhibitions in London and Paris. By the mid-twentieth century it was, in Bradford's terms, the "holidaymaker's Channel", "a ribbon of water at the doorstep, decorative but not defensive" (1966: 107). However, such physical domestication has not—as Anglo-French tensions over the Sangatte camps have recently made clear—dissipated the Channel's symbolic force. In describing its "lasting peculiarity", Rainsford states that "[the Channel] can be constructed, at times, as neither French nor English; not necessarily neutral or a no-man's land; but rather a territory in which identities, sovereignties and reputations are forever up for grabs; where individuals, alliances and nations have to prove themselves" (2002: 12).

That the Channel may be seen as interstitial in this way is highlighted by Julian Barnes in the collection of short stories that constitute *Cross Channel*. In describing the armies of Irish and British labourers constructing the railways of northern France in the mid-nineteenth century, he alludes to the emergence of an interlingual Anglo-French *patois*—perhaps more accurately, in linguistic terms, an *argot*—that becomes the language of this Channel zone, a concrete illustration of the reflection underpinning a number of contributions to this volume: despite the nationalist rhetoric and its popular manifestations, English and French identities remain overlapping and even interdependent; despite political splits, the increasing traffic of people and ideas and goods transformed the Channel zone into a space of transnational exchange, even at time of political hostility (Barnes 1996: 33). Pichot's description of the Paris to Rouen railway, the focus of Barnes's short story, reveals this blurring of national boundaries, resulting in an ambiguity that can easily trigger a resort to the vocabulary of latent menace and imminent invasion, as may be seen regularly in the press on both sides of the Channel: "On the railway from Paris to Rouen, you might think you were in England as soon as you leave the rue Saint-Lazare. It's an English railway: the engineer is English..." (Pichot 1850 quoted in Gury 1999: 67). This shift from site of exchange to site of rivalry is often an imperceptible one, and the persistent reassertion of the Channel as a site of Anglo-French competition can be seen in key crossings: Captain Webb swam from Dover to Calais in 1875, allegedly with the sound of *Rule Britannia* in his head; Louis Blériot's crossing by air in 1909 was presented in the London press as a direct challenge to British sovereignty (on Webb, see Watson 2000).

Such rivalry, as already suggested, translates into respective national traditions of representing and relating to the Channel, the distinctiveness of which is clear in the differing nomenclature applied to the straits. The proprietorial "English" of the "*English* Channel" reflects an assumption of ownership wholly absent from *la Manche*.

> No country can own the sea beyond the three-mile limit of its territorial waters; yet few Englishmen, I suppose, do not in their private imagination claim the Channel for their own. [...] No Frenchman so far as I know has ever wished to give it so possessive a name on his country's behalf [...]. It is not their Channel: it is ours. (Selincourt, 1953: 1-2)

This clear reflection of the influence of geography on history and on identity serves to emphasize British insularity and isolationism to such an extent that one might ask (as does Aubrey de Selincourt, 1953: 1) whether becoming an island—through the erosion of the Channel—was in fact the first distinctive event in British history.

Different symbolic values

There is no French equivalent to the rich British tradition of books devoted to the Channel itself and privileging the frontier it represents, for, as Rainsford writes (2002: 132) "[t]hc Channel coast is, [after all], just one of several 'natural' frontiers or boundaries that have for centuries been enlisted in debates about the rightful shape and extent of the [French] nation, and, these days, the Channel coast is just one side of the 'hexagon', that newer image of France that implies symmetry and cohesiveness." Moreover, British interest in the Channel has, it could be argued, increased in the late twentieth century—again in response to political developments, and to anxieties regarding the integrity and sustainability of an imagined "national" identity. Two of the earliest cross-Channel narratives—Caesar's *Conquest of Gaul* and the Bayeux tapestry—are, after all, stories of conquest, and it is perhaps not surprising that at moments of acute national identity crisis, the Channel, symbol of the "myth of Albion, inviolate since 1066", becomes a privileged site of reflection (see Unwin 2003: 131). In Gaby Dellal's recent film *On a Clear Day* (2005), the protagonist Frank Redmond (played by Peter Mullen), made redundant by a Glasgow shipbuilding firm "rationalized" after a foreign take-over, recovers his self-esteem (and, by extension, that of a post-industrial Britain) by swimming the Channel. Aubrey de Selincourt reflects on this specific relationship: "The Channel Shore and the waters which wash it are woven so closely into the consciousness of Englishmen, that it is as difficult for them to imagine a time when they did not exist as it is for a child to believe his elders when they tell him that once he 'was not'." (Selincourt 1953: 1).

De Selincourt's historically nostalgic lament, part of one of a series of similar essays on the Channel published in the 1950s, was written at a time of post-war identity crisis, in response to a sense that Britain was as a country in decline, a decline most evident at its extremities. Yet it represents the construction of a certain type of Englishness—not to do with Wales, Scotland, even the North of England itself—defined in relation to continental Europe. In the remainder of this chapter, we shall reflect on the ways in which a recent account of a "voyage around and across the English Channel", Sebastian Smith's *Channel Crossing*, may be seen to react to this tradition of instrumentalizing the Channel in English reflections on national identity. It is our contention—and this is potentially, of course, a larger study in its own right—that the respective national traditions of representing the Channel reflect the evolution of Anglo-French relations. At the same time, the traditions indicate the very different ways in which travellers engage with and textualize this space, presenting it (as is often the case in French accounts) as a hindrance to travel or a threshold to be crossed rapidly, or (more commonly in English accounts) as a site worthy of closer exploration in its own right. Although travel in and around the Channel plays a role in a number of contemporary French travel narratives (such as Hamon 1997 and 1999), this stretch of water does not appear to possess the same symbolic capital as it does in a series of English-language texts. In Jacques Gury's anthology of French travellers' journeys *outre-Manche*, for instance, the Channel itself plays a relatively minor role: it represents a fleeting experience and an experience of necessary international passage (see "Franchir la Manche", Gury 1999: 66-107). The sea is an obstacle, its crossing a rite of passage whose often harsh physical conditions serve as preparation for the shock of an encounter with British alterity:

> If the "journey to England" arouses apprehension, it is not because of the distance, difficulties or dangers, but because of the need to "cross into England", to embark on a ship. It is simply a matter of getting across a sound, but the obstacle is linked less to the seven leagues of the Straits of Dover than to the prospect of having to face another world. On the other side of the Channel, England is an elsewhere entrenched in its insularity. It has to be tackled without the benefit of familiarity permitted by a slow approach across marches and margins. A few days by road, a few hours at sea, and soon you are in London, in a totally foreign country, a week after having left Paris. (Gury 1999: 66)

The Channel does not appear, however, to be invested with the same symbolic value present in works by contemporary British travellers, and it is striking that with the increasing traffic across the Channel from the 1850s onwards, Gury's examples peter out. Indeed, by the later nineteenth century, the crossing has become the subject of *littérature d'anticipation* (science fiction): Michel Jules Verne's "Zigzags à travers la science" (1888) anticipates more recent post-tunnel literature in its emphasis on the amelioration of travelling conditions, and on the domestication—or even obsolescence—of the Channel this implies. The narrative begins: "On September 25th 189-, I was catching the 6.40 evening express from Boulogne to London. A three-and-a-half-hour journey, including one hour crossing the famous twenty-four mile bridge which for the last three years had linked France to England" (Verne 1888: For a discussion of this, see Rainsford 2002: 115-18).

A "forgotten, bypassed world"

Verne's narrative is of interest for it foreshadows works such as Smith's *Channel Crossing*, written over a century later, which is itself a travel narrative written not only shortly after the opening of the Channel Tunnel, but also in the context of a rapidly changing Europe (Smith 2002). Smith's aim is to learn to sail a Wayfarer dinghy in order to cross the Channel in a vessel that appears wholly inappropriate not only in terms of size, but also in relation to other possible means of transport (i.e. ferries, or the tunnel). The resulting account may be read as part of a tradition of "domestic" journeys exploring the spaces of home, but is to be seen at the same time as an attempt to draw on the conventions of adventure travel to re-invest the Channel with traces of its historic and strategic significance. Smith accordingly seems to respond to Rainsford's bleak assessment of the redundancy of conventional Channel crossing:

> The opening of the Channel Tunnel has made it possible to travel between France and England with minimal discomfort and hardly any thought. Eurostar passengers are barely called upon to notice that the Channel is there. They descend into the earth on one side and emerge from it at the other, and the only water that they see comes in bottles, at an exorbitant price. It is like a prolonged ride on the Tube or the Métro, with better seats and fewer interruptions. (Rainsford 2002: 46)

Two questions arise from Smith's project-based approach to Channel crossing, both of which are linked to the future of the literature of the Channel: why bother to sail? and, why bother to describe any journeys still undertaken there, given the Channel's democratization (for certain travellers at least…) as a space of transit?

Smith's journey and its subsequent account are a response to these points, a reaction to the sense of melancholy and loss that pervades the opening of the text (and the reflection on the last British lighthouse keeper on which this focuses). In describing this Channel crossing as a search not for "the Channel of Eurostar", but for a "forgotten, bypassed world" (Smith 2002: 23), Smith appears to present the nostalgic recovery of the past that characterizes much travel writing (and in particular perhaps that of recent British travellers seeking a certain idea of rural France), analysed by Chris Bongie in his *Exotic Memories*:

> Dire visions such as these [those of Claude Lévi-Strauss in *Tristes Tropiques*], however, most often resemble each other not only in their pessimism but also in their propensity for deferring the very thing that is being affirmed: although humanity is settling into a "monoculture", it is at the same time still only *in the process of*, or *on the point of*, producing a "beat-like" mass society. (Bongie 1991: 4)

Smith adopts the strategy of differentiation, seeing his journey as project (he needs to learn to sail), and presenting his trajectory as an instance of extreme travel (he constructs a very clear sense of solitude; he crosses shipping lanes in a seemingly inappropriate vessel). On the one hand, therefore, there is clear nostalgia, for previous modes of travel and for earlier understandings of space (and, with this, an implicit critique of modernity). At the same time, however, the work represents a reflection on the nature of travel: it describes the exploration of a place seen increasingly in terms of Marc Augé's notion of the anonymous *non-lieu* (non-place) through which people pass in a hurry to get elsewhere, in which people make no personal investment (the ferry on which at one point he travels is "more motorway service station than ship", p. 87), but where, through deceleration and proximity, history and other travel stories begin to emerge. The cross-Channel ferry has inspired little in the field of cultural representation. Serge Gainsbourg's "69 année érotique" nevertheless takes the journey as its central theme: "Gainsbourg et son Gainsborough / Ont pris le ferry-boat / De leur lit par le hublot / Ils regardent la côte / Ils s'aiment et la traversée / Durera toute une année" ("Gainsbourg and his Gainsborough / Caught the ferry / From their bed through the porthole / They looked at the coast / They made love and the crossing / Lasted a whole year"), and an exploration of the potential of Channel crossing as a site of sexual encounter and self-exploration underpins Catherine Breillat's *Brève Traversée* (2001) in which Thomas (played by Gilles Guillain), a sixteen-year-old French boy, meets Alice (played by Sarah Pratt), a much older British woman, on a ferry from Le Havre to Portsmouth.

Smith's account thus enacts the reversal of emphasis seen on the maritime chart, where—unlike on a conventional map—the land itself is empty of geographical features and the sea is represented in extreme detail. The narrator's aim is to map this territory, a process evident in his preparation for a journey that is in itself very brief: the crossing begins on page 216 of a 240-page volume, and is concluded very quickly (within only 14 pages). This focus on preparation permits the reinscription of adventure—"this sea might be narrow, but the path across was long" (p. 64)—and serves as a response to Smith's desire to be a "real" sailor (p. 111). At the same time, however, the emphasis on journeying *around* as opposed to solely *across* the Channel—learning to sail; travelling to other parts of the straits, to France on a trawler, to the *îles anglo-normandes*; listening to other travel stories—permits a proximity to spaces increasingly absent from what Emily Apter (2002) dubs a "literature of the Chunnel zone". This close engagement with space has two principal implications. Firstly, it reflects Smith's attention to travel and border crossing, and to the ambiguous role of borders such as the Channel (described as "the place between, the interruption, the nowhere land", p. 219) in the contemporary, globalized world. His claim that he is a "citizen of the Channel" (p. 231) reflects Rainsford's observation that, for certain travellers and thinkers, this zone responds to the "need for something other than their home nation and its equivalent, opposite numbers":

> The Channel lets fresh air and water into a particular part of the world, but it symbolizes the invigorating effects which might be associated with borders everywhere: geographical moments where identities were interrupted or exchanged, but, for a while, not taken for granted, and open to supplementation and renewal. (Rainsford 2002: 159)

Secondly, this notion of interruption and exchange is linked to the narrative's challenge—through the recognition of alternative accounts and experiences of the Channel—to its narrator's own self-performance and associated self-distinction. For much in the same way as the fictional author of Barnes's *Cross Channel*, in the final story of the collection, sees himself, on his crossings, gathering, sifting and grafting memories ("his memories, history's memories", 1996: 210), so Sebastian Smith describes himself "sailing among the Channel ghosts" (2002: 203), travelling among those phantoms, both historical and current, real and fictional, by which the symbolic value of the place has been elaborated and freighted:

> On the night ferry back to Portsmouth, I waited until we were under way and took a turn of the deck. There was nothing to see in the dark other than a glimpse of white wake. Most passengers were asleep, except for some at the bar, which would soon close. But when I looked out, the Channel teemed with stories. (Smith 2002: 182)

As recent reports appearing in the UK press make clear, for refugees seeking to cross the Channel, this narrow stretch of water continues to mark a real difference: the democratization of mobility to which we have alluded remains a distant hope, and Smith's silence on these parallel "travellers" presents a point at which his own account might be prised open. What *Channel Crossing* does not include is an awareness of these other migrant travellers, whose role in the symbolic reassertion of the Channel in recent years cannot be underestimated.

To conclude, in what direction might the research agenda we have sketched out go next? To understand the Channel as a site of travel, tourism *and* migration, these alternative journey accounts must be recovered and read contrapuntally against a corpus traditionally and conservatively defined as "travel writing". Traces of these alternative stories are currently recovered and preserved not so much in literature as in a series of recent films, such as Pawel Pawlikowski's *Last Resort* (2000), with its focus on asylum seekers housed in a decrepit tower block in Margate, Michael Winterbottom's *In this World* (2003), which concludes with its young protagonist's successful negotiation of the Channel tunnel balanced on a lorry's back axle, Henri-François Imbert's *No Pasaràn* (2003), whose epilogue creates connections between Spanish Republican refugee camps in 1930s France and the more recent camps for asylum seekers at Sangatte, and Nick Broomfield's *Ghosts* (2007), which shows Chinese migrants crossing the Channel hidden behind a compartment in a van. It is these stories that recall James Clifford's admonition in "Traveling Cultures" (1997: 38): "if contemporary migrant populations are not to appear as mute, passive straws in the political-economic winds, we need to listen to a wide range of 'travel stories' (not 'travel literature' in the bourgeois sense)." Perhaps it is only with a contrapuntal awareness of these contrasting modes of mobility that we become aware of the full complexity both of travel and of its most privileged, complex sites, such as the Channel itself.

Bibliography and References

APTER Emily (2002) "From literary Channel to narrative Chunnel," pp. 286-93 in Cohen & Dever.

—. (2006) "'Je ne crois pas beaucoup à la littérature comparée': Universal Poetics and Postcolonial Comparatism," pp. 54-62 in Haun Saussy (ed.), *Comparative Literature in an Age of Globalization*, Baltimore: Johns Hopkins University Press.

BARNES Julian (1996) *Cross Channel*, London: Picador.

BOLDRINI Lucia (2006) "Comparative literature in the twenty-first century," *Comparative Critical Studies*, 3(1-2), pp. 13-23.

BONGIE Chris (1991) *Exotic Memories. Literature, Colonialism, and the Fin de Siècle*, Stanford CA: Stanford University Press.

BRADFORD Ernle (1966) *Wall of England: The Channel's 2000 Years of History*, London: Country Life.

CLIFFORD James (1997) *Routes: Travel and Translation in the Late Twentieth Century*, Cambridge MA: Harvard University Press.

COHEN Margaret & DEVER Carolyn (eds.) (2002) *The Literary Channel: The International Invention of the Novel*, Princeton & Oxford: Princeton University Press.

FALVEY Robert & BROOKS William (eds.) (1991) *The Channel in the Eighteenth Century: Bridge, Barrier, and Gateway*, Oxford: Voltaire Foundation.

FONVIELLE Wilfred de (1882) *Les Grandes ascensions maritimes: la traversée de la Manche*, Paris: Auguste Ghio.

FOUCRIER Annick (ed.) (2005) *The French and the Pacific World, 17th–19th Centuries: Explorations, Migrations and Cultural Exchanges*, Aldershot: Ashgate.

GIBSON Robert (1995) *Best of Enemies: Anglo-French Relations since the Norman Conquest*, London: Sinclair-Stevenson.

GILROY Paul (1992) *The Black Atlantic: Modernity and Double Consciousnes*, Cambridge MA: Harvard University Press.

GLISSANT Edouard (1969) *L'Intention poétique*, Paris: Seuil.

GURY Jacques (ed.) (1999) *Le Voyage Outre-Manche: anthologie de voyageurs français de Voltaire à MacOrlan du XVIIIe au XXe siècle*, Paris: Laffont.

HAMON Hervé (1997) *Besoin de mer*, Paris: Seuil.

—. (1999) *L'Abeille d'Ouessant*, Paris: Seuil.

LACARRIERE Jacques (1998) "A propos de la Méditerranée," pp. 33-35 in Michel Le Bris & Jean-Claude Izzo (eds.), *Méditerranées*, Paris: Librio.

MANGOT Joseph (1888) *Traversée de la Manche de Cherbourg à Londres*, Paris: Imprimerie du 'Spectateur militaire'.

MARSHALL Bill (ed.) (2005) *France and the Americas: Culture, Politics, and History*, 3 vols., Santa Barbara CA: ABC-Clio.

MATSUDA Matt (2005) *Empire of Love: Histories of France and the Pacific*, New York: Oxford University Press.

PICHOT Amédée (1850) *L'Irlande et le pays de Galles*, Paris: Guillaumin.

PRATT Mary Louise (1992) *Imperial Eyes: Travel Writing and Transculturation*, London: Routledge.

RAINSFORD Dominic (2002) *Literature, Identity and the English Channel: Narrow Seas Expanded*, Basingstoke: Palgrave.

ROJEK Chris & URRY John (eds.) (1997) *Touring Cultures:Transformations of Travel and Theory*, London: Routledge.

SELINCOURT Aubrey de (1953) *The Channel Shore*, London: Hale.

SEVIN Olivier (1999) "Propos introductif", pp. 7-10 in *Les Méditerranées dans le monde*, Arras: Artois Presses Université.

SMITH Hillas (1994) *The English Channel: A Celebration of the Channel's Role in England's History*, Upton-upon-Severn: Images Publishing.

SMITH Sebastian (2002) *Channel Crossing: A Voyage around and across the English Channel*, Harmondsworth: Penguin (first published 2001, London: Hamish Hamilton).

UNWIN Peter (2003) *The Narrow Sea: Barrier, Bridge and Gateway to the World: The History of the English Channel*, London: Review.

VERNE Michel Jules (1888) "Zigzags à travers la science," *Le Figaro, supplément littéraire*, 16 June 1888.

WATSON Kathy (2000) *The Crossing: The Curious Story of the First Man to Swim the English Channel*, London: Headline.

WILSON Keith (1994) *Channel Tunnel Visions, 1850-1945: Dreams and Nightmares*, London: Hambledon Press.

CHAPTER EIGHT

FROM "CHAMOUNI" TO CHAMONIX: THE BRITISH IN THE ALPS

CHRISTINE GEOFFROY

When Turner went to Chamonix in 1802, his first trip to the continent, he travelled in relative comfort: thanks to the generous support of a number of benefactors, he was able to undertake the journey in a light convertible carriage along with a Swiss valet-cum-guide and a gentleman-artist who organized the expedition and looked after the finances. Nevertheless, it took him twelve days to get from London to Geneva. The journey included a windy crossing of the Channel, with a perilous landing in small boats at Calais due to weather and sandbank problems (in clear contrast to more recent conditions mentioned in the previous chapter). It then took almost three more days to reach Chamonix (Hill 1992), which was at that time only accessible to travellers riding on a mule or walking. Today, British people can complete their journey from London to Geneva in less than two hours, on any one of a number of daily flights offered by low-cost airlines. In 2005 over nine million passengers used Geneva airport, the nine millionth being a regular passenger on an Easyjet flight, whose arrival was celebrated in December. The annual report issued on June 1st 2006 showed a year-on-year growth of 9.5% in passenger traffic. Many of the flights link Geneva with twenty different British airports, and a system of shuttles, most managed by British operators, provides transport from Geneva to Chamonix in just over an hour. The "small town in the mountains" is changing under the influence of its growing British population, composed of tourists, seasonal visitors, peripatetic visitors, and temporary or permanent residents (categories defined by Karen O'Reilly, see page 145).

Chamonix-Mont-Blanc, a focal point for international tourism comparable to the French Riviera or the Caribbean islands, seems to have attracted great numbers of British people ever since the eighteenth century. Then, young aristocrats on their way to Italy on their Grand Tour would make a detour via "Chamouni" and its "glacières", as they called them. The bold British conquerors of the Alpine summits attained worldwide fame in the golden age of mountaineering, from 1854 to 1865. At the end of the nineteenth and beginning of the twentieth century, tourism in this area grew hugely thanks to the massive arrival of British people taking advantage of the newly extended railway networks. Comparable to that mass tourism initiated by the railways is the influx today of a new wave of British people, encouraged by the fast and cheap transport to take a break from work. We have previously analyzed the reasons why this small town attracts British people today, as well as the demographic, social and economic impact on the locality (Geoffroy 2005, 2007). In this chapter, we shall address the links that can be traced between the travellers or tourists of yesteryear and today's migrants or, to use the sociologist Glick Schiller's term, "transmigrants" (1992).

Travellers and tourists of yesteryear

What are the distinctions between the traveller and the tourist? Both of them move physically in space (Urry 2000), the latter choosing to see particular places and objects out of interest or for pleasure. Hence it is the tourists' "gaze" (Urry 1990) that distinguishes them from travellers, with a marked evolution in their vision of mountains in the eighteenth century, a time when there was a change from the terror caused by "those dreadful heights" to an ecstatic delight at the sight of "those sublime heights" ("Ces monts affreux...": Engel & Vallot 1934, "Ces monts sublimes...": Engel & Vallot 1936). The travellers who undertook the Grand Tour, particularly those who at the end of the eighteenth century and beginning of the nineteenth century were accompanied by artists, painters, or writers, not only coined the very term "tourist" but also heralded the transformation of status from that of traveller into that of tourist. The way they looked at the places they chose to visit or the landscapes they chose to cross and paint or describe, differentiates them from those who travelled from place to place for reasons from which pleasure or emotion were absent. Representations of mountain scenery in the middle of the eighteenth century were essentially composed of topographic works, totally devoid of emotion and purely descriptive. They were followed later in the century by a few works produced by British artists, among whom Cozens in particular stands out. The way he saw the Alps when travelling there, in 1776 and 1782, initiated a fundamental change in the representation of relations between sky, water and rock (Schama 1999: 538-541). The effects of light, his treatment of perspective and his drawing of relief differed from the first alpine maps drawn by his predecessors. Turner, a young student at the time, was able to study Cozens' watercolours by trying to copy him and it was then that he began to toy with the idea of alpine subjects. Turner's first journey on the Continent in 1802 and his crossing of the Alps occasioned a true revelation, which was to mark a decisive turning-point in his painting. His rapture can be perceived in all the works he brought back from this expedition. The spectacle offered by Chamonix glaciers in particular, the experience of his intimate union with nature and the ice on which he settled to paint the Mer de Glace, made him transgress all the rules of pictorial convention and the academic norms followed in his time. The Alps had created the first of the "Modern Painters" (Ruskin 1843) by profoundly changing the vision of this famous traveller.

But it was also the personal appearance of the travellers that made them tourists, both through the way they were perceived by the local inhabitants, and through the care with which the travellers themselves constructed their own appearance. Take, for example, the outfit Pococke wore when bivouacking in the meadows near Sallanches on his first expedition to the Mer de Glace with Windham in 1741. Having donned a magnificent caftan and turban which he had brought back from his expeditions to the Orient, Pococke asked a servant to mount guard with drawn sword at the front of his tent (Schama 1999: 528). One can easily imagine the anxiety felt by the guides who accompanied the "explorers", and the amazement of the local shepherds at the sight of an Arab sultan appearing in their midst.

In the context of people looking at each other, nineteenth-century tourists who tried to ape local clothing habits laid themselves open to ridicule. In 1825 a visitor to the Alps thus related his amazement at the sight of an English tourist:

> We beheld a description of an animal rather frequent in the mountainous regions—not a chamois nor a lammergeyer but an Alpine dandy. He was fearfully rigged out for daring and desperate exploit, with belt, pole and nicely embroidered jerkin—a costume admirably adapted for exciting female terror, and a reasonable apprehension, that some formidable hillocks and rivulets would be encountered during the day, before the thing returned to preside over bread and butter at the vesper tea-table. (De Beer 1949: 167)

The way the person of the tourist was seen became even more differentiated with Rodolph Töppfer's descriptions. This Swiss schoolmaster, founder of a boarding school in Geneva and forerunner of summer camps, completed more than twenty walking tours in the Alps with his wife and his students each summer from 1823 to 1842 (De Beer 1932). In his travel stories he never failed, like many non-anglophone contemporaries, to make fun of the British tourists. They appeared to be so unwilling to engage in conversation that he had given them the name of "yes and no tourists". In his typology, which ranged from the "tourist *père de famille*" to the "tourist epicure", from the "solitary tourist" to the "experienced tourist who knows everything and looks at nothing", he readily contrasted them with the "German tourist who does nothing but smoke" or the "French tourist who talks incessantly" (Töppfer, quoted in De Beer 1932: 194-195). The tea-time ritual remained a favourite of Töppfer's, in his caricatures:

> The pekoe tourist, always an English one, sits at a separate table with his ladies. Clean-shaven, meticulously well-groomed, disdainful of everything but his supply of finest tea, he divides his time with equal seriousness between the ritual of tea and the reading of the Galignani [*Galignani's Messenger*, a daily paper printed in English], between the delicate practices required to preserve intact the aroma, and the victories of China or the disasters of Afghanistan. Meanwhile the ladies nonchalantly run their beautiful blue eyes over the continentals who come in, have supper or go out, until, once the brewing is completed, they just as nonchalantly administer themselves cup after cup and slice after slice. The whole thing is extremely solemn and twenty-six pekoe tables assuredly make less noise and fewer speeches than a single Frenchman with Madam his wife having fat broth on the corner of a table. (Töppfer, 1864: 98)

The expansion of mountaineering in the second half of the twentieth century gave the mountain additional attraction. Inns started to be crowded with English people visiting the tourist sites of Montenvers and the Mer de Glace, or watching the bold conquerors of Mont Blanc through telescopes. The cannon was fired to salute the heroes returning to Chamonix each evening. So we can distinguish between different visions of the mountains: that of the tourists who came to contemplate the alpine landscapes, of those who came to make the physical effort that would lead them to the top of the highest summits, of those who came to watch the exploits of the mountaineers, and of those who came to be seen and to be able to say when back home that they had been there.

Social differentiation showed in these different approaches and visions. Aristocrats and gentlemen who believed themselves to be the only ones to possess a natural taste for appreciating the mountain were alarmed at the "vulgarity" of the newcomers. What a shock to hear a cockney accent: "How can such people ever have thought of such a journey!" exclaimed a certain Brockedon in 1833 (1833: 36). In the second half of the nineteenth century, Albert Smith ardently employed himself to further spread the craze for the mountains among all social classes. An Alpine enthusiast since early childhood, even learning French so as to be able to translate the writings of Horace Benedict de Saussure, his dream came true at the age of 35 in 1851: he was a poor climber, yet half sick and carried by his guides for the greater part of the climb, he finally reached the summit of Mont Blanc. As soon as he was back in England, he set his mind to putting his adventure on stage by means of a diorama reproducing mountain scenery. The show of his journey to Chamonix and climb up Mont Blanc, constantly renewed and adorned with exotic details—live alpine animals appearing on the stage, peasant-girls or milkmaids in traditional costume—was a tremendous success for six successive years. Queen Victoria herself attended two private performances, and the Prince of Wales, the future Edward VII, travelled to Montenvers accompanied by Smith in 1857. The "man of Mont Blanc" had started the phenomenon known as "Mont Blanc mania" which was to enthral the country for several years. Thousands of children played a snakes-and-ladders board game called "The New Game of Mont Blanc", while their parents danced to the music which had been composed for the show: "the Chamonix Polka" or "the Mont Blanc Quadrille" (Fitzsimons 1967, quoted in Fleming 2000). Smith had come at the right time, just when the railway across France had brought the Alps within easy range of the new English tourists.

This democratization of travel initiated changes in the social status of the former elite travellers (Urry 1990). Thereafter, if most people could travel thanks to the development of the railway networks and the "package holidays" proposed by companies such as that of Thomas Cook, distinction of taste, in Bourdieu's meaning, was no longer operating according to whether people could afford or not to travel, but according to what they had come to see or to seek.

Travellers and tourists today

Are today's tourists so different from yesterday's? Careful observation would no doubt lead back to the typology established by Töppfer with so much humour. The elements which our analysis, based on the ways yesterday's British tourists saw and were seen, are also to be found in our contemporaries today. Rapture in the face of nature's wonders, the experience of just "being there", immersed in this landscape of mountain and ice, can be perceived in the discourse of the British people interviewed in over fifty semi-directive interviews conducted in the

Chamonix Valley between June 2004 and December 2005. To this qualitative survey was added a quantitative one using the 85-item questionnaire devised by the French University economist Marie-Martine Gervais-Aguer for her own survey in the Aquitaine region.

All of them confessed to their fascination for the site. L. confided that she contemplates Mont Blanc at length every morning while M. told about the first time she had come to Chamonix and how she could not detach her gaze from the scenery, spending hours sitting on a balcony and "just looking". The mountain makes her "feel inspired", she concluded. E. said that after climbing various mountains all over the world, he has always come back to Chamonix: "nowhere else can you find mountains like here," he explained. N. spoke of the "visual extravagance" of the site and S. said that "everything is different here", both of them expressing the need to experience the extraordinary in contrast to the ordinariness of everyday life (cf. Urry 1990). R., who practises hiking in the Chamonix Valley, conceives of walking as a means of access to places from where she can observe and think.

But through these visions, appears a differentiation of taste and social distinction, recalling those we have underlined in the travellers of the nineteenth century. L., born of British gentry, enjoys being lost in contemplative meditation over the landscape. She confided that she does not mix with those she and her friends call the "city boys". "They come to Chamonix only to be able to say they have been here when back home," she said. She despises the way they dress: "they have all that fashionable gear but don't even know how to ski!" Here we are not too far from the description of the alpine dandy of the nineteenth century, nor from the contempt for those tourists who came and invaded a space seen as the preserve of a certain elite. The "package holidays" organized in the resort called "Chamonix Chic" or "Snowy Mecca" (*French Magazine*, 23 January 2005), have been the rage for the last few years among a category of holiday-makers concerned about their own image and the idea of staying in the resort that was "the" must of the winter. The development of cheap airline fares has also allowed other tourists those festive weekends of binge drinking, which they will boast about when meeting their less fortunate friends who remained in their home country.

In contrast, the most elaborate vision was met in a British student carrying out academic work on her relation to the landscape and her identity as a tourist. Here is the description she gave of herself and her friends when getting off the train at the Montenvers station before setting out for a walk:

> Our intentions are revealed by what we wear. Walking boots, tee-shirt and

fleece, backpacks, with picnic, water, maps and waterproofs stowed tightly within, telescopic poles neatly tied to the outside. We are ship-shape, purposeful, already visibly declaring that we will not linger at the Terminal, but signal in our dress, and perhaps our manner, that we mean to strike out, beyond. (Roots 2004: 19)

From tourism to residence: early returning residents

Ruskin would have preferred the Alpine gaze of the tourist to remain contemplative, even mystic, in the face of "these great cathedrals of the earth, with their gates of rock, pavements of cloud, choirs of stream and stone, altars of snow, and vaults of purple traversed by the continual stars" (Ruskin 1860). He went so far as to accuse climbers of violating these cathedrals just as "the French revolutionists made stables of the cathedrals of France", and of transforming them in recreational space: "You have made race-courses of the cathedrals of the earth" (Ruskin 1865). But some of these climbers were able to combine the new way they looked at the mountains with their private intimate aesthetic experience. Such a famous alpinist as Leslie Stephen (1832-1904), father of Virginia Woolf and Vanessa Bell, the title of whose book *The Playground of Europe* reveals at once a certain way of looking at the Alps, was also able, like his contemporary Alfred Wills (1828-1912), to move in the company of climber-artists who had acquired the ability to blend diverse visions. The experience of "being there", of corporeal and intimate communion with the place of recreation or entertainment, the sharing of this experience and spectacle with companions, far from debasing the vision, seems on the contrary to increase its intensity:

> Twenty-one years ago we climbed Mont Blanc together to watch the sunset from the summit. Less than a year ago we observed the same phenomenon from the foot of the mountain. The intervening years have probably made little difference in the sunset. If they have made some difference in our powers of reaching the best point of view, they have, I hope, diminished neither our admiration of such spectacles, nor our pleasure in each other's companionship. (Letter to artist and alpinist Gabriel Loppé, in Stephen 1894, Preamble) [see Fig. 8-1]

Mountain sports, when not undertaken solely in order to achieve exploits, thus enrich sensory experience. The birth and development of new mountain leisure activities in the nineteenth and twentieth centuries—climbing, walking, skiing—participate in this adventure of the senses and in the building of a new relationship with nature. What the eye sees can be completed with tactile and kinaesthetic sensations for hand-to-hand combat between climbers and rock. Walkers, immersed in the scenery, become permeated with the odours of the forest, of the rain or the snow, perceive the rustling of leaves, the murmur of a stream or the rumbling of a cascade swollen by a rainstorm. Cross-country skiers leave their traces on virgin landscapes where only the hissing of their sealskins or the sliding of their skis on the snow break the silence of the passes and small valleys as they cross them.

Fig. 8-1. Gabriel Loppé, *Sunset over the summit of Mont Blanc, 6 August 1873*, Les Amis du Vieux Chamonix.

The richness of the multi-sensory experience in a universe in which time seems to stand still, creates new commitments, described by John Urry as "place obligations" and "time obligations" (Urry 2002). An intermittent contact of the tourist with the selected place is no longer enough to meet these obligations. The pursuit of direct immersion in this ideal space, and access to these quality-time intervals, all forms of "co-presence" will only be satisfied by prolonged residence. The nineteenth century saw artists and mountaineers settling in the valley of Chamonix and its neighbourhood for stays of increasing duration. It may be argued that these prolonged stays had alpine physical training as their only goal. But this hypothesis can be seen to be only partially valid if we consider the case of alpinist Alfred Wills, for instance. How can we believe that he could build his "Eagle's nest" chalet on an isolated plateau at the heart of the wild "Fer à cheval" cirque in Sixt, only to satisfy his passion for climbing?

> It was in the month of August, 1857, that I first saw the Plateau des Fonds. I was descending from the summit of the Buet in company with Balmat and an English friend. The scenery struck us as uncommon in character and unique in beauty, and as we stood at the edge of the level ground, it passed through my mind what a glorious site it would be for a chalet. A day or two afterwards we both wished to revisit the spot, for we could neither of us call to mind in our Alpine experiences a view that had pleased us equally. Finding that our second visit did but strengthen our impressions of the rare beauty of the scenery, the passing thought of the former day returned, and began to assume the character of a definite wish. (Wills 1860: 95)

It was indeed the quality of his vision and the feeling that he had to be there which drove Alfred Wills to undertake his project of building a chalet on this particular site. The Wills family came to stay there every summer from the end of June until the end of September and an annex had to be added to welcome children, relatives and friends. The photos in the family albums reveal a modern and comfortable chalet, strangely situated on a plateau surrounded with precipices, cascades and passes. Up to twenty people can be seen standing, sitting in armchairs or on the grass, reading or drawing, while other characters are leaning out of the windows in an attitude of contemplation of the landscape [See Fig. 8-2].

The pictures show us a quietly flowing life spent in walks and picnics, reading and drawing, or gardening. The letters describe a country-like life beside the peasants who make hay or bustle about corn fields, in a resounding concert of cow and goat bells. But the chalet inhabitants' gaze invariably returns to the scenery. Wills's second wife Bertha— his first wife Lucy had designed the plans of the chalet but was never to see it, as she died before its completion—wrote in a letter to her mother-in-law in August 1862: "There are plenty of lovely strolls that suit my capabilities within easy reach. Every turn is full of beauty." Further on she added: "We lose the sun soon after six, and often see the surrounding rocks lit up by the beautiful rosy rays which rest on them for a short time before it leaves us altogether" (Wills collection). The fittest of the guests would climb at night by candlelight to reach one of the nearest passes and have "a fine view of Mont Blanc" in the rising sun.

Fig. 8-2 "The Eagle's Nest", photo John Wills' private collection.

From second home to full residence

Many British people today feel the same urge, the same obligation to return to the famous valley of Chamonix periodically and meet these sensations of intense pleasure given by the contemplation and immersion in its wonderful landscapes. The desire to "be there" is comparable to that which drives others among their compatriots to buy a house at the seaside or in the countryside of Aquitaine or Normandy, places which certainly promise as richly sensory an experience. Encouraged by transport facilities, television programmes boasting of the continent as a little paradise and the alluring articles to be found in magazines specializing in property business, how could they possibly avoid being tempted with the dream of living at the heart of an exceptional place!

The process of transformation of the tourist into a resident is then naturally set in motion: one first tastes the pleasures of staying in the valley, next the visits gradually become more frequent as the seasons and years pass, so reaching the point of wishing to extend even more one's presence. The final option is that of moving to permanent residence. For some this will mean transforming their second home into a permanent residence, while others will pass directly from renting to buying a property. Over ninety percent of the people interviewed in our survey who had settled in Chamonix or its neighbourhood in the past five years, had all been previously visitors to the valley. S. typically related her own progression:

> We have known the area for several years. We rented a place here in the season for seven years with all our friends. We started coming at the weekends and then came more and more often. Then we decided to buy a chalet and we came to live here permanently one year ago.

When asked about the push-and-pull factors which drove them to change their life, a majority mentioned "the quality of life" as a priority, which means a relationship with time, space and nature they deem totally different from that of the life they had in Great Britain. The sensory experience therefore appears to come first in the process of deciding where to live, and in the desire for a "co-presence" with the extraordinary, which will eventually become the everyday ordinary.

The dream they entertain becomes a reality due for the most part to the development of airline carriers, but social differentiation is in fact operating in the process, as it already was in the preceding centuries. For who indeed could afford long stays in the mountains in the nineteenth century? Those who, like Alfred Wills, occupied privileged professional positions. A high magistrate at the Royal Court, he could on the one hand interrupt his activities for several weeks and, on the other hand, meet the expenses of his travels to France, the building of his chalet and its maintenance. Officially, one had the "best and noblest" reasons to come and stay. One was not, indisputably, to be confused with those fashionable figures who were invading hotels and inns, nor with the "package holiday" customers, "Cook's hordes and vandals" (Brendon 1991, quoted in Urry 1990) who, after travelling by train from London to Dover, the ferry to Calais, train to Geneva and charabanc to Chamonix, were gathered in packs of fifty people to walk or ride a mule to the Montenvers and be able to take a glance at the Mer de Glace.

Who nowadays can afford to reside for more or less extended periods of time in Chamonix? The distinction still operates through occupational categories, income levels or economic motives. A certain social elite with high professional skills has appropriated the variables of travel, tourism and migration and invented new modes of mobility and dwelling. Blurring the notions of distance and frontiers, these modern nomads organize their professional life and their private life in a transnational space, which enables them to work "virtually" in London, Liverpool or Manchester from their alpine home, or to physically work in a country while living in another. They too do not want to be confused with casual visiting compatriots, too noisy, too gaudy and who "do not come for the right reasons", nor with property speculators or tourist "racketeers" who launch businesses renting chalets, often with all services provided. Even if the flight fares from London, Birmingham or Edinburgh to Geneva offer unbeatable prices, the place itself operates a distinction of taste. The way they see the mountain landscape, the feeling of deep communion with the elements that are its constituents, as a certain British fringe group felt or sensed yesterday, and feels and senses today—sometimes with a touch of arrogance—are not devoid of a cultural construction linked to class. "Being drawn to the idea of Chamonix isn't enough, one has to get committed to the Valley," said C., who went on to quote articles published in the British press promoting huge estate development projects in the Valley, without a word on how important it is "to get to know the place, develop a reason to be there, and eventually buy because one has formed an attachment with place and people."

Relations with the locals

The Chamonix local people themselves have fully understood what is happening. Yesterday they looked benevolently on those of the British tourists and visitors who had won their respect and with whom they had developed deep bonds of friendship. Well-read aristocrats, enlightened bourgeois, magistrates, scientists, artists, all of them curious intellectuals and lovers of nature, actually cast on landscapes, geology, wildlife and flora, a gaze echoing that of the hunters and crystal seekers who had become their guides. François Devouassoud had been Douglas Freshfield's faithful companion and guide in all their mountain expeditions. Here is what this eminent member of the Royal Geographical Society and President of the Alpine Club said of his guide:

> He knows equally well when to efface himself and when to come forward. His conversation is original and entertaining. He combines the varied interests, the power of observation, and more than the ordinary power of expression of an educated man with the simplicity and breadth of view of a peasant philosopher. (Cunningham 1888; 106)

In the name of this friendship, some English clients invited their guides to hunt on their land, or received them in London to advise them on business matters. Lord Sinclair initiated the project of converting Couttet's boarding house into a grand hotel in 1859 (Borgeaud 2002). The "king of Chamonix guides" François Couttet, nicknamed "Baguette", had until then offered lodgings to numerous English climbers in a house lacking most conveniences. Invited to London by Sinclair, "Baguette" was introduced to several of the aristocrat's friends who helped him design the project of a more modern hotel in line with his prospective clients' requirements. We must also evoke here the links uniting Alfred Wills with his guide Auguste Balmat. Wills accommodated Balmat, on the verge of death, in his own "Eagle's nest" chalet and sat at the bedside of his suffering guide for more than three weeks:

> Indeed, I can't help being a good deal touched at their simple faith and trust in me, and the way in which they seem to count fearlessly on my sympathy and aid. [...] Then, he [Balmat] retains his old predilection for me. He will take double as much food from me as from his sister even, and they say he never fails to hear me and notice what I say, when he is deaf to every other voice; and so, she said, even if he were already half dead, she thought he would hear and listen to the voice of "monsieur", and so she prayed me not to be absent when his last hour should come. Stephen kindly promised to sit up with me the first part of the night, and I was to be called instantly in case of any symptom of death coming on. (Alfred Wills' letter to his mother, September 7, 1862: Wills Collection)

What is left today of all those great demonstrations of friendship? They seem to have grown scarce and distorted under the influence of estate and commercial speculation. The local people in Chamonix, whose children can no longer meet the expenses generated by the purchase of property or the inflating inheritance taxes on their parents' chalets, feel that they are being dispossessed of their own land. The bitter feelings about their loss sometimes prevent them from spotting those of the British people who, like P., still share their concerns today: "The people who made the Chamonix Valley special are pushed away from the place of their origin so that they are forced to commute back (to their previous) 'home' to work [...] The constant push for development, fed and fed upon by UK journalism, does not attempt to address this problem." Or those, more discreet and adept at downsizing, who chose to lead a simpler life whilst still building today an attachment to the place and a close friendship with its inhabitants: "My family took a drop in income of seventy-five percent," said G., "in order to come and live here and both to have more free time to be together and also take advantage of the surroundings."

But even in these last two cases, social differentiation is revealed through cultural features: the construction of the vision, the capacity for thinking, for educating, for asking oneself questions or doubting, remain the essential elements of the passage from the status of tourist into that of resident. Having some savings and buying one's home in a place selected in a magazine or discovered while watching a television programme is not enough: "We've sold up, packed up, said our farewells and we're heading across the Channel en-route to our new lives in South-West France. Why are we doing this?" Tony Jackson wonders, as he sails away on the ferry to France (FrenchEntrée.com). By deciding to leave one's country, it is both one's own vision and other people's vision of you that change: "It's also your whole world-view unexpectedly changing. You start to see your friends and everyday events through the 'moving permanently to France soon' veil [...]. Anyone who even vaguely knows you now sees you uniquely as 'the family going to live in France' ". The soon-to-be migrants, identified with television programme characters invading British screens, perpetuate in their compatriots' imagination the live myth of a hoped-for new life in an ideal natural French environment:

> You soon realize with some alarm that you are also carrying with you the hopes and dreams of the entire *Place in the Sun* viewing audience (most of Britain), who would be going like a shot themselves were it not for Grandad/Work/Kids, Schooling/Health/Other reason (delete as appropriate). Your expedition is a talking point whether you like it or not, and let's face it, for many of us the ups and downs of someone's else's madcap adventure are always worth watching in preference to doing it yourself. (FrenchEntrée.com)

Vision or illusion?

It would have been tempting to close our analysis with a comparison of the processes to be found in the British of the 2000s and those of the neo-rurals of the 1970s or the British city-dwellers of the 1980s and 1990s (Fée 2003). One would indeed find the same justifications of a mobility based on the nostalgic quest for a countryside offering calm, security and quality of life. The case of Chamonix, however, illustrates that this quest belongs to an earlier process, initiated by the eighteenth- and nineteenth-century travellers to the mountains. By widening the scope of our research to the origins of tourism in the Alps, we have been able to demonstrate the continuum of British mobility to this area, underpinned by an evolution in the traveller's vision which, moving from neutrality to emotion, has built that of the tourist. The traveller's eyes, which slid across the landscape without gaining a firm hold, will in the tourist fasten onto the same landscapes, to try and "better see, and understand, after some surprise, some terror, some beauty, an ordinary peculiarity which attracts our attention" (Le Breton 2006). The vision of the landscape, at first contemplative, meditative, even ecstatic, is enriched, in parallel with the evolution of mountain leisure and sports, with an intense multi-sensory experience, a true union with nature and the environment. This vision will commit the tourist, in order to savour the place for longer, to invent new forms of mobility and dwelling. Initiated in the nineteenth century with the transformation of the tourist into a second-home resident, the obligation of "co-presence" in time with the place so extraordinarily different from everyday life, leads nowadays to the next step: the transformation of the second-home resident into semi-permanent or permanent resident. In a continuum of fluid mobility, it then becomes possible to select one's place of residence, distinct and distant from one's working place.

But if, as in the nineteenth century, the democratization of leisure activities, accompanied by the development of fast and cheap transport, gives the illusion—strengthened by the dream-merchants of the international property market—that "the flavour of the world" (Le Breton 2006) is within everyone's range, a tendency towards social cleavage is always apparent, reproducing the class distinctions of the past centuries. Giving oneself up to one's senses, total immersion, the "embracing posture" with the natural world (Le Breton), cannot avoid confrontation with meaning. By confusing the mountain or any other seaside or countryside landscape with a product or a commodity, by turning a blind eye to economic, psychological, social and affective realities involved in any migration, there is a great risk of seeing one's hope for a better life turn into frustration and failure.

Parallel to the British migrants described by Karen O'Reilly (2007) in Spain, the Chamonix valley is witnessing the emergence of socially excluded residents who cannot emulate the lifestyle of a transnational elite, mobile and well-off, heirs to their rich elders' traditions of mobility. The shutters of D. and P.'s chalet have been closed for a year: financial problems, school difficulties with their teenage children, difficulties in adapting to the place and the people, have not given them the opportunity to see, taste, feel and understand their relationship to the mountain and their new life. They have joined the increasing number of people who silently return to Great Britain, without any media or statistics mentioning this fact.

Bibliography and References

BORGEAUD M.-N. (2002) *Gabriel Loppé, Peintre, photographe et alpiniste*, Grenoble: Editions Glénat.

BROCKEDON W. (1833) *Journals of Excursions in the Alps*, London: James Duncan.

CUNNINGHAM C.D. & ABNEY W. (1888) *The Pioneers of the Alps*, London: Sampson Law, Marston, Searle and Rivington.

DE BEER G.R. (1932) *Alps and Men*, London: Edward Arnold & Co.

—. (1949) *Travellers in Switzerland*, London: Oxford University Press.

ENGEL C.E. & VALLOT C. (1934) *"Ces Monts affreux..." 1650-1810*, Paris: Librairie Delagrave.

ENGEL C.E. & VALLOT C. (1936) *"Ces Monts sublimes..." 1803-1895*, Paris: Librairie Delagrave.

FEE D. (2003) "La campagne anglaise: valeurs et conflits," pp. 13-53 in Monica Charlot (ed.), *Nouvelles valeurs dans l'Angleterre d'aujourd'hui*, Paris: Presses de la Sorbonne Nouvelle.

FLEMING F. (2000) *Killing Dragons*, London: Granta Books.

FrenchEntrée.com. www.frenchentree.com/living "Real Life, On the ferry, leaving England behind, An emotional account of one family's French move."

GEOFFROY C. (2005) "L'immigration des Britanniques à Chamonix," online www.univ-paris13.fr/CRIDAF/TEXTES/ChGeofChamonix.pdf

—. (2007) (forthcoming) "Chamonix Chic?" in *Les étrangers dans les campagnes*, Clermont-Ferrand: Commission de Géographie Rurale & Rural Geography Research Group publication.

GLICK SCHILLER N., BASCH L. & SZANTON BLANC C. (1992) "Transnationalism: a new analytic framework for understanding migration," pp. 1-24 in Glick Schiller N., Basch L. and Szanton Blanc C. (eds.), *Towards a Transnational Perspective on Migration: Race, Class, Ethnicity, and Nationalism Reconsidered*, New York: New York Academy of Sciences.

HILL D. (1992) *Turner in the Alps: The Journey through France & Switzerland in 1802*, London: George Philip Ltd.

LE BRETON D. (2006) *La Saveur du monde. Une anthropologie des sens*, Paris: Editions Métailié.

O'REILLY K. (2000) *The British on the Costa del Sol*, London: Routledge.

—. (2007) "Intra-European migration and the mobility-enclosure dialectic," *Sociology*, 41(2), pp. 277-293.

ROOTS C. (2004) *Bivouac*, MA Cultural Geography Dissertation, Royal Holloway, University of London.

RUSKIN J. (1843) *Modern Painters*, vol. I, London: Smith, Elder & Co.

—. (1860) *Modern Painters*, vol. IV, London: Smith, Elder & Co.

—. (1865) *Sesame and Lilies*, Part III, *Sesame: Of Kings' Treasuries*,

London: Dutton and Co.
SCHAMA S. (1999) *Le Paysage et la mémoire*, Paris: Editions du Seuil. [First published 1995, *Landscape and Memory*, New York: Alfred A. Knopf Inc.]
STEPHEN L. (1894) *The Playground of Europe*, London: Longmans & Co. (The Silver Library).
TÖPPFER R. (1998) [1864] *Nouveaux voyages en zigzag*, Geneva: Editions Slatkine.
URRY J. (1990) *The Tourist Gaze*, London: Sage.
—. (2000) *Sociology beyond Society. Mobilities for the Twenty-First Century*, London: Routledge.
—. (2002) "Mobility and proximity," *Sociology*, vol. 36, n° 2, pp. 255-274.
WILLS A. (1860) *The Eagle's Nest in the Valley of Sixt*, London: Longman, Green, Longman & Roberts.
WILLS COLLECTION. John Wills' private collection of the photographs and letters of his forbear Alfred Wills (1828-1912). The letters are deposited in Chamonix at the library of the "Amis du Vieux Chamonix". The author wishes to express particular thanks to John Wills for his kind assistance, and for allowing free access to the collection including reproductions of his photos.

Chapter Nine

British Migration to the Midi-Pyrenees

Catherine Puzzo

The 1999 general census recorded 18,500 British immigrants living in the Midi-Pyrenees region, to which should be added about a thousand Irish people living in and around Toulouse. But since 2004, EU migrants do not need to register, and so now it is difficult to obtain official figures. The region has not seen any sudden growth due to the massive arrival of the British, who are nothing like as numerous as earlier European migrants such as the Spanish, Portuguese or Italians. Unlike other French regions, where British migrants are concentrated in particular areas, like the Dordogne with its famous "Cordes-Gaillac-Monestiès golden triangle, a real English enclave" (*Dépêche du Midi*, 28/08/03) or Chamonix (see above, chapter 8), the Midi-Pyrenees—at 45,348km^2 the largest of the French regions, and as large as Denmark—is mostly rural, with tiny villages, and has a low population density (58.17 inhabitants per km^2). Apart from some districts in the Toulouse conurbation, it has no British enclave. Although the media have sometimes reported on British migration in Europe, there have been too few academic studies of British migration to the French regions (the most recent include Gervais-Aguer 2003 and 2004). The present chapter, based on a questionnaire together with primary and secondary sources, provides updated and detailed data and a portrait of British migrants to the Midi-Pyrenees region.

Four sources

The sources on which this chapter is based were: (1) An anonymous questionnaire addressed to British residents, with twenty questions under five headings—their status, their arrival in Midi-Pyrenees, their reasons for leaving Britain and choosing France, their life in France and their possible return to the UK. The people questioned were selected either on the basis of their residence (Toulouse and suburbs, rural villages mainly in the Haute-Garonne, Lot, Ariège and Gers), or of their professional activity (the Airbus group). Despite the limited number of questionnaires returned (forty-seven), quantitative data were extracted from the analysis of the answers and some significant trends could be discerned. (2) A corpus of about seventy articles from the local press provided a good source of secondary data (*Décrire et prescrire* 2005). (3) Selected publications on British migration to France and the South-West in particular, incorporating a variety of disciplines: geography, sociology, tourism, and English studies. Each discipline, with its own research demands, tested hypotheses and adopted different approaches to migration. (4) Internet resources for the British in France or thinking of going to France (forums, blogs, B&B web pages, British shops and estate agents): although such sources are to be treated with caution, they provided a sometimes almost indiscreet view of direct, spontaneous, private data.

The results presented below stem from these different sources, with the survey as a starting point to formulate hypotheses, either confirmed or denied by the replies and supplemented by the other sources.

The stories of British migration to the Midi-Pyrénées

Unlike nearby departments or towns in Aquitaine like the Dordogne or Pau or the spa towns on the Atlantic coast, there is no historical English presence in the Midi-Pyrénées (cf. Cassen 2004 & Fouhety 2004). On the occasion of the one hundredth anniversary of the Entente Cordiale (2004), the local press recalled how British people had interacted with the local population, but no real presence of a British community has ever been felt as was the case for other migrant communities who have influenced Toulouse and its region, like the Spaniards who fled Franco's regime or Italians from Venice and Piedmont arriving in the 1930s. As already stated, the absence of recent figures makes it impossible to quantify trends exactly, but from the survey it emerged that British residents could be divided into sub-categories according to certain defining characteristics and with different chronological landmarks:

– The idea of a peaceful retirement in South-West France, which first attracted foreigners to the Dordogne at the end of the 1950s, extended to the Midi-Pyrenees in the 1980s. These newly-retireds were on the whole less well-off than earlier ones, and chose the Aveyron, the Ariège or the Haute-Pyrenees for their authentic rural idyll. Also included in this category are those who share their time between Britain and France and have a home in both countries, as well as those spending only a few months in the region, potential future full-time residents but not yet qualifying as immigrants.

– Economic considerations were very important for working migrants to the Midi-Pyrénées. Managers, engineers and technicians have regularly been sent to the Toulouse site of Airbus, with detachments and transfers from the Filton and Broughton sites in Wales (1996-97, and again since 2000). Those posted to the region tend to live in the suburbs of Toulouse in specific areas where there is a higher concentration of foreign residents. Migrants who came alone seem to face more difficulties in integrating and often envisage returning home whereas those who came with their families have adapted better to the French way of life and do not contemplate returning to the UK.

– In parallel to these two categories, since the end of the 1990s and particularly since 2003, the new type of intra-European migration from the North to the South already observed elsewhere in France and Europe and much publicized by the media, has been drawn to the region. Still working or recently retired, these British migrants have come in search of a more relaxed lifestyle they knew they could not find at home: a big house in the countryside, a simpler life in contact with nature and animals but close to urban centres and airports. The Gers, particularly popular with British people, is nicknamed 'The Gascon Tuscany' and it symbolizes this new phenomenon:

> We (my wife and I) are travelling to Gers in the half term week to see if the area looks and feels as good as it sounds. We are planning to buy a permanent home in France and have been to quite a few parts of the country but never to Gers. [...] What we're looking for is what most people are looking for of course: a rural idyll, good weather, food, walking and plenty of cultural interest and property at reasonable prices… (Internet Forum *French Property*)

– Finally there are all those who do not fit into these categories and who for various reasons arrived one day in the Midi-Pyrénées and have stayed there ever since. Many of these have French partners and so do not stand out or attract much media interest.

What triggers migration?

Almost a third of the respondents (29.5%) were retired, 25% being already retired when they arrived in the Midi-Pyrénées. This finding contradicts journalistic stereotypes where all British residents seem to be retired. The majority of respondents were relatively well-off: over half owned their French home and had skilled or highly skilled jobs; 22% of them worked for the Airbus group or one of its sub-contractors, 18.8% were teachers, 4.5% worked in tourism, 6% in research, and 11% were professionals (translators, journalists).

The survey questions on motives for migration were multiple-choice but it was possible to add personal comments, and it was in fact under the heading "other reasons" that many respondents chose to express themselves. It was perhaps no surprise to find the British climate as the most frequently quoted reason for leaving Britain (46.5%); just under one third (30.2%) mentioned the economic, political and social context in Britain, and 23.25% said they based their decision on the cost of living in Britain and better economic conditions in France. 63% mentioned factors ranging from the French health-care system and welfare state in general (13.6%), to the absence of violence and day-to-day stress, and a better transport system, to name the most quoted. The higher population density, notably in the south of England, also seemed decisive, and the overpopulation of the British Isles was a recurrent theme. Unaffordable property prices in Britain compared with those in the Midi-Pyrenees often contributed to their decision. Most lived either in the suburbs or the country, with the exception of mostly unmarried respondents living in flats in town.

The mild climate (60%) and the geographical location of Toulouse and its region (39.1%) were most frequently quoted reasons for opting for the Midi-Pyrénées. Many stressed they were attracted by the cultural diversity of the area, and the proximity of the Pyrenees, the Atlantic Ocean, the Basque Country and Spain. Unlike the south of Spain, the contrasting seasons with their mild winters, and year-round skiing or walking in the Pyrénées were reasons why the region appealed. The other decisive factor was the possibility of finding a genuinely rural environment (58.6%), especially when compared to the south of England. This corresponds to the stereotyped image of an idyllic rural past that Barou & Prado (1995) and Hoggart & Buller (1994) have already analyzed and that is illustrated by the comment of one interviewee: "There is no traffic, stress or violence. The region reminds me of the England of my youth." For a third of the interviewees (33.8%) French food was among the relevant elements in their decision, and for just under a quarter, a better social life (22.7%). Despite the growing popularity of shops selling teas, beers and British food, South-West specialities were appreciated, wine in particular. Of course, for people working in the Airbus aeronautical group, decisive criteria were opportunities to improve their career coupled with the possibility of improving the standard of living of their families (lower living and housing costs). For others it was the perspective of a different daily routine more in accordance with family life, with less stress, less pollution, and little or no commuting.

A large majority of respondents (73%) moved directly to the Midi-Pyrenees, between 1970 and 2005. There was a sudden influx in 1996-97 due to the Airbus plan to build a new European jet: moving to Toulouse was for some the only way to avoid redundancy, while for others it constituted a great opportunity to speed up the advancement of their careers (Truc 2003). In the Aveyron department, most of the respondents settled at the end of the 1990s, after buying a second home there. The figures for that department tripled between 1989 and 2001, most of the residents coming from London and its region, and the south of England (Georges 2003). In our survey, taking 1999 as a base year, the number of people arriving in the Midi-Pyrénées as a whole had multiplied by five in 2001 and by nine in 2003, but clearly slowed down in 2004. These regional figures compare with the evolution of British emigration monitored by the Office of National Statistics: 1994 (125,000), 2000 (161,000), 2002 (186,000), 2003 (361,000) (*The Guardian,* 5 November 2004).

Adapting to life in France

To evaluate the level of insertion into French life, the questionnaire used two criteria: knowledge of French and regular contacts with French and/or British people. Other possible criteria are involvement with local clubs, knowledge of local habits and local food, or even participation in politics. Additional information on these aspects was provided by blogs, forums and publications.

Only about a third (32.5%) thought their level of French was excellent, usually those with a French partner. However 20.9% of them considered their French fluent, while 37.2% admitted to an intermediate level and 9.3% only a basic knowledge. There are two possible explanations for these discrepancies: the arrival date in France and the professional background. Some British residents regretted that the most recent arrivals in France do not speak good French. The longer established residents had often paid many visits to France before settling, or even had had a second home for holidays). Yet a surprising finding among the newly arrived residents was that 55.8% did not know the region before settling. Some residents claim to have bought their house by telephone or via mail (*La Dépêche du Midi*, 7/04/04). Paradoxically, some of these migrants assert that they love France and French culture, while not knowing much about it. Hence the great popularity of forums in English, created by British residents for British people, such as *Ariegelife.com, MidiPyrénéesinfo, Midi-life.com., French-property.com, Sunseekershomes.com.* Also the professional environment may not have encouraged some of them to learn French: this seemed to be the case for the Airbus staff (50% with only a basic knowledge). They were keen to stress that they do not need to know French for their work or even outside, because of the international atmosphere they live in. The universality of the English language is for others to be used to find a job in Toulouse, without any need to learn more than basics of French. Of course it is widely recognized that a good command is necessary for all those who are required to use both languages on a daily basis, like teachers, translators, professionals or journalists.

As for interaction with people outside the work context, 51% said they saw only French people, 16% only British people, and 32% both. Two trends emerge: some want to live where contacts with compatriots will be easier and they can become part of an ex-pat community. This is the case in the small towns which are part of the Toulouse conurbation: Pibrac, Colomiers, Lèguevin and l'Isle-Jourdain (where there are pubs and an international high school, and where St Patrick's Day and Halloween are celebrated). In more rural areas in the Ariège, Aveyron or Gers *départements*, some groups of British migrants have created networks for communication, mutual aid and social life (a women's group in Ariège, a gardening club in Escanecrabe). A British couple living in the Gers described their situation as follows:

> There's quite a strong ex-pat British community but it represents only a tiny proportion of the populace, so there are no English ghettoes. [...] We are fortunate to belong to an internet group called "Dreaming of South-West France". This group has been invaluable in answering all the inevitable questions that arise, and frequent gatherings of real people have occurred both in France and the UK where lasting friendships formed on the screen are confirmed in the flesh. (iangillis.chez-alice.fr)

Others have on the contrary refused any kind of contact with other British residents which would have reminded them of the society they have left behind. They selected the location of their new residence in order to meet French people, to immerse themselves in life in the nearest village:

> I do not want to build up an ex-pat network where we all sit around quaffing wine and discussing the differences between UK life and France. I (and every one else I knew for that matter) had enough of that when I was in the UK. (www. french-property.com)

Finally, forums and blogs give us a glimpse of their life in France and provide details not supplied by the questionnaire, like the pleasure of going to local open markets and chatting with the stallkeepers, village festivals, contacts with neighbours and participation in local life (the harvest, the local patron saint's day, ferias...). These exchanges via the internet are more reliable accounts than articles in the local press, which often deal with British residents without really letting them speak, seeing them through the filter of what a French readership wants to hear. The following quotation is one example:

> We came here with our eyes open, and intent on making ourselves part of the local community. We live in a tiny village thirty minutes from Foix, and can't imagine anywhere better. Give me "la vie Française" any day. (Simplybritishshop.com)

Returning to Britain?

Links between these residents and the mother country were evaluated through the frequency of visits to Britain, their length and the motives. The first conclusion is that these visits are short, on average about a week, ten days at the most. Many (46%) only go back once a year (Christmas, Easter, summer vacations or special occasions such as weddings) but 20% go back two or three times a year in connection with their work. The well-known phenomenon of commuting professionals, working in London during the week and living in the region during week-ends (Napoli 2004), was not as significant in our survey (5%) as in neighbouring regions such as Languedoc-Roussillon (daily flights between Carcassonne and Stansted) or Aquitaine (Bergerac-Midlands, Pau-London). The ties with Britain seem tenuous, especially for the children of the long-term residents, born and educated in France and who do not feel at home in Britain.

The last part of the questionnaire concerned the desire to return to live in Britain, in the medium or long term. A majority (62%) did not envisage returning, while those who would like to go back (18%) were almost as numerous as the "don't knows" (20%). Except for the Franco-British couples whose desire to stay permanently in France is more or less taken for granted, the reasons given by those who want to stay were broadly similar for all the interviewees and cover the push and pull factors mentioned above. A comfortable adaptation to local life, economic considerations (the same living standards are not available in Britain), the feeling they belong in France (home and work) and the presence of children born and educated there exclude the idea of returning to Britain. Some more personal comments are worth quoting:

> "Too crowded, too much traffic, social injustice. We are very happy with our French life and are able to spend more time together in congenial and relaxed surroundings."
> "Apart from family and friends in the UK, I cannot think of one reason to visit that country!"
> "Never! I'm much better off here!"
> "We've made our lives here and built our home. We belong here."

Reasons for returning, whether for the undecided or those who intend to go back, were connected either to personal circumstances (old age, moving closer to children who remained in the UK, children going to a British university) or to their current difficulty in adapting to the French way of life and culture. So we did not find any "myth" about returning, as we might have expected to, for this population which was not forced into emigration, but on the contrary freely chose to leave Britain and could afford to change their minds (features which distinguish this population from other immigrant populations).

A plurality of migrations

This chapter has demonstrated that there is not one but several coexisting British migrations to the Midi-Pyrenees. The differences are explained by size and geographical diversity of the region, the date of arrival and the different motives. Conversely, the profile of the migrants was not so diverse: coming from the south of England and especially Greater London, English, a relatively high socio-economic status. But from a sociological perspective we cannot talk about a real British community. There are some pockets with more or less significant concentrations of British residents, where gregarious behaviour can be observed. But at the regional level we cannot talk of a community spirit or British networks. However, recent arrivals and the prospect of a future wave of migration may modify these conclusions: this British migration to a European destination may structure itself along more visible and official, institutional lines.

Bibliography and References

BAROU J. & PRADO P. (1995) *Les Anglais dans nos campagnes*, Paris: L'Harmattan.

CASSEN Bernard (2004) "Au cœur de la Dordogne anglaise," *Le Monde Diplomatique* (August 2004).

FOUHETY H. (2004) "Dordogne, terre britannique," *Pour* n° 182 (June

2004).
DÉCRIRE ET PRESCRIRE (2005) "'Décrire et prescrire': la différence dans l'information locale." Report by the Laboratoire des Sciences Sociales du Politique (LASSP), part of the project "Comprendre et agir sur les professionnels de l'information en région," March 2005.
GEORGES A. (2003) *British People Living in the Aveyron: A Case Study in the Villefranche Basin*, Masters dissertation, Université de Toulouse-le-Mirail, département d'études du monde anglophone.
GERVAIS-AGUER Marie-Martine (2003) *Ces Européens qui bougent: recherche à partir des migrations entre le Royaume-Uni et la France*, Research Report for the Conseil Régional d'Aquitaine. Ierso-Ifrede. Université Montesquieu Bordeaux IV (June 2003).
—. (2004) *Les Fondements de l'attractivité territoriale résidentielle: les enseignements d'une recherche portant sur les résidents britanniques en Aquitaine*, Université Montesquieu Bordeaux IV: Cahiers Ifrede-Ierso 2004 n° 25.
HOGGART K. & BULLER H. (1994) *International Counter-Urbanization. British Migrants in Rural France*, Aldershot: Avebury.
NAPOLI J. (2004) "The phenomenon of low cost airlines and its impact in France," paper delivered at the Universal Forum of Cultures, UNESCO, 14-16 July 2004, Barcelona.
TRUC V. (2003) *The Expatriate Spouse in and around Toulouse*, Masters dissertation, Université de Toulouse le Mirail, département d'études du monde anglophone.

CHAPTER TEN

THE INTEGRATION OF BRITISH MIGRANTS IN AQUITAINE

DAVID SMALLWOOD

This chapter examines the process and the level of integration of a sample of the British resident population of Aquitaine, with particular reference to the role of language in this process. By integration is meant the degree of interaction between the British residents and the French population, and of acceptance by the two populations of each other. The empirical part of the research was based on a series of twenty-six semi-structured interviews of approximately 45-60 minutes duration, carried out in as informal a situation as possible, usually in the home of the interviewee. The subjects represent a wide range: the age was eight to seventy-two years, the length of residence in France from six months to thirty-one years, and the geographical location was based statistically on data taken from a survey of the British residents of Aquitaine (Gervais-Aguer & Smallwood 2003).

A typology emerged from these interviews and could be summarized as follows:

– a group of well-integrated subjects, often in mixed French-British couples, who regularly interact professionally and socially with French natives, who are relatively demanding, and slightly frustrated by their inability to be regarded as totally French, but who are nonetheless satisfied with their situation;

– a large group of non-integrated subjects who do not seek integration, as their initial ambitions to integrate have been modified and who have found the life-style they seek within the confines of a British expatriate society; they are generally undemanding and satisfied with their situation;

– a third group of non-integrated subjects, who are seeking integration; they are demanding and extremely frustrated by their inability to master the language; they are not prepared to seek refuge in the English-speaking community and their attempts to settle end in failure, often with a feeling of resentment towards "the French".

In this chapter we will show how these typologies emerge, and then analyse the importance of the interplay between identity and alterity in the integration process. It has become clear that the conflict between the representations of self and of other, between familiar and strange, plays a role in how migrants accept the indigenous society and how it accepts them. There are sound sociological reasons which may help to explain the relative lack of integration of many of the British migrants in France. One of the basic concepts of the notion of alterity indicates that individual identity is constructed with reference to the attitudes of the Other to the individual. Culture and differences of culture are intrinsically significant in this construction, as stated by Marc Augé: "If identity is only discerned at the boundary between the self and the Other, this boundary is itself essentially cultural. It defines all the problem areas of a culture" (1994: 80). "Cultural alterity" is the process by which societies and cultures exclude particular people on account of their otherness. The argument posited is that the British migrant is confronted with a host society which does not share similar attitudes; this creates confusion in the construction of identity, and tends to push the migrant towards a social group that *does* share similar attitudes. The reflection of one's own self thus produced is more in line with expectations and the construction of identity can continue without confusion. Furthermore, the confirmation of this group is manifested in its exclusion of the host society, thus affirming its cultural alterity.

The importance of language

One major reason for carrying out this research was the decision taken by many people to migrate to a country where they don't speak the language. In the interviews, reactions to the importance of the language in the process of integration vary and are sometimes surprising. Those who spoke the best French and were ostensibly the most integrated were the ones who expressed the most concern about their level of French and its negative role in their perceived integration. One bilingual teacher was concerned about her English accent and that it betrayed her origins ("You never lose your accent, do you?"). She also stated that she felt a change in her relationship with French members of the administration when her accent made them realize she was English: "They become more aggressive when I open my mouth and treat me differently because I'm foreign." These same interviewees also, unanimously, said that their character and sense of identity changed depending on the language they were speaking.

One said he felt more aggressive in English, perhaps because he felt that his French was not sufficient to express the same aggression, subtly or with the same personal satisfaction. One bilingual stated that he always spoke French in the family with his native wife and children, "unless I get angry, and then everybody understands me!" Another felt he was more likely to be the life and soul of the party if he were speaking in English, but found it difficult to express humour in French, despite being bilingual.

Other people declared themselves to be rather less than competent in the language but expressed relatively high levels of satisfaction with their level of French with comments such as "I get by", "I make myself understood", "after five years, I can ask for bread now" (said, it has to be admitted, with a certain amount of humour!). Some thought that language was not an important factor in the degree of integration; others thought it critical, "an incredible obstacle". Quite a few complained that they don't get the opportunity to speak French or to mix with the French because they have their own, English-speaking, social group and on mixed social occasions, the French locals want to speak English. This barrier becomes insurmountable when the initial urge to be accepted and to avoid the other "Brits" dissolves into apathy. "You start out with good intentions but then you give up and just mix with the other Brits", which in its turn creates or increases the dependency on other British residents in the region, and reduces the desire to be integrated with the indigenous society.

The interviews included one particularly poignant example of the importance of language in the process of integration. Kevin and Karen moved to France, at the latter's suggestion, to further Kevin's career. The interview with Karen was very emotionally charged; many of her comments showed that the lack of relationships with French natives was causing fairly deep-seated concerns for her: "I have had to try and learn and it has not gone the way I thought it would go. I thought I would learn it a lot quicker than I have done and I am probably more disappointed that I haven't, so it is actually quite frustrating and it caused confidence problems ... it has caused this sort of, you know, yes, serious confidence problems." Her inability to form relationships at the level she desired was eventually, during the course of the interview, blamed on the French, who would not help her to integrate.

She spoke at one point of preferring to live in Spain, even though her knowledge of the language was as rudimentary as her knowledge of French. Her preference derived from a perceived notion of Spanish people being more welcoming than the French. This notion was based on several holidays spent in that country, but her perception of the French had also been that they were warm and friendly before she came to live in France.

This perception had changed dramatically after a year of actually living and trying to be accepted as a resident in the country, to the point where she felt that the French were actually ridiculing her because of her attempts to speak their language. "Spanish people are really open and friendly and I don't think people here are openly friendly … I felt very comfortable in Spain. People are all warmer, there is a different way of being … I am not aware in England of coming across foreigners and ever, ever, ever taking the mickey out of them. You … help them and I feel that here it's different … sometimes people here treat you like you're really stupid and I'm not stupid!"

At one point in the interview she started to consider what the concept of "home" meant to her. At first, this meant where her family was, but then, as her family is dispersed around the country, and, as her father was Austrian, even in other countries, she finally decided that "home" was where her friends were. "Home is where my friends are, friends that I have had for a long time that I can just go and see … *people who just know what you're about* … wow, that's big!" – DS: "So if I ask you what you miss, if anything, in England?" – K: "It's my friends, oh yes, my friends." It became clear that she had already made the decision to abandon her attempts to integrate because of this constant malaise at being "out of it", not included in social groups. She consciously refused to go and look for English friends in France, a decision based on her pride at not wanting to admit that her attempts to integrate were a failure: "No I would never fall back on the British . No, very definitely."

She started to speak of living in France in the unreal conditional tense ("I wouldn't live in France"*)*, even though her life at that moment was in France. Her husband was working successfully, but she projected herself into an unreal future where her decision to settle in France would be different: "It's funny because I always thought I would be able to live anywhere, but I don't feel that this is my place to live, it doesn't feel right to me. I wouldn't live in France. I might live in other places in the world but not France. I have learnt a big lesson by coming here. [Very pensive] I thought you could go and live anywhere." Her malaise was so great that she confided that she had applied for a job in the UK without her husband's knowledge, in an attempt to hide her angst from him. "I actually did apply for a job with the National Trust—I didn't tell Kevin—but that obviously didn't come off. But I would have gone back; I would definitely have gone back. Oh yes!" Two months after the interview, Karen returned to the UK, at first without Kevin, who joined her there when he had sold his business.

At the other end of the linguistic scale, several "bilingual" interviewees—all of whom were part of mixed Anglo-French couples—stated varying degrees of alienation regarding their acceptance in French society. Day-to-day contact with French-speaking interlocutors was not a problem: what they observed was that on a much deeper level, they felt that their "otherness", the fact that they were different, made it difficult to feel *totally* integrated into the host society. Their malaise was far from being as deeply felt as that of Karen, but it existed nonetheless, and created a *perceived* level of integration lower than their *actual* level. Their respective partners all felt that their English husband/wife was entirely accepted by and integrated into French society, yet there was a doubt hovering in the minds of the English partners.

Linguistic or cultural barriers?

Aspects of culture in its general sense were often cited as areas of difficulty. Humour was mentioned on a number of occasions. Alison, perfectly at ease in the host language as she has lived in Bordeaux for 31 years and was married to a French man for most of them, made the following point: "There are lots of things in French humour that just do not amuse me at all and it's something in which you immediately feel at ease with English speakers or rather other English people because you are on the same wavelength … you can translate these things into French but somehow they don't understand what you're getting at." This inability to capture the nuances of foreign humour and to express one's own identity through this medium was expressed by another interviewee, Rupert, who is in a similar situation to Alison: "My character when I talk to French friends is not the same as when I talk with English friends, basically because when I am with my English friends I can be the life and soul of the party but in French I can't because I'm too slow and I don't have the same sense of humour to be able to run the show, so to speak, and I'll never be able to speak French *perfectly*." The last word is stressed because this is at the heart of the disillusionment expressed by this category of interviewee. As one can never be totally accepted as being French, one can never be totally integrated into French culture and society. Rupert looks English and, although speaking French perfectly adequately, has a strong English accent when he speaks.

Whether the barrier is linguistic, as stated by Rupert, or cultural, as implied by Alison, the barrier to "total" integration still exists. Rupert commented, not without a tone of regret, that he is constantly being reminded by French contacts that he is English: "My way of life is entirely French but I still consider myself to be English but ... everybody around me also thinks I'm English even though I speak fluent French ... they keep reminding me that I'm English."

Notions of Otherness

How we see ourselves is very dependent on the way others see us. Both the identity and the integration of a British resident in France depend on how he or she is seen by the French. But how far is Englishness a barrier to integration? Can one be regarded as English in France, and yet be integrated? If we consider the "otherness" one has in one's own society, Scots working in England will sometimes flaunt their otherness, and this was made clear by a Scottish interviewee who was proud of his different origins when in England, but not in France. His accent marked him out from other English-speakers in the UK and he was happy with his otherness. He was different but accepted. In France however, his accent was just vaguely "British" and so he was made aware of his alterity, but the distinction was not made between his Scottishness, of which he was proud, and his Britishness which just made him feel different—and possibly not accepted.

This appeared to be the case with many of the British residents interviewed—their difference was remarked upon and this otherness affected the way they were accepted or not, probably in a negative way. Why is this so? Many interviewees, when asked the specific question as to what extent they felt integrated in French society, replied that they were always regarded as being British. So, does this necessarily exclude you from the host society? The notion of "otherness" is perhaps more important in terms of identity than in terms of integration, but it does appear from the answers given during the interviews that one's sense of identity has a strong bearing on the degree of integration.

We certainly found in our analysis of the interviews that we could define several categories of people within this context of integration, in terms of *desire* to be integrated and also of *level* of integration. If we add to this the distinction between the *perceived* level of integration and *actual* level of integration, the conclusions are far from simple. Let us take two examples.

The first case was a retired interviewee who stated, after several years of living in the area, that he could now manage to order his bread at the local *boulangerie* and felt that he had been accepted by the *boulanger*, a fact which to him was symbolic of a kind of integration, or positive acceptance at the local level. The small degree of acceptance was a big step forward, and was thought of as being a very positive phenomenon. He did not seek a greater level of integration and so was happy to be accepted even at such a basic level. His perceived level of integration was quite high, as was *his* notion of command of the language. He did not seek to be considered as a French native—an impossible feat given his limited command of the language. Ordering his bread was a highly symbolic achievement for him. His life was spent either in his garden or with other English people, and he was content with this situation. He chose when to confront his otherness, when to make contact with the natives. His feeling of Englishness had not been eroded by living in France, but, to him, this was not a problem. His otherness was not a negative phenomenon.

The second was a bilingual Englishman, Robert, living in Bordeaux, professionally active, married to a French woman and working almost exclusively with French people, but who stated that he would never be accepted by the French because he would always be thought of as being English. Between these two extremes, there is a huge range of possibilities. In the latter case, constant contact, socially and professionally, with French people makes the interviewee more aware of his difference, his otherness; he seeks, perhaps not consciously, a much greater level of integration, an acceptance of himself as a person, not as an *English* person, and he is disappointed with his failure to be *totally* accepted. His perceived level of integration was disappointing, even though, if asked, his French contacts would consider him to be well integrated. He felt in limbo between two cultures and identities, and he was not alone in stating this; he has lost his essential Englishness, but at the same time is not accepted as being French, so is neither one thing nor the other.

Several interviewees expressed a feeling of being uncomfortable, again because of their otherness, when returning to the UK after living in France. One said that when she goes "home"—her own word, meaning in this case where her parents are—she is treated as an outsider. She sees them doing "very English things" and her family thinks she does "very French things", which makes her different. But this does not make her feel alien to that culture because it is *her* culture. Once again, this person stated that despite "fitting in" in France, being part of the parent-teachers association at her children's school, and standing for election to her local *conseil municipal*, she felt different in France too, a kind of "no fixed abode". It is the degree of acceptance that causes the problems. The question of degree of integration becomes important when one finds oneself in a culture which is not one's own, and in which one feels much more insecure. This problem of culture, as pointed out in the quotation above by Marc Augé (page 120), is undoubtedly an important factor in the process of acceptance. "Culture is definitely the biggest barrier to integration", stated one interviewee. The longer one stays in France, the more one feels that one will never be totally accepted into the culture and, at the same time, the more one feels alienated from one's original culture.

In answer to the question "How do you feel when you go back to the UK?" several answers confirmed this hypothesis: "Strange really", "a bit like a foreigner", "stressed, really stressed", "I don't feel comfortable going into an English bank. I don't bank in England"; "I don't really feel connected to the UK any more ... but I feel English generally, culturally." Most interviewees didn't see this as "a problem" but it was remarked upon by several; there seemed to be a certain cultural ambivalence in many of the people spoken to. They felt part of both cultures but not fully "integrated" in either. This takes us back to the question of how far natives of a country are culturally "integrated" in their own culture? Are we not aware of being culturally different only when we find ourselves in a strange culture, and wanting, striving to be accepted?

This notion of not being part of a society, even when apparently well integrated, was astutely analysed by one of the interviewees. The person in question had been involved in local politics while living in England, but had also spent a large part of his life in other countries. When confronted with a problem in the host society, for example, he says: "In the UK I would get annoyed and I would get the feeling that I ought to be doing something about it whereas in France I can rather hypocritically say 'Well I'm not from here; it's their problem and I'm not going to change it anyway' ". He went on to say that he feels far less involved in life in France, even though he is, and feels, well-integrated. He can watch French football teams and appreciate the sport, but he would not feel fanatical about any particular French team like he does about the English team he supports. He can observe French politics but not feel passionately involved in the arguments; his involvement is intellectual and reasoned, whereas in the UK he would have much stronger, more committed views.

The relationship between identity and Otherness

In *Identity and Alterity in Sociological Perspective*, Franz Welz states that "it has become much harder for individuals to develop the sense of continuity and consistency of self in the course of life-changes and in the various areas of life which are commonly described as *Identity* (Döbert *et al.* 1980: 9), that is the affirmation of who we are in contrasting our way of life with that of others" (Welz 2000). There is a sense that the construction of identity is becoming more difficult due to the increase in social and geographical mobility because the consistency of remaining in a familiar social group is lacking. This phenomenon is necessarily present and seems even exaggerated in the case of British migrants settling in France. Welz makes the point that "the creative first-person subject [...] self-identity [...] is available in its component parts in the attitudes of others towards me. But do I belong to a clearly-fixed group, whose attitudes are equivalent to my own?"

Clearly, for typical British migrants, the host society does not have attitudes equivalent to their own. In addition, their difference is constantly being iterated, as we have seen from the comments of many interviewees; they are not allowed to feel "similar" as they are confronted, on a daily basis, by their own otherness. Some sociologists tend to agree that otherness is always important to identity in a *static* way. But what comes out of the interviews is that for people who migrate, the relationship between identity and otherness is important in a much more *dynamic* manner—simply because each individual concerned has to deal with this relationship on a direct and daily basis. The behaviour and attitudes of the Other are the origin for each particular identity, according to the perspective of *symbolic interactionism*, particularly in the work of George Herbert Mead. So if the Other is constantly reiterating the individual's difference, this affects the construction of identity and pushes the individual into a social group that is understood and reflects more clearly the construction of identity, due to the cultural and social similarities to be found in this group. This reinforces the cultural bonds of the group as they all find themselves in a similarly disorienting situation.

According to Pierre Clastres, "It is part of a culture's essence to be ethnocentric, precisely to the degree to which every culture considers itself the culture par excellence. In other words, cultural alterity is never thought of as positive difference, but always as inferiority on a hierarchical axis" (2002: 889). The constant iteration of the individual's difference, when confronted with French people, forces the migrant to take refuge in a familiar cultural environment for a more positive reflection of self. The group consoles itself in its cultural alterity and regards its culture as being superior to that of the Other. British people commented, with an almost colonialist verve, that they had collectively improved the environment in which they had decided to settle: "We have kick-started the local economy", "Without us this region would be dead", "All these houses were falling to pieces and the people were just peasant farmers", "We come and do up the houses and the French see it and think 'they look good' and so they do it as well and the whole village looks better now since we got here." Several critical remarks were made on this attitude by interviewees, and one person made particularly relevant comments. This quotation is from a former secretary of the European Socialists in a large town in Aquitaine, and who wished to remain anonymous: "The British have a strange mind-set which excludes them from becoming integrated into French social groups. They form exclusive groups themselves and because they have too much time on their hands, they tend to gossip a lot. They spend all their time organizing parties so that they can criticize the French together. They stick together because the French don't help them to integrate. I don't know why they're here." She seems to be saying that they mutually confirm the superiority of their culture compared to that of the host population. It is interesting to note that the person in question had spent a lot of time in the United States and, according to her, "of course this changes things". In the context, this seems to mean that her attitude towards integration and the assumed French reluctance to help migrants integrate easily should be seen in comparison with the American open-arm attitude that she felt there. They have a similar attitude to her and therefore integration was easier. And of course, they speak the same language!

Clastres' notion of cultural alterity and the assumption of superiority are important. It could explain the "ghettoization" mentioned by another interviewee who felt that the British in south-west France formed ghettos, "but rich ghettos, not like the other ones in England". Perhaps not like the "other ones" financially but, according to this theory, ones formed for the same reasons! Clastres suggests that all groups have a tendency to develop normative expectations which they share: some people don't meet those expectations, and become Others—in this case, ironically, the host population, the French. In addition to that, whenever we define an In-group, we automatically create an Out-group: those who aren't included. During the course of building solidarity for our In-Group, of establishing our norms and boundaries, group self-esteem and pride is nurtured by reacting against outsiders. Sociologists talk about the need we seem to have for consensus or "belongingness". That need has led us to believe that if we can come to a consensus amongst ourselves, then we have achieved something worthwhile as a social group. That consensus then becomes normative and our expectations tend to be based on it. When our expectations are not met, we consider the other who doesn't meet them "deviant", not like us, Other. So it is that our concept of Other is always judgmental, always implies a value difference in which our values are superior to those of the Other. Every now and then the "professing of radical alterity passes over into 'ethnocentric xenophobia' " as Aleida Assmann writes (1994: 29). The thus safeguarded integration of society by means of an "already existing" shared cultural pre-understanding no longer seems to be universally or wholly relevant to the social structure the migrant discovers in France. There exists a form of cultural fundamentalism which provides a justification for excluding the "alien" singular and therefore also the "alien" plural (Stolcke, 1994: 58). It arms itself in advance against a reified understanding of cultural difference, a kind of essentialized interpretation of cultural identity, which is intrinsic to cultural relativism.

A classic scenario

A classic scenario emerges from the interviews, of the British migrant arriving full of good intentions to avoid all fellow Brits ("If I'd wanted to meet Brits I'd've stayed in England!"*)*, ready to try very hard to be integrated into the host society, learn the language and become part of this wonderful life that had been witnessed before taking the plunge to "emigrate", but gradually finding that they can take advantage of the best parts of the life—the weather, the wine, the food, the "life-style"—without actually mixing with the French, and "after all, the language is very difficult to learn at my age". They do try, and consciously avoid contact with other British migrants. However, they feel that little contact is being made with French people and this contact is superficial and unrewarding. Whenever they try to speak French (or even sometimes before), the French revert to English, assuming that their English, however rudimentary, is better than the migrant's French and of greater value on a global scale, and so no progress is made. The level of understanding, for the migrant, is very low and a certain feeling of resentment starts to creep into dealings with the Other, who seems condescending, to speak French too quickly, to make no effort to help integration. All of these "criticisms" have been taken from transcripts of the interviews; they were made at least twice by different interviewees and were mentioned by other English-speakers when spoken to off-the-record.

The migrants don't like how the Other sees them, or they don't understand how the Other sees them. At the same time, almost despite themselves, they are being introduced to other ex-pats, who, in their turn, introduce them to a fairly established circle of British residents, who invite them round for drinks, golf, tennis, walks, barbecues, bridge evenings, the local English club's whist drive and before long the social calendar is full of splendid, culturally comforting occasions, almost exclusively with English-speakers. Thanks to earlier earnest attempts to be integrated, the migrants feel that they have made an effort to meet French people but the latter don't seem to want to help. The French, the Other, are criticized, consensus is reached and, in the terms of Clastres, something worthwhile achieved: a sense of belonging, of feeling comfortable; the Other does not share the same attitudes, they don't understand anything. The way we do it is better! Our new migrants feel good about all this, and if we apply some of the ideas from above we see why: they can understand this group, they share a similar way of looking at things and interaction is more positive, deeper, more rewarding and constructive. They are integrated into this group, without any effort. The reflection of self is much as anticipated and the identity can continue its construction without the confusion felt with the Other. Thus the social group has become almost exclusively British, all attempts to learn the language are abandoned and life is spent around their English friends' swimming pool, sipping aperitifs and talking about the French, usually critically, and feeling pretty good about things and especially about themselves.

Three categories of migrant

To summarize, the first group in our typology is the most integrated, often in culturally and linguistically mixed couples with a Franco-British family, professionally active and working easily within the French community. Significantly, they are usually very demanding and want to be regarded as a French native. Due to these very high expectations, they generally express a hint of frustration over the fact that they are always spotted as being English, and therefore not *totally* integrated, but on the whole very happy with their situation, with no thoughts of going back to the UK.

The second category is the migrants who are not particularly well-integrated, but who are now in a situation where they are not looking to be integrated. They may have started with ambitious intentions to learn the language and mix with French people, but have now resigned themselves to the fact that the life-style can still be enjoyed without making a great effort to be integrated into the indigenous society. They are far less demanding than the first group and therefore totally satisfied with their situation, despite the almost total lack of integration. This group is by far the largest of the three.

The third category is of those who, by their own definition, are not integrated at all, who feel totally isolated in the society despite enormous efforts to adapt, to learn the language, to mix with French people, to work in France and to make French friends. These people are demanding, extremely frustrated by their inability to learn the language and thereby to be accepted by French society, and are often bitter about the French because they feel that they haven't helped them in their efforts to be integrated. With a huge sense of failure, they generally abandon their attempt to fit into French society.

Bibliography and References

ASSMANN Aleida (1994) "Zum Problem der Identität aus kulturwissenschaftlicher Sicht," pp. 13–35 in Rolf Lindner (ed.), *Die Wiederkehr des Regionalen. Über neue Formen kultureller Identität*, Frankfurt am M/New York: Campus.

AUGÉ Marc (1994) *Le Sens des autres. Actualité de l'anthropologie*, Paris: Fayard.

CLASTRES Pierre (2002) "Ethnocide," pp. 888-890 in *Encyclopædia Universalis*, volume 8, Paris.

DÖBERT Rainer, HABERMAS Jürgen & NUNNER-WINKLER Gertrud (eds.) (1980) *Entwicklung des Ichs*. Königstein Ts: Athenäum (2nd edition).

ERIKSON Erik H. (1973) *Identität und Lebenszyklus*, Frankfurt-a-M: Suhrkamp.

GERVAIS-AGUER Marie-Martine & SMALLWOOD David (2003) *Les Fondements de l'attractivité territoriale résidentielle*, Bordeaux: Éditions Université Montesquieu Bordeaux IV.

MEAD George Herbert (1967) *Mind, Self and Society from the Standpoint of a Social Behaviorist*, Chicago: University of Chicago Press.

STOLCKE Verena (1994) "Kultureller Fundamentalismus," pp. 36–63 in Rolf Lindner (ed.), *Die Wiederkehr des Regionalen. Über neue Formen kultureller Identität*, Frankfurt am M/New York: Campus.

WELZ Frank (2000) "Identity and alterity in sociological perspective," paper presented at JNU-Freiburg Sociology Workshop on "Culture and Society in the Era of Globalization", Jawaharlal Nehru University, New Delhi, 12 October 2000.

CHAPTER ELEVEN

A PECULIARLY BRITISH SPIRIT OF ADVENTURE? THE DISCOURSE OF EMIGRANTS

MICHEL BRUILLON

From the late nineteenth century, when tourism grew in popularity and became differentiated from the Grand Tour, the British often travelled to southern Europe, to France, Spain, and Portugal. More recently, over the last thirty years, there has been considerable migration to these countries as huge numbers of British tourists have decided to settle there, as the previous three chapters illustrate in the case of France. The decision to leave one's home country reflects a certain state of mind—for example the idea that elsewhere the grass is greener—and it is this attitudinal aspect of migration that the present chapter explores.

With migration on the increase, regional authorities are beginning to show an interest, and statistical studies, surveys and interviews have become commonplace. Our research is based principally on a number of interviews, which will be approached here from an original angle: dealing with the narratives both of individual lives and of families who share a past, a common culture, life stories, etc., our aim is to move from the "reality of facts" to the "reality of discourse". It is the discourse of these new migrants that provides the keys to understanding their mentalities. We will firstly suggest reasons why British people now go into voluntary exile, then analyse their discourse on this subject and identify the main themes, before attempting a re-reading of the interviews.

"The British spirit of adventure"

Today, the British move to France to leave behind a lifestyle which no longer fulfils their aspirations. They find what they believe is no longer available in Britain: a better quality of life and a feeling of security which the Welfare State provided until the 1970s. So, somewhat paradoxically, the move abroad reflects the deep attachment to the traditional values that are part of their identity. They feel that over the years, their country has become a less pleasant place to live in. The environment has deteriorated and there are no more open, uncluttered spaces, unlike in France. They discovered France's regions as tourists, and experienced a feeling of liberty, with no social pressures. These moments of respite encouraged them to develop projects for the future, or even to dream. Dreaming implies the existence of a model, as is indeed the case here. These new migrants are ready to swap their previous model of social success for a new one. This new model paints life as an eternal holiday, perhaps a lifestyle reminiscent of the leisured gentry which the migrants attempt to imitate. This is a quest for identity in which the migrants are ready to face the adventure of an exodus.

During the interviews, the expression "spirit of adventure" came up time and time again. When it was first used, it seemed well suited to the reality described. One interviewee—a young woman—used it to explain her decision and her attitude, comparing herself to other compatriots who had made the same choice:

> [...] and it's a little bit the spirit of adventure of the English, coming to a place that not many people knew and starting from the beginning...
> Q: The English?
> A: I think it's a very important factor in the English mentality, this spirit of adventure, discovering, maybe colonization...

This implies a firm belief that this attitude comes naturally to the British and that it is part of their culture. Similar notions are to be found in a work on the colonial period in Africa from 1900 to 1960, consisting almost exclusively of accounts by Colonial Office staff. One woman described her state of mind as follows:

> [...] in those days to be British was, in our minds anyway, to be absolutely top of the world. Such self-confidence, together with the knowledge that you were luckier than your contemporaries back home made it easier for young innocents fresh from England to put up with the most extreme conditions. (Allen 1982: 131)

Of course, other peoples migrate as well. Yet the British interviewees seemed to feel that the capacity to leave everything behind and move to another country was part of their identity. Moving abroad does not necessarily mean turning one's back on one's own culture to adopt another, nor does it mean taking on another identity, as is implicit in the previous chapter. On the contrary, it means preserving traditions at the heart of British culture, as this extract from an interview shows:

> And I think that's ... you know, I mean, you know Gary Parker, the man who started the aircraft, it's that sort of blind belief in yourself, (laugh) blind arrogance, (laugh) which keeps you going, it says I'm going to do it whatever. And he's done it, and he failed, and he comes back again he's on another flight ... and this is a bit like that...

This indicates an attitude that the interviewees consider an integral part of their identity. They are capable of adapting to a variety of situations—they believe that they can get used to anything. This confidence in their own abilities is reflected in much of their discourse and similar attitudes were identified in a number of interviewees. They saw this in terms almost of a belief. In fact, the above use of the adjective "blind" indicates that there is something irrational here. The terms "belief" and "arrogance" likewise express aspects for which there is no logical explanation. One of the people interviewed explained thus:

> So there is a tremendous imperative ... which drove us … and that again is not unparalleled in my view ... which is something perhaps which isn't instinctively French which if you were to look at, if you are looking at why it should be the English who would come here and do it, you have to have what makes us enterprising, arrogance, confidence, a dream—all these things; it is of course very British. They might not have the possibility to do it, but you believe you have (laughs), which is wonderful, I mean, you know, quite stupid but it works, it might work, yes...

This phenomenon is held to be the work of the subconscious, a peculiarly British instinct. They believe that a French person would not be able to react in the same way. This is revealingly indicative of a typically British belief which constitutes a myth in the ethnological sense of the term. While many peoples could justifiably claim to have the pioneering spirit and that they can succeed in life having left their home country, the British seem to see this as part of their basic cultural identity—what they see as the reasons causing them to act or react. The first example is an interview with a retired couple whose words resembled an account of an epic adventure.

Travelling through the Lot, I stopped in a hamlet, where I met a recently retired couple who were restoring an old house. They were being helped by two other British people who did not live there. Most of the restoration work was complete and the couple were proud to show me round. Once I had explained that I was conducting a study into the lifestyle of British expats in the south-west of France with interviews as part of my research, they agreed to talk to me. They owned a number of sports shops in Scotland. They were both aged around fifty and had taken early retirement. The man and woman took turns to speak, sometimes contradicting one another but without ever undermining the main thrust of the ideas developed. The interviewer suggested themes in his questions; only rarely did the couple introduce themes themselves. Overall, their discourse was rather defensive and controlled, with little room for more spontaneity, at least not openly. The discourse prompted by the questions is focused on two countries—France and Britain—and two nationalities—French and British. Language and money play the role of intermediaries linking these four poles. France is associated with beauty and pleasure, almost a land of milk and honey where houses cost next-to-nothing. To enjoy one's possessions, all it takes is to be able to make oneself understood and to understand others, even on the most basic of levels. The housing market is fluid and attractive because the region they have set their heart on is poor. ("The Lot is a pleasure for the eyes, We feel at home, a magnificent French place. Houses cost next to nothing. Our French really isn't very good but it comes to the same thing"). While abroad—in this case, in France—the migrants choose where to live and move from day to day, thereby defining a type of Britishness which recalls the recurrent motif of the spirit of adventure. In Britain, on the other hand, choices appear more definitive and have weightier consequences, housing prices and the cost of living remaining consistently high. However, Britain also holds the key to the migrants' social identity, such as being a taxpayer or even in some cases the recipient of unemployment benefit. It is interesting to note the desire, or even the necessity, of maintaining a clear distinction between the two countries in terms of possessions and language. Britain remains a bolt-hole, a place to return to in case anything goes wrong—and here the migrants mention the possibility of a world-wide recession.

They talk of their compatriots in negative terms, and in France, as potential rivals. Compatriots are identified as their own kind, but arouse very negative feelings because they are too dangerous. They are perceived as ridiculous when they try to learn French. The interviewees wished to keep them at arms' length when participating in activities that we identified as being akin to predation. ("I don't like being with other British people, I don't want to be reminded of Britain here. They think that they're more important just because they're British. If they can't speak the language, it's to our advantage"). The French are perceived as kind and easy to get to know in just a few words. They are service providers, and easy to deceive because they mistake exchanges for friendliness. The interviewees consider them to be poor and unaware of the potential of their home region, as they have let their houses—the principal focus of British desires—become run down. We have here all the historical conditions of a conquest: a powerful hero who controls both money and language, discovering a peaceful country whose inhabitants are ignorant and poor yet cheerful, and aware of the gains to be made from their possessions. The hero comes from a strong, stable country where the feeling of identity is constantly reinforced by a rigid social organization. The hero has paid his dues in his home country in the form of obligatory work, and has earned the right to his leisure. In this case, leisure is identified as the conquest of new lands, with house-hunting playing a major part. This quest implies facing a series of risks—the jealousy of their compatriots, loss of identity due to the softening effects of too much leisure, the loss of the possibility of returning home. Our heroes use a range of strategies to combat these dangers—disguise (speaking French in front of other English people), constantly moving from place to place (making them hard to pin down), work (which positions them as having a mission to accomplish), restoring their home and, indeed, the country as a whole to its former beauty. Like all conquerors, they confiscate the land and the local language holds no interest. These conclusions raise two essential points. Firstly, the existence or otherwise of a British community in the region: the interviewees deny the existence of any such community, not wishing to be associated with it, while implicitly acknowledging its presence. Compatriots are potential rivals trespassing on their own territory. Secondly, their attitude towards French indicates that the language is used a bare minimum, just enough to get by; a deeper knowledge of French language and culture is seen as superfluous. There is no desire for integration, as they wish to remain independent, not subjected to any social rules. Success is measured in terms of house-buying. Home ownership is a sign of going up in the world, as if the family could not exist *per se* if it did not own its own home. Learning a foreign language and the notion of the spirit of adventure both seem to be part of this British identity. These interviewees firmly believe that being British in itself gives them the opportunity to succeed.

Hard work and constant effort

The second interviewees, unlike the first, were not yet retired. Diana and her partner live a few kilometres from Bergerac, a medium-sized town. She explained in her interview that three years ago, she opened a hotel and restaurant. The couple entirely restored an old farmhouse, choosing to employ local craftsmen. I was once again warmly welcomed and spent a pleasant weekend at the hotel sampling the owner's cooking and interviewing this new style of hotel manager! She answered my questions readily and often hardly needed prompting, as she had plenty to say, as if she wanted her experience to be of benefit to others.

I met Diana just as her project was beginning to take shape, after she had faced her first difficulties which she attributed to her ignorance of often complex French administrative procedures. The success of the project was still far from assured. She was cautiously forward-looking—the attitude of someone who has come too far to back out but who still has a long way to go. She made the usual comments about the beauty of the landscape and how it is easier to buy a home in France than in England, but her discourse was more emotional. She was more forthcoming than the first interviewees about what led her to leave Britain, and spoke about England in more mythic terms. When I met her, she was focusing all her investments on her efforts to succeed, which meant that questions of identity were not at the forefront of her mind, as her identity was at that time bound up with the project. The project arose at a time of existential crisis, which doubtless made her discourse more emotional, characterized by the heavy use of verbs expressing states rather than action. The project had arisen as the children grew up and left home, work became a mere routine, with less margin for creativity, and her husband was threatened with unemployment despite his managerial post. The initial impetus for the project came during a trip to France, prompted by the difference in house prices. Diana thought about renting out bungalows with her husband. But back in England, the project appeared too ambitious.

At this point, Diana drew on the most characteristic theme of the emigration myth: the way the home country has betrayed their expectations, so that after a lifetime's hard work, the parents are unable to guarantee a well-deserved degree of comfort for their children. She and her husband had worked hard in well-respected social positions. They believed that when the time came to retire, they would be able to enjoy the fruits of all their hard work. They believed they would be well off, but this turned out not to be the case; they feel let down by their country which has not protected their children against easy access to credit which means anyone can join the housing ladder. To escape sliding towards poverty, the couple decided to try a new professional venture which they refer to not in terms of conquest, but of saving their lives. They are giving themselves another ten years before they take stock of their lives. However, they are already confirming their decision by talking about how it is possible to live in France without being wealthy, while they consider that doing so in England would be humiliating. Behind the notion of failure is the idea of an easier life in exile, as if their home country had rejected them. They thus refer to France in terms of security which they sum up by saying "Here, I feel at home". However, for the time being, they are working extremely hard, and Diana expanded on a theme close to her heart, explaining that she believes that because women are seen to make more effort to learn French, they carry a greater part of the responsibility for ensuring the new life is a success, while once men are settled in their new country, they tend to stick together and relax. She suggested that some men thus risk making their new lives a failure, while their wives and children adapt better. She also suggested that men are more sensitive to the effects of sliding down the social scale, such as when her husband, a financial manager, went on to work in the service sector managing a restaurant. The perception is that once the "conquest" is over, men are more prone to nostalgia. Because women are in charge of the children's education, they are more likely to get to grips with the new situation and to settle in better. She is very keen to earn recognition in France, making every effort, for example, to get her hotel into the best-known tourist guides such as Michelin or Logis de France.

Although she attributes different roles to men and women, the way to succeed is clear—hard work and constant effort. Making money is seen as an alternative to their failed project to live off their estate in retirement due to the declining value of their property in Britain. However, their British identity is still present. They believe that all this has only been possible because of their typically British qualities—blind faith in oneself and a certain arrogance which compels them to keep going. The theme of other British emigrants recurs time and time again—those who are less lucky or less well off and who, in the more or less short term, will have to return home. Diana, who sees work as all-important, referred to other British emigrants with no profession or particular skills. In her eyes, the greatest threat is from the British unemployed working class who might once have emigrated to South America but who nowadays might well prefer to settle in France as so many of them have done in Spain.

Diana's myth can be summed up as follows: she used to live in a country where people of a certain social standing, or the well-born, worked to earn a comfortable fortune which they would enjoy in retirement. Formerly, the well-off could count on the value of their property which enabled them to spend part of the year living on the Riviera. However, there was a large influx of immigrants after the Second

World War, and the British government, unaware—as Diana sees it—of the consequences of such a policy, encouraged these people to purchase their own properties, something that hitherto had been the sole province of the wealthy. As a result, Diana, who had believed herself wealthy, found she no longer was. However, she was granted a second chance by starting over again with a new job and a new property in France. At no point does it occur to her that she is now in the shoes of an immigrant benefiting from favourable circumstances and undermining the financial situation of the local population. This indicates that above and beyond the truth of her claims, her position is based on the notion of foreigners coming to take away her property. This belief echoes the earlier interview.

To each their own myth

The series of interviews as a whole is a fascinating collection of portraits, as each interviewee related their own experiences and compared them to those of their compatriots, often making comments that give revealing glimpses of unconscious attitudes. The first story, common to all, is how they came to abandon their home country where life has become too hard, with the different reasons given forming a myth. Formerly, there was a good standard of living in Britain and if one worked hard one could enjoy a comfortable retirement. These days, for this group of people, these conditions no longer exist, whether because of inflation, a fall in purchasing power, the threat of unemployment or the loss of job security. Whatever the cause, all feel the same need to emigrate. Yet although they have undeniably emigrated, none of the interviewees actually used this term. They see their emigration in terms of a quest in search of their lost ideal of a comfortable life.

Depending on their age, the interviewees refer to the 1930s, the 1950s, or the Welfare State. To each their own myth! They sell up, leave the United Kingdom, making a break with their past to set up home and work in a region where they believe anything is possible. In some cases, the project is based on different motivations closer to the notion of the conquest of new territory: we must defend our interests, so we must try to take power. These are pioneers, emigrants who leave in search of adventure and who hope to found a city or a province that reflects their native culture. Perhaps the shared history and culture of the British—generations of emigrants, the exploration of new territories, and the establishment of colonies—inspire these new emigrants in turn to try a new adventure.

Of course, anyone moving to a new country intends to make a success of it and enjoy a better quality of life. The distinction is above all cultural. In the case of the British emigrants interviewed, their self-assurance and self-confidence were the result of their upbringing. The onlooker has the impression that this self-assurance is a means of avoiding the difficulties that might arise when moving to another country by avoiding getting too deeply involved in life there. Some emigrants show an interest in the local culture and lifestyle, without, however, joining in themselves. They fall for the illusion that it is possible to settle in another country with no investment other than financial, as if the Other—the local population—did not exist.

The notion of conquest is perhaps too aggressive, but it was implicit in the interviews on several occasions. Of course, British emigrants do not use terms such as "colonist" or "colony", and yet they implicitly behave as conquerors, since the human dimension—contacts with the "natives"—are always a secondary consideration and have little influence on their project when the decision is taken to move. They often refer to the similarity of cultures between France and Britain, yet the notion of conquest is apparent in their restoration of old buildings. They see it as incumbent upon themselves to save the region's heritage because the locals are incapable of doing so. This form of appropriation is at the heart of the projects of many British settlers.

The terms they use to refer to their contact with their fellow countrymen are also worthy of note. On several occasions they made unflattering reference to some of their compatriots. If the underlying notion of the conquest of a new territory is indeed present, relations between compatriots are economic in nature and each British emigrant is a potential rival and a threat to the future development of one's projects. However, these relations are not only economic in nature, since solidarity comes to the fore when British cultural identity is threatened. Despite elements of contradiction in the discourse of the interviewees, Britain remains the point of reference, a haven in case of difficulties. Depending on individual circumstances, returning home remains a possibility. These emigrants never totally break off all links with their roots. They have a luxury not accorded to all emigrants—the possibility of going home.

Bibliography and References

ALLEN C. (ed.) (1982) *Tales from the Dark Continent*, London: Futura.

ALTHABE G., FABRE D. & LENCLUD G. (eds.) (1992) *Vers une ethnologie du présent*, Paris: Editions de la Maison des Sciences de l'Homme (Ethnologie de la France, Cahier 7).

ARIC (Association pour la Recherche Interculturelle) (1989) *La Recherche interculturelle. Actes du deuxième colloque de l'ARIC*, 2 vols., Paris: l'Harmattan.

BRUILLON M. (2003) "Le séjour des Britanniques en France à l'époque victorienne," pp. 97-111 in Marielle Seichepine (ed.), *Le Départ à l'époque victorienne. Actes de la journée d'études du 22 mars 2002*, Metz: Centre d'Études de la Traduction, Université de Metz.

DUBUISSON D. (1993) *Mythologies du XXe siècle*, Lille: Presses Universitaires de Lille.

DURAND G. (1996) *Introduction à la mythodologie*, Paris: Albin Michel.

FERRAROTTI F. (1990) *Histoire et histoires de vie*, Paris: Meridiens Klincksieck.

GHIGLIONE R. & BLANCHET A. (1991) *Analyse de contenu et contenus d'analyses*, Paris: Dunod.

GHIGLIONE R. & MATALON B. (1991) *Les Enquêtes sociologiques, Théories et pratique*, Paris: Dunod.

KOTKIN J. (1992) *Tribes*, New York: Random House.

LEVI-STRAUSS C. (1958) *Anthropologie structurale*, Paris: Plon.

MacFARLANE A. (1978) *The Origins of English Individualism*, Oxford: Blackwell.

MANGAN J. A. (ed.) (1990) *Making Imperial Mentalities, Socialization and British Imperialism*, Manchester: Manchester University Press.

SAID E.W. (1994) *Culture and Imperialism*, London: Vintage.

PART III -

TOWARDS NEW FORMS OF INTERNATIONAL MOBILITY

CHAPTER TWELVE

EMERGING TOURISM FUTURES: RESIDENTIAL TOURISM AND ITS IMPLICATIONS

KAREN O'REILLY

North Europeans, particularly the British and Germans, have been migrating to Spain's coastal towns in increasing numbers since the 1980s. They have been attracted by the weather, the relative cost of living, and the slow pace of life. They are aided by portable pensions and the increase in expendable wealth experienced by some northern Europeans in recent decades. And the migration or mobility is eased by the existence and development of reasonably-priced and regular transport routes, cheap airlines, and a good local infrastructure that was developed initially for tourism. Key areas of North European settlement in Spain are the Costa Blanca, the Costa del Sol, Mallorca and the Canary Islands. These "immigrants" now form a large minority group. Officially, the largest groups of migrants in Spain are Moroccans (500,000), followed by Colombians, Ecuadorians, Romanians, then migrants from the United Kingdom (220,000), followed by Germans (120,000). However, it is almost certain that these figures, from the Spanish Institute of National Statistics, seriously underestimate the actual numbers of settled or partly-settled European migrants. Several experts have estimated (and our own survey confirms) that only about one in three settled UK migrants actually register as resident at their local town hall.

Fluidity

Of course, the term "migrating" makes one think of people who have moved, but the difficulties of separating tourism and migration in terms of contemporary mobilities are now well-rehearsed (Williams & Hall 2002). Where the term tourism was once used for temporary travel for business or pleasure, with a return home expected within a year, migration was taken to involve nothing less than settlement in the destination. Tourism has been defined in terms of what it is not (not work, home and so on), as a change in scenery or lifestyle, or an inversion of the "normal" (Graburn 1978, Smith 1978, Urry 1990). Migration then becomes a new "normal" life. Contemporary forms of mobility have, however, undermined this distinction, and not least where north-south European migrants are concerned.

Researchers have used various forms of terminology to capture what they consider a new phenomenon and have therefore explored *retirement migration* (Casado-Díaz *et al.*, 2004; King *et al.*, 2000; Rodríguez *et a*l., 1998), *intra-European migration*, *second-home owners*, *residential tourists* (Aledo & Mazón, 2004) and *seasonal visitors* (Gustafson, 2001). With our focus on a community rather than on a trend, we identified four key migrant groups, who were not—or were something more than—tourists: *full residents*, who live in Spain full time; *returning residents*, who return to the UK regularly, but consider their main home to be in Spain; *seasonal migrants*, for whom home is in the UK but who seasonally move to Spain; and *peripatetic migrants*, who move back and forth between countries in unpredictable ways, treating both places as home (O'Reilly 2000). In reality, though, people find ever more creative ways of living in more than one space at a time: migrating, circulating, oscillating and touring, altering migration patterns and legal status apparently at will.

Julie and Richard, for example, moved to Spain in 2003 when Julie was fifty and Richard was sixty years old and had recently retired. Richard had spent much of his working life as an expatriate, taking up international assignments for large employers. Julie was trained as lawyer and worked in the UK apart from when she took time out to move abroad with Richard. On Richard's retirement, Julie wanted to commit herself more fully to her career but Richard did not want to settle back in the UK. So, they bought a house in the countryside near Alhaurin el Grande (in Málaga province) from where Julie is able to conduct most of her work as a lawyer by email, post and telephone, returning to the UK from time to time for meetings and court appearances. Julie lives *de jure* in the UK and *de facto* in Spain, while Richard simply lives in Spain. Charlie and Mary are a very different example: they moved to Spain with their two children in 2004 when they were fed up with the rain, the cold, and the lack of prospects in the UK. They had both worked as entertainers, Charlie as a comedian and Mary a singer, but they were finding it difficult to make ends meet and were worried about the future prospects for their children. "If we stayed in that town much longer the only thing was certain was Jody (their son) was going to get into trouble with the police," said Mary. Like so many of these migrants, they see Spain as much safer for children and believe they will have more freedom as well as being less likely to grow up into a life of crime. They lived in a council house in the UK so had no property to sell and have simply rented a caravan near Fuengirola, in Málaga, where they now live full time. The children go to a local school and Mary is a "caravan-wife" (as she calls it). Charlie, on the other hand, goes to the UK and to other parts of Europe to work as an entertainer intermittently, perhaps for four weeks at a time, earning just enough to fund their new lives in Spain.

However, not only is this a very flexible migration trend, it is also difficult to disentangle migration and tourism here: many people were tourists first, prior to settling a little more permanently; they settle in holiday places; they spend time on a daily basis with holiday-makers; most go "home" during the year for weddings, funerals, or to visit the family (which seems more a return to the normal than an inversion of it); a huge majority have visitors spending time with them throughout the year for the purposes of a holiday; many live on urbanizations—concentrated developments of holiday homes or second homes—and they share social spaces, newspapers, magazines, shops, and even workplaces with tourists (O'Reilly 2003).

"Residential tourists"

Here it is proposed to develop a way of conceptualizing these migrants (in the dictionary sense of the word migration, which is to move from one place to another) that recognizes they are part of a broader trend of people moving from affluent to less-affluent parts of the world. This might comprise: Northern Europeans moving to Spain (Rodríguez et al. 2005), including British (O'Reilly 2000), Germans (Aledo 2005; Schriewer & Jimenez 2005), Finns (Karisto 2005), Norwegians (Helset *et al.* 2005), Swiss (Huber & O'Reilly 2004), Swedes (Gustafson 2001) and Scandinavians in general (Casado-Díaz 2006); North European retirement migrants to Malta, Italy, Portugal, Greece and Turkey (Ackers & Dwyer 2004; Casado-Díaz *et al.* 2004; Warnes *et al.* 2005); European and US second home owners in Croatia, especially Istria and Dubrovnik (Božić 2006); British people moving to France (chapters 8 to 11 above, and Geoffroy 2006); the Dutch in France (Ginet 2006); Europeans in Romania; North Americans migrating to Mexico (Rojas & Thankam 2006); Europeans, especially French, going to Marrakesh (chapter 13 below) and Québécois to Florida (Tremblay & O'Reilly 2004).

The examples listed above are capitalizing on the differences in property prices and cost of living between home and host countries, in search of a better quality of life, and are moving either part-time or full-time, temporarily or permanently, to places that have previously been developed for, or signify, tourism and leisure. We propose the term *residential tourism* as a way of distinguishing a key aspect: the affluence that enables them to turn tourism, to some extent, into a way of life, and to construct fluid, leisured lifestyles betwixt and between places, and in which even when they ostensibly try to settle they still remain in some ways outside or above the community they have moved to. "Residential tourism" is a term being used increasingly by estate agents and council officials in Spain, by the Spanish tourist board, local newspapers and some Spanish academics (Aledo & Mazón, 2004; Casado-Díaz, 2001). It remains to be adequately defined but generally refers to property ownership and short-term residence of North-Europeans in tourist areas, residence that falls short of full migration. We have criticized the use of the term in the past, because its association with the leisure and temporary aspects of tourism means that the more permanent or long-term impacts and implications of this tourism-related migration are overlooked. However, it may offer potential in the fact that it is, and describes, an oxymoron.

Residential tourism is the result of a convergence of factors, so that explanation has to separate the historical and material preconditions enabling the phenomenon from what migrants want to do—the motivations for migration—and how this is achieved in practice. To look firstly at the historical and material conditions, this section draws on the "migration systems theory" approach, which has emerged in recent years in response to failings of traditional uni-dimensional migration perspectives, by attempting to cover all dimensions of the migration experience and which views migration as the result of interacting macro- and micro-structures (Castles & Miller 2003).

The relevant historical developments and material conditions for residential tourism can be summarized as follows: globalization, increased interconnectedness and the increased sense of the world as a single place; the development of mass tourism, in which more people visit more places than ever before, and now the travel, fluidity, flow and flux that arguably characterize modern life (Urry 2000; Papastergiadis 2000); the spread of mass communications, and time-space compression (Giddens 1990); rising living standards and unprecedented rises in property values in some parts of the world, especially relative to other parts; flexibility in labour markets, the ability to live and work in different places, and with these, increased leisure time in affluent societies, extended holidays, early retirement, and flexible working lives; and finally migration chains, in which, through the construction of networks, migration movements, once begun, become self-sustaining social processes (Castles & Miller 2003). We must also acknowledge the role of intermediaries—estate agents, financial institutions, mass media—promoting and enabling migrations. In other words, citizens of northern and western countries, or relatively affluent peoples, are freer to move, are more aware of the world as a single place, have more opportunity for travel and more free income to fund such a move than ever before. They are more likely to retire early or to manage extended holidays or to work flexibly, and therefore to have time to spend in holiday or second homes, to visit friends and family who have settled elsewhere, consolidating the international networks, and to be able to communicate rapidly and cheaply with home, family or work while doing so.

For the purposes of this chapter (though not for all purposes) we can treat residential tourism as a single whole phenomenon, and can then place one of its representatives at the centre of the discussion to exemplify the phenomenon. Residential tourism in Spain has been subjected to more studies than any other tourism-related migration, is perhaps the most important trend numerically, and is indicative of the broader trend in terms of material conditions. While Spain was, at the beginning of the twentieth century, a country of net emigration, still contributing 2.2 million Spaniards between 1960 and 1970 to the massive labour migration of that decade, by 1975 it had become a country of net immigration, with return migrants and immigrants from the economicly less-developed countries of Africa, Asia and South America contributing to a net positive migratory balance (King & Rybaczuk 1993). This immigration continued to grow during the 1980s and was increasingly supplemented by the migration of Europeans to Spain. Here, we cannot ignore the role of the development of mass and package tourism during the 1960s and 70s, in which Spain was a favourite destination, and the consequent development of certain coastal regions specifically for mass tourist consumption (Burkart & Medlik 1974). The phenomenon of the all-inclusive, package tour was critical in this growth of mass tourism and its Europeanization during the 1960s and 1970s (Shaw & Williams 1994), while the success and spread of tourism are partly explained by the simultaneous increase in real disposable incomes of northern Europeans, the increase in leisure time and paid holidays experienced by workers across the social scale, and developments in transport which made travelling long distances cheaper and more comfortable.

After Franco's death in 1975, more and more North Europeans visited Spain's coastal areas and islands each year as tourists, some staying longer, returning, and eventually buying businesses and homes there (King & Rybaczuk 1993). Later, the development of the European Community and the European Union, and the subsequent 1992 shaping of legislation which made it easier for Europeans to purchase property, to reside, to work, and to move freely within Spain, have been major contributory factors. We cannot ignore the active encouragement, during the 1980s and 1990s, on behalf of Spain's administration, of foreign purchase of land and property in order to compensate for the seasonal and regional nature of tourism (Valenzuela 1988); the relative cost of property and land in Spain; and massive growths in the property market in the UK and other European countries (at different periods in this history). They combine with longer holiday entitlements and the growth in early retirement in some North European countries, encouraging longer stays and retirement to the homes bought relatively cheaply. For later waves of migrants, the existence of a settled and informed community made a move easier and smoother, and offered employment opportunities for newcomers. This was followed rapidly by the growth of intermediary individuals, institutions and organizations facilitating more and more flexible migration trajectories by offering a full range of services and products for the European migrant. These factors continue to be supported by the more general developments associated with globalization and outlined above: increased interconnectedness, mass telecommunications, cheap air travel, and increased mobility. These conditions both enable and promote the increased mobility of certain affluent groups, and the phenomenon in various forms is being developed in several parts of the world.

Motivations for migration

The motivations for residential tourism are clear in many pages of this book (particularly chapters 2, 5, 8 to 11, and 13), and in our own research (see research note below). The main reasons these migrants give for moving are: "quality of life", a slower, relaxed rhythm; the climate/ sun (which enables health and relaxation); the cost of living, cheap property (enabling early retirement and/or a better lifestyle); a business opportunity (to fund a better life); a better life for the children; the culture (which includes community, respect for the elderly, safety, and less crime); closeness to home, and other ties and connections; the desire to leave their home country (because of high crime rates, and too many immigrants!, or to escape the rat-race, failing businesses, unemployment, or the political situation); and to go somewhere where "you can be yourself".

Overwhelmingly, respondents in our research projects cited quality of life, a relaxed way of life, or a slower pace of life as reasons for moving. It is difficult to be sure what they mean by this. Rodriguez and colleagues (1998) summarize it as "the relaxed and informal way of life". Respondents in our ethnographic studies phrased it as follows:

> "I would definitely say there is less stress here." (Alice, retired, sixties)
> "(It's) a better way of life I suppose, but that sounds so vague, it doesn't mean anything. Really I mean a more relaxed way of life." (Jane, part-time working mother, forties)
> "It's more relaxed here. Even if you've got to work, it's easier." (Lyn, self-employed, thirties)
> "The Spanish way of life, really. Yes, they're very laid back here." (Annie, retired, seventies)
> "I think people come here because they want to get away from it all, start a new life." (David, working, fifties)

A review paper that pulls together research projects on North European retirement migration in Tuscany, Malta, the Costa del Sol and the Algarve (Casado-Diaz *et. al.* 2004), notes that four out of five migrants cited the climate as one of their top reasons for migration. However, in the expanded comments collected qualitatively, references to climate are enigmatic, with interviewees referring to health, lifestyle, morale and even financial aspects as if these are somehow connected to the climate. The Mediterranean life (encapsulating cuisine, wine, a slow pace of life, and outdoor living) was also commonly cited, along with the cost of living. For Rodriguez *et al*'s (1998) European respondents the most common reason for moving was also climate, then lifestyle, followed by cost of living, and then geographical proximity to home. Madden's business owners on the Costa del Sol, when asked why they moved, listed climate, quality of life and lifestyle before business opportunities: "to many of the business owners, opening a business in the Costa del Sol is also a way of funding a different lifestyle" (1999: 33). Catherine Puzzo's British emigrants to France explain their migration in terms of escape from a hectic way of life, to a better pace of life and better cost of living (chapter 9 above). The relative cost of living comes up over and over again.

Some are looking for sun and others for the rural life. King *et al* (2000) separate out, among their retired British migrants in Southern Europe, those who are looking for a relaxed life in the sun from those who seem more motivated by the search for the *rural idyll*. Andreas Huber and Karen O'Reilly (2004) note how this search for the rural idyll includes a search for *heimat* (home, belonging and community), the perceived loss of which marks contemporary western lifestyles. Nearness to home remains a common theme. Rachida Saigh Bousta (chapter 13 below) argues that the attractions of Marrakesh, for its European residents and second home owners, are its nearness to Europe, followed by its infrastructure (which has been developed for tourism), its heritage, the weather, and relative cheapness. The search for the rural idyll and a new home, or somewhere not too far from home, includes a gaze in which the new community is exotic and strange. Gustafson (2002: 9) demonstrates the way his seasonal migrants had a tendency to "construct Spain as idyllic, exotic and at times a bit backward when compared to Sweden".

Finally, it is common for residential tourists to describe their reasons for moving in the context of comparisons with the home country. In other words, they will outline what the new place has to offer that their own country has not. So, Finnish migrants escape high taxes, high prices, unemployment and a poor climate (Karisto 2005); Germans in the Balearics obtain a more peaceful and more secure quality of life than they had at home (Salvá Tomás 2005); Norwegian migrants talk of how they do not want to grow old in Norway (Helset et al 2005); and British residential tourists describe their move in the context of escape, from stressful jobs or the threat of unemployment, but also from high crime rates, run-down inner city areas, and dangerous neighbourhoods. They worry about their children's futures and want to give them a better start or they are anxious about the quality of retirement that was looming ahead. They express doubts about the real value of UK pensions, or the ability to rely on sickness or unemployment benefit in times of difficulty, and expected to gain better quality of life for less money in Spain (O'Reilly 2007). Many residential tourists use language like "getting out of the trap" or making a "fresh start" and "new beginnings". It is not difficult to see the connections between these motivations and the theme of the rural idyll, so common in counter-urbanization literature, but also the themes of leisure, pleasure, refuge, escape from the banal and routine, and the idea of journey or pilgrimage in search of the authentic (or some imagined past) that are so common in the field of tourist studies.

It is important to examine patterns that are developing in order that we might foresee how these will impact on the future. At the time of our initial research into what we are now calling residential tourism it was a fairly new phenomenon affecting parts of Spain, Portugal, France and Italy, and it was sensibly captured with the terms "retirement migration" and "second-home ownership". Now the phenomenon is growing, it includes younger migrants with families, and in Spain is moving inland as people search for cheaper properties and the rural idyll they can no longer find on the coastal strip. There is some irony in the fact that the very people who have encouraged massive over-development of some of these tourist areas are now complaining that they are too crowded or spoiled. One British man living in Spain said he was looking to move elsewhere, perhaps Croatia or Romania, and added without apparent irony: "there are too many Brits here now." But the appetite for cheap, pretty, warm places where life is simple seems insatiable, and more Northern Europeans are now settling, or buying property and investing in emerging property markets, in places such as Romania, Bulgaria, Croatia and even Morocco and South Africa, while in the US residential tourism spreads ever further south.

Future scenarios and questions

The search for possible future scenarios includes the following proposal. Residential tourism begins with a few people buying second homes somewhere where there are regular cheap flights, a pleasant environment and some tranquillity—probably somewhere they, or someone they know, or perhaps the property developer or estate agent, has previously visited as a tourist. As they become more settled so others visit and decide to join them. Those who are less brave will prefer to go to places that have been tried and tested to some small degree. These first migrants are probably seasonal visitors or retirees, but as time goes on and a community of residential tourists becomes established, so other, younger, migrants decide to go and offer services for the tourist and residential tourist, thus funding a lifestyle they could not have afforded without work of some sort. The more who move to the area, the more crowded it gets, the more polluted, the more traffic on the roads and the less remote and exotic it feels. At the same time it becomes less and less easy to integrate socially and culturally with the local community as the migrant community becomes increasingly visible. As more people are attracted to the area, so property prices rise and then other prices associated with the general cost of living rise too. Eventually the perceived simplicity, remoteness and tranquillity of the place are lost, the crime rate rises with the population rate, and residential tourists are no longer attracted to the area. Those who are there want to move on. What happens to the place that was initially developed for tourism remains to be seen: Marbella (in the Costa del Sol) has retained its elite status and high prices, while Torrevieja (in the Costa Blanca), with plummeting house prices and rising crime rates, has become somewhere people are desperate to leave.

Residential tourism raises several questions, especially in relation to its fluidity and flexibility. How sustainable is this sort of fluid movement at the level of individual lives? Can people cope with such fluidity? Can governments and apparatuses of state cope with it? In a recent paper we looked at the extent to which people who had moved to Spain more permanently could be considered integrated in the new society (O'Reilly 2007), taking integration in as broad a way as possible to include social, cultural, political and economic integration. What we found, for some people, was exclusion. Social exclusion is generally seen as a combination of adverse social situations, for example unemployment, unfavourable market situation, low earnings, poor health and/or living conditions, plus the inability to build social networks. Or, indeed, social exclusion is "the dynamic process of being shut out [...] from any of the social, economic, political and cultural systems which determine the social integration of a person in society." (Walker and Walker, 1997: 8)

Our research revealed extensive evidence of British migrants working in the informal economy, paying no income tax or national insurance contributions, relying on emergency state health provision or inadequate private insurance, who are confused about what they are supposed to do to be legal residents, who are neither registered with their town hall nor have residence permits, who do not know who to turn to in times of difficulty, who cannot speak the language adequately and come unstuck when they need to call the police or an ambulance. There are those who, having moved to Spain, no longer have the right to use the National Health Service in the UK, have severely reduced their entitlements to UK pensions and social service benefits, yet are not addressing this through private or Spanish provision. Many migrants do not know whether their homes in Spain are legally built, do not have deeds to their homes, or bought land without proper planning permission. There are families with children in private, international school who struggle to afford the fees, families with children in Spanish school who are not managing to learn the language or integrate, and families with children who are not even in school. These migrants are trying to live the good life in the sun that wealthier migrants are managing, but have stretched their finances a little too thinly in the process and at the same time are victims of the contradiction and tension between tourism and migration that impacts residential tourism so effectively (O'Reilly 2007).

Research needs to explore the impact of these migration trends on the migrants and on the local communities, and to consider environmental and social sustainability. We also need to explore the links and interactions between these migrations/mobilities and others. For example, Polish people are now migrating to the UK in large numbers in search of what UK citizens consider low-paid work while, conversely, British people are buying up the cheap houses in Poland that the Polish cannot afford. Here, researchers would benefit from employing the concept of the stratification of mobility. There is also an entire potential research programme in "new fluid living patterns", because while some residential tourists are giving up and going home, others successfully manage flexible lifestyles. While some areas deteriorate, or are abandoned, others remain buoyant with high property prices and tourism, residence and residential tourism coexisting peaceably. There ought to be research undertaken on questions of integration, on the impact of residential tourism on local communities (especially the impact of high property prices), and researchers need to have a keen eye directed towards the places that are now becoming affected by residential tourism.

Finally, we need to ask how theories and conceptual developments are helping in this research programme. What use can we make of the concepts of transnationalism, cosmopolitanism, neo-colonialism, globalization, mobility, or even world systems? We agree with Beck (2006) that a cosmopolitan vision is needed, to look beyond borders and boundaries at what is happening across and between, but often theories and empirical research do not go hand in hand. Research must keep an eye to movement and change but also to structures and constraints and their ability to reproduce and re-create themselves and to keep certain people in and others out.

Research note: The author's research in Spain has spanned nearly fifteen years. In 1993 to 1994 she undertook fifteen months intensive ethnographic fieldwork with the British community in Fuengirola and Los Boliches, in the Province of Málaga, and conducted over 300 informal interviews. Between 1994 and 2002 she made return visits to Spain of between two weeks and six months duration. During this time she became a second home-owner in Andalusia and later a peripatetic migrant to the area, for four years living part of each year in Spain. Between 2003 and 2005 she conducted a new project exploring issues of integration for British and other north-European migrants in Spain (funded by ESRC grant R000223944). This involved fieldwork in Alhaurin el Grande, Mijas, Fuengirola, Cártama and Coín in the Málaga province; a 53-item questionnaire survey of 340 migrants; qualitative interviews with 65 (mostly British) migrants and Spanish individuals who have regular contact with European migrants (ten of these interviews were with children aged between 11 and 16 years); eight group interviews—two with migrants and six with children of mixed nationalities—and the collection of 48 student essays on the topic of living in Spain, from children of mixed nationalities aged between 12 and 14 (O'Reilly 2000, 2003, 2007).

Bibliography and References

ACKERS L. & DWYER P. (2004) "Fixed laws, fluid lives: the citizenship status of post-retirement migrants in the European Union," *Ageing and Society* 24(3), pp. 451-475

ALEDO Antonio Tur (2005) "Los otros immigrantes: residents europeos en el sudeste español," pp. 161-80 in Fernandez-Rufete & Jimenez 2005.

ALEDO A. & MAZON T. (2004) "Impact of residential tourism and the destination life cycle theory," First International Conference on Sustainable Tourism, Segovia, July 2004.

BOZIC Saša (2006) "The achievement and potential of international retirement migration research: The need for disciplinary exchange," *Journal of Ethnic and Migration Studies*, 32(8), pp. 1415-1427.

BURKART A.J. & MEDLIK S. (1974) *Tourism, Past, Present and Future*, London: Heinemann.

CASADO-DIAZ M. Á. (2006) "Retiring to Spain: an analysis of difference among North European nationals," *Journal of Ethnic and Migration Studies*, 32(8), pp. 1321-1339.

CASADO-DIAZ M. Á., Kaiser C. & Warnes A.M. (2004) "Northern European retired residents in nine southern European areas: characteristics, motivations and adjustment," *Ageing and Society*, 24, pp. 353-381.

CASTLES S. & MILLER M. (2003) *The Age of Migration*, Basingstoke & New York: Palgrave Macmillan (3rd edition).

CERAMAC (2006) *Les Étrangers dans les campagnes*, Rural Geography Research Group Conference, Université Blaise-Pascal, Vichy, 18-19 May.

FERNANDEZ-RUFETE José & JIMENEZ Modesto (eds.) (2005) *Movimientos Migratorios Contemporáneos*, Murcia: Fundación Universitaria San Antonio.

GEOFFROY C. (2006) "Chamonix-Chic?", CERAMAC 2006.

GIDDENS A. (1990) *The Consequences of Modernity*, Stanford CA: Stanford University Press.

GINET Pierre (2006) "The Dutch real estate purchasing in Thierache, or the Randstad Holland perimetropolization of a margin space,"

CERAMAC 2006.

GUSTAFSON P. (2001) "Retirement migration and transnational lifestyles," *Ageing and Society* 21, pp. 371-394.

—. (2002) "Tourism and seasonal retirement migration," *Annals of Tourism Research*, 29(4), pp. 899-918.

HELSET Anne, LAUVLI Marit & SANDLIE Hans Christian (2005) "Jubilados Noruegos en España," pp. 167-194 in Rodriguez *et al.* 2005a.

HUBER A. & O'REILLY K. (2004) "The construction of *Heimat* under conditions of individualized modernity: Swiss and British elderly migrants in Spain," *Ageing and Society*, 24(3), pp. 327-352.

KARISTO Antti (2005) "Residentes Finlandeses de Invierno en España," pp. 195-220 in Rodriguez *et al.* 2005a.

KING R. & RYBACZUK K. (1993) "Southern Europe and the international division of labour: from emigration to immigration ," pp.175-206 in R. King (ed.), *The New Geography of European Migrations*, London: Belhaven Press.

KING R., WARNES A. M. & WILLIAMS A. M. (2000) *Sunset Lives: British Retirement to Southern Europe*, Oxford: Berg

LORD Michaela (2006) "Becoming significant: the appropriation of the French rural space by British migrants," CERAMAC 2006.

MADDEN L. (1999) "Making money in the sun: the development of British- and Irish-owned businesses in the Costa del Sol," *Research Papers in Geography 36*, University of Sussex, Brighton.

O'REILLY K. (2000) *The British on the Costa del Sol*, London: Routledge.

—. (2003) "When is a tourist? The articulation of tourism and migration in Spain's Costa del Sol," *Tourist Studies*, 3(3), pp. 301-317.

—. (2007) "Intra-European migration and the mobility-enclosure dialectic," *Sociology*, 41(2), pp. 277-293.

PAPASTERGIADIS N. (2000) *The Turbulence of Migration: Globalization, Deterritorialization and Hybridity*, Cambridge: Polity Press

RODRIGUEZ V., FERNANDEZ-MAYORALAS G. & ROJO F. (1998) "European Retirees on the Costa del Sol: A Cross-National Comparison," *International Journal of Population Geography*, 4 (2), pp. 91-111.

RODRIGUEZ Vicente, FERNANDEZ-MAYORALAS Gloria, DIAZ Maria Ángeles Casado, HUBER Andreas (2005) "Una perspectiva actual de la migración internacional de jubilados en España," pp. 15-46 in Rodriguez *et al.* 2005a.

RODRIGUEZ Vicente *et al.* (eds.) (2005a) *La Migración de Europeos Retirados en España*, Madrid: CSIC.

SALVÁ TOMÁS P. (2005) "La inmigracion do Europeos retirados en las Islas Baleares," pp. 221-234 in Rodriguez *et al.* 2005a.

SHAW G. & WILLIAMS A.M. (1994) *Critical Issues in Tourism. A Geographical Perspective*, Oxford: Blackwell.

SHRIEWER Klaus & JIMENEZ Modesto García (2005) "Entre europeos: acerca de una possible conciencia europea. El caso de residents europeos en Espana," pp. 181-204 in Fernandez-Rufete & Jimenez 2005.

SMITH V. (1978) "Introduction," pp.1-14 in V. Smith (ed.), *Hosts and Guests. The Anthropology of Tourism*, Oxford: Blackwell.

TREMBLAY Remy & O'REILLY Karen (2004) "La mise en tourisme des communautés transnationales: le cas des Britanniques en Espagne et des Québécois en Floride," *Tourism Review* 59(3), pp. 20-33.

URRY J. (2000) *Sociology Beyond Societies. Mobilities for the twenty-first century*, London: Routledge.

VALENZUELA M. (1988) "Spain: the phenomenon of mass tourism," pp. 39-57 in G. Shaw & A.M. Williams, *Tourism and Economic Development. Western European Experience*, London: Belhaven Press.

WALKER A. & WALKER C. (eds.) (1997) *Britain Divided: The Growth of Social Exclusion in the 1980s and 1990s*, London: Child Poverty Action Group.

WARNES Tony, KING Russell & WILLIAMS Allan (2005) "Migraciones a España tras la Jubilación," pp. 47-68 in Rodriguez *et al.* 2005a.

WILLIAMS A. M. & HALL C. M. (2002) "Tourism, migration, circulation and mobility: the contingencies of time and place," pp. 1-60 in A. M. Williams & C. M. Hall (eds.), *Tourism and Migration: New Relationships between Production and Consumption*, London: Kluwer Academic Publishers.

CHAPTER THIRTEEN

NEW FORMS OF MIGRATION: EUROPEANS IN MARRAKESH

RACHIDA SAIGH BOUSTA

Anyone living in Marrakesh for the last ten years or more will not have failed to notice that a new category of foreigner is becoming increasingly visible. This population, which does not have the same concerns as the traditional tourist, has the same profile as the resident and goes about its business in a similar way. These "new residents"—meaning foreigners who stay permanently, or continuously for periods during the year as seasonal residents—are to be found everywhere, in the newly-opened supermarkets, in the alleys of the popular souks, entrenched in places previously known only to well-informed locals. They can be found in architects' offices, or in travel agents, hardware shops, modern or traditional furniture-makers and furniture bazaars. In banks as in public offices, it is obvious that the town is attracting newcomers from the northern shores of the Mediterranean, with the probable intention of settling in this space so highly prized by westerners.

Amongst these residents settling in the "red city", there is an increasing French presence. It is very difficult to get accurate figures, but whereas there are 215 Italians, 150 Spaniards, 100 Belgians and 100 British registered in consular centres in Marrakesh, the French Consulate has registered more than 3,500 permanent residents, to which should be added more than 7,000 individuals having a resident's permit issued by the Moroccan authorities (interviews 2006). Not included in these figures are temporary residents (up to two months), mixed French-Moroccan couples who are not systematically listed, and the French of Moroccan origin who live as residents between Morocco and France.

Many of the new residents were initially just passing through, looking for exotic experiences during a short stay organized by a travel agency. Others came to explore and taste the socio-cultural environment, ready to eventually invest or settle. The French represent over eighty per cent of these new temporary or permanent "migrants". Certain figures for 2005 (cf. Oberlé 2006)—and our own research confirms that they continue to rise—are very telling:

– 800,000 French people visited Marrakesh;
– 33,018 French people were registered on consular lists;
– about 17,000 French people owned a property in Marrakesh.

Since the 1990s there has been a great enthusiasm for Marrakesh, which shows no signs of diminishing. This continually growing phenomenon is most visible amongst French "clients". Many have past attachments to the city—some lived in Morocco as children, or were there as an alternative to military service; others have family or close contacts who have lived in Morocco. There are those who fell under the charm of the "pearl of the South" during a tourist visit, and those who are investors or businessmen, especially in real estate.

Before and after *Capital*

Some observers believe the numbers really started taking off in 1999, when the French television series *Capital* showed a spectacular programme on Marrakesh (Penna 2006). This programme stressed investment possibilities in the Medina and elsewhere, and emphasized the attractive property prices compared to Europe. Apparently, this had a real kick-start effect, setting up the infatuation with the city. Yet although this media coverage undoubtedly excited people's imagination, the interest had started less spectacularly a few years before, and the early 1990s did see some developments. But the real take-off came after a series of administrative and legal measures and reforms, which had the effect of attracting foreign investors because they offered a privileged socio-economic environment and guarantees of security for capital. In fact, since 1999 many decisive factors in the growth of foreign investment have resulted from profound changes which have affected the socio-economic climate in Morocco (1999 was the year of accession of Mohammed VI, which in itself represented a strategic political turning-point, leading to reforms considered attractive to foreign capital). Firstly, Morocco has embarked on "a strategic vision of competitive modernization" which will directly affect the tools of development and will re-position Morocco in the context of globalization. Administrative procedures, which are a real obstacle for the investor, are being simplified, and a vast infrastructure modernization programme has also been launched (ports, airports, motorways; privatizations; housing projects…). This process is also connected to a regionalization strategy. Banks are taking on board the new strategies and authorizing more and more loans, fairly easily, to foreign investors, which had not always been the case. Although the proximity of Morocco to Europe is certainly the background to all this, it is above all the new geopolitical, economic and socio-cultural environment which has played a decisive role in the dynamic which has led some Europeans to switch from being tourists to being residents, temporary or permanent.

It is important to stress that many attractive aspects of the city and its surrounding countryside remain valuable assets in the eyes of westerners—the quality and accessibility of its closer-to-nature consumer products, and a certain purity dear to mechanized or super-industrialized societies: the more societies modernize and the more they move away from a spontaneous life-style, the more mankind seeks ancestral principles and human values which have not been corroded by the demands for stereotyped models. Marrakesh has profited from the rejection of a modernity which determines people's acts to the detriment of listening, communication and spontaneity. Marrakesh is no more than three hours from most European capitals, especially since 2004 when Moroccan airspace was opened to European companies, creating many new regular and occasional flights thus increasing both tourist numbers and the number of migrants, which in turn attracted investors to acquire a seasonal residence. This prime destination offers a very attractive environment. Endless sun, a magnificent material and non-material heritage—especially as an "exotic" change of scenery—an infrastructure of hotels and other residences for every budget, a particularly high-quality life style for western pockets… all very important assets.

Considering its historic past—Morocco was a French Protectorate from 1912 to 1956—the linguistic proximity is a considerable extra asset. The traditions of cooperation between the two shores and especially the relations between the two countries in the areas of geopolitics, economics and culture, have been important. Any individual effort can build on a solid platform, and further ties—albeit of a different kind—can be created.

Foreigners can obtain considerable income-tax reductions, particularly for pensions that have been transferred, and investors are offered advantages by the Moroccan authorities, notably the Regional Investment Centres, which give appreciable assistance and facilitate the launch of businesses. Thus many promoters and individuals have realized that they can qualify for privileges and opportunities, real advantages amounting to more than just an escape from modernity or the quest for a better quality of life.

Nevertheless, there are unpredictable harmful effects, such as extremists and other immature excesses. It is important not to exaggerate these. If

Marrakesh—like the rest of the world—cannot claim to offer cast-iron guarantees, it does present a reassuring face to westerners: the representative of the *Union des Français de l'Étranger* in Marrakesh stated that the French say overwhelmingly that they chose Morocco because the country makes them feel safe (Saigh 2003 & 2004). There are well-established traditions of hospitality, in a culture both ancient and modern. Life in Marrakesh is seductive and very pleasant, with guaranteed exoticism and a dream within reach. This is at least what seduced the first famous French settlers who chose to make their holiday homes here in the late 1980s and especially the early 1990s (Saigh 2003 & 2004). Their love of the city took them beyond the walls of the Medina and towards the vast spaces of the Palm Grove district (*la Palmeraie*), with its irresistible charms, and they then moved elsewhere in the city and its surroundings. As the first pioneers were part of an elite, they started a fashion which was emulated, easily enough when the socio-economic and strategic conditions were right.

More mobile travellers

If tourism has always benefited from these many advantages, some occasional travellers are becoming more mobile, either partially or more permanently, on account of changes in Europe and more general changes in mentalities. This is feeding the exponential phenomenon of an increasingly regular seasonal migration which is developing in Morocco, notably in Marrakesh, in different ways. The most obvious are:

– companies financed either by French or mixed capital, investing mostly in hotels, restaurants, foods, textiles and decoration (about fifty companies, according to figures from the consular agencies);

– increasing acquisitions and conversions of the Ryads (traditional Moroccan residences mainly in the old Medinas; the Ryad is generally built around an interior garden or patio, with four small courtyards separated by pathways, and converging on a small fountain or pond; the rooms around the patio open onto this space and create an intimate kind of lifestyle, convivial and allowing communication between the terraces, but with a jealously guarded private life); many of these residences are being bought by Europeans (the figure of seven hundred foreign-owned Ryads has been suggested) who stay for short periods or turn them into commercial outlets; some of them decide to settle;

– the proliferation of second homes, with several prestigious properties belonging to Europeans who remain for three to six months a year;

– the migration of young promoters who set up companies in Morocco, given the incentives mentioned above;

– the new and growing phenomenon of the recently retired who buy or rent accommodation in Morocco and settle there permanently, seeking a better quality of life for their income compared to what they could have in their own countries.

From a purely economic point of view, the most affluent members of this last category have chosen to live in Marrakesh, taking the opportunity to invest and to live a different life. Those with comfortable incomes can enjoy a better life style with the same income. Those with smaller pensions get by and many avoid the insecurity that they would have to face in their countries of origin. In every case, this category, which probably represents the majority of the more or less permanent migrants, make the most of a pleasant socio-cultural environment, a life style which would be unavailable to them in France with the same means, and above all—for some at least—the chance to live out their lives far from retirement homes and in a perfectly preserved and warm personal environment. For many of them, it is like an extended holiday.

According to Oberlé (2006), the Party for Justice and Development (PJD–Islamic tendency) is adopting a particularly favourable policy towards pensioners and foresees a migration of almost a million people by 2020. This objective is apparently based on the fact that "old Christians" would bring in guaranteed income which would stimulate employment and reduce clandestine emigration. According to the same source, this category has the advantage of not radically altering the culture as they are, given their age, less likely than young migrants to create situations of cultural confrontation.

It is perhaps too soon to assess the accuracy of this point of view. There is also the emergence of marriages between young Moroccan women and pensioners from the Northern shores, looking for young wives, even very young wives, with other attractions (some, although they would not admit it, are apparently seeking docile or even submissive wives). The increase in marriages between pensioners in their fifties and young Moroccans (aged eighteen to thirty) is sufficiently great not to go unnoticed. The new wives, from modest or very modest backgrounds, appear to be attracted by the relatively high incomes of their suitors who are seeking partners who sometimes are the same age as their grand-daughters. These women are of course tempted by the dream of acquiring a nationality which, in their imagination, will open doors to freedom and to the utopia of financial security. All this in exchange for real pleasure in a hopefully not-too-distant future, in their intimate relations and those of their immediate family. So many inexpressible but easily imaginable dreams blossom in the imagination of these companions.

Generally speaking, the migratory movement which stems from tourism has generated real economic activity. Flats, houses, villas or luxury residences are rented or bought. Moroccan investors, and especially foreign investors, have quickly understood the trends of this demand. In addition, residential complexes are being built, as well as medical and leisure establishments, in a pleasant and attractive environment.

The rush for the Ryads

Another, quite large, category of clients has chosen to keep closer ties with their country of origin, while making the most of a more pleasant autumn and winter climate. They make the choice of a double residence. This allows them to get away from harsh seasons and to retain the possibility, when necessary, of staying for shorter or longer periods in the "red city". If it is difficult to give precise figures for these migratory movements, it is certain that the phenomenon is almost exponential, and it is beyond question that it gets much of its momentum from tourism.

The rush for the Ryads has been a most spectacular phenomenon. It has grown with amazing speed. In certain Western imaginations, the Ryad is a place where one can penetrate the myth of the Orient, in the steps of the many famous characters who were the first wave of immigrants. The Ryads were literally snatched up. A vast and insidious marketing operation was launched by certain estate agents who started by discreetly identifying the Ryads which might go on the market and then targeting the owners with incentives and temptations. The result was outrageous, radical and often savage speculation. It should be pointed out that many owners were trapped or even cheated. So much so that anyone walking down the narrow streets of the Medina cannot fail to notice the number of Ryads that have fallen into the hands of foreigners, or been converted into guest houses catering for foreign clients, at least in certain areas of the Medina. In 2002 it was estimated that out of five hundred converted Ryads, three hundred and eighty were French owned (Véran 2002). Out of more than seven hundred Ryads that are now foreign-owned, at least a third of the new owners are residents, permanent or temporary, and mix with the locals. The rest have been converted into guest houses and are therefore devoted to tourism.

The foreign resident, like the tourist, sees in this the dream come true of living in a palace, albeit a miniature one. It is a totally unreal experience which gives one the feeling of the secret world of Arab-Berber or Muslim culture, with its strong attachment to both the material and the immaterial.

The Ryad perhaps suggests living life as one imagines the Other does... A large number of foreign owners, seduced by the traditional architecture and the craftwork of the decorations, very quickly start renewal work on their dwellings, which in some cases were close to ruin. These foreigners have means beyond those of the locals. In addition, in the case of Ryads converted into guest houses, the owners often improve the small street near the Ryad. They are very concerned about the cleanliness of the district. Some owners make their neighbours even happier by taking on staff. The owner often creates a community spirit by answering the expectations of the locals, who show courtesy and respect to their new neighbours.

In fact, when the Ryad is used for tourist residences, the situation is quite unusual. In this type of neighbourhood, the locals, who are discreet, tend to remain silent in their way of seeing the Other. If you ask them, they feel uncomfortable about expressing their views and especially their criticisms. More often, they will express their lack of comment by subtle insinuations. In fact, for them tourists tend to exhibit cultural traits which are not in keeping with Moroccan traditions and rituals. Tourists sin through ignorance. Their status as tourists means that their behaviour attracts attention, surprises, offends and shocks through certain excesses, all of which creates underground tensions, even if these very rarely come out as open, direct reactions.

Nevertheless, with a certain amount of patience and skill, one can get some significant comments. By way of example, even if in the opinion of the locals it is agreed that TV and the cinema are responsible for the shift in behaviour, in the Medina it is recognized that the most important changes in behaviour of the young locals came about with the emergence of the Ryads as guest houses. According to the parents, the young from districts increasingly inhabited by foreigners have become more demanding. They point out changes in their way of speaking, acting and thinking. The changes in dress code are the most striking. The young are believed to be fragile as they try to imitate the manners of the foreigners. In certain respects, for the parents and older people, the presence of foreigners is considered essentially as a threat to the material and immaterial patrimony of the Medina. For some native Marrakeshis, the sheer number of foreigners makes it a kind of pernicious colonialism, or neo-colonialism. Lapses in behaviour are very quickly pointed out. It is said that the Ryads are sites for pornographic films. Others say that it is a hiding place for sexual and homosexual practices. Some newspapers report that in certain guest houses there are "pedophile networks", "male and female prostitution", "swingers clubs" and "filming of pornographic films" (*L'Economiste* 2002). This surely only concerns a minority, even if the effect cannot be measured quantitatively.

In terms of tourism mutating into various forms of migration, what stands out is the important economic activity arising from this global situation. This is evident in the creation of employment in sectors such as construction and connected activities. Craftwork also does well, not only because it and its values are much more visible, but also because of the emergence of new forms and uses of traditional practices. We can see designs which derive from a secular life-style, or which are remodelled and combined with a western approach. Certain aspects of this craftwork—wrought-iron work, woodwork, carpet design, ceramic mosaics, jewellery, pottery—are laboriously recreated and adapted, especially for export, which is expanding and developing at an unusual rate. One may however wonder how far these new influences are a threat to the nature of this heritage by dragging it into a world of financial pressure. One might also wonder about the extent to which fair trade practices apply. The town and the region are going through a boom in estate agents, hotels, guest houses, bed-and-breakfasts, apartment blocks and all kinds of restaurants. We can also see an increase in new shops aimed at the new clientele and often created by foreigners. Art galleries, deluxe bakers, stylists and decorators, exporters of revamped craftwork, factories making domestic linen, manufacturers of remodelled kitchen- and table-ware, etc. All these and more set up business and offer products which could be called "modern".

For a large number of these new residents, Marrakesh is still an Eldorado where one can have an exceptional lifestyle and start a business which has every chance of succeeding. Artists, great creators and the rich are delighted by their homes constructed in several hectares of palm trees or in the ancient luxuriously renovated palaces and Ryads. So many dwellings mock the luxury hotels not only by their unique and exceptional splendour and refinement, but even more by the exclusivity of their exoticism and their existence in a world sometimes worthy of the *Arabian Nights*. Everyone competes for the most splendid view of the Atlas, sometimes majestically wrapped in its blanket of snow, or set against a sky of crystal blue.

To conclude, it is undeniable that we are seeing socio-cultural changes which could prove deep and sustainable in the long term, but whose importance we can still not measure. The migratory phenomenon could be considered as a direct or indirect source of economic input. Firstly, with the introduction of currency, but also by putting Morocco in the shop window, which can only be positive for the image of the country, a country of tolerance, of safety and of conviviality. In the long term, and keeping things in proportion, this could produce a chain reaction which could only be beneficial for the economic development of the country. On the other hand, we are seeing property prices increase dramatically. This could have perverse effects, firstly on the local population who could see themselves squeezed out of the house market, but also in the Medina where the Ryads have seen their prices go up to meet the increase in foreign demand, a situation which creates an incentive to sell. If this trend continues at the same rate as today, the Medina, which is prized for its lifestyle and material and non-material heritage, is in danger of becoming an annex to the hotels and so losing its soul and essence (Bousta 2003 & 2004). It is not necessarily the new owners who would be to blame, but the opening of their Ryads to tourists, who are only passing through and are sometimes totally unaware. The impact on the socio-cultural environment could be particularly disastrous, leading to the disappearance of the very atmosphere and lifestyle that the tourists come to find.

Bibliography and References

BOUSTA SAÏGH Rachida (2003) "Voisinage des ryads maisons-d'hôtes dans la Médina de Marrakech: résultats d'une enquête réalisée en mars 2003," pp. 179-201 in Bousta R. (ed.), *Communication interculturelle, patrimoine et tourisme*, Marrakesh: Université Cadi Ayyad, Centre de Recherche sur les Cultures Maghrébines.

—. (2004) "Le ryad maison-d'hôte, esquisse d'une réflexion sur le phénomène et ses retombées," pp. 157-169 in Bousta R. (ed.), *Le Tourisme durable: quelles réalités et quelles perspectives*, Marrakesh: Université Cadi Ayyad, Centre de Recherche sur les Cultures Maghrébines.

L'Économiste (Moroccan business paper) (2002) "Enquête: 6.500 dh la soirée « chaude » dans un ryad à Marrakech," 22 April 2002, p. 3.

OBERLÉ Thierry (2006) "Marrakech, terre promise des retraités français," *Le Figaro*, 8 March 2006, p. 4.

PENNA Armandine (2006) "A qui appartient Marrakech?" *Le Nouvel Observateur*, n° 2157 (9-15 March 2006), *Spécial Maroc, portrait d'un royaume en movement*, pp. 16-18.

VÉRAN Sylvie (2002) "La bataille de la Médina," *Le Nouvel Observateur* June 2002, p. 55.

CHAPTER FOURTEEN

BACKPACKERS: NEW NOMADS, OR ESCAPISTS?

ANNA DLUZEWSKA

Tourism is one of the most quickly evolving forms of leisure. Apart from satisfying the need to learn, to explore the new, or the need for recreation, totally new functions of travelling have emerged, such as simple snobbery or even habit. Furthermore, participants in particular types of tourism often criticize other tourists and even feel animosity against them: for example an individual tourist looks down on organized groups of tourists and mass resorts, while tourists from organized groups cannot stand individual tourists. Since tourism ceased to be an elite activity and became a mass activity, new types of tourism satisfy those who are searching for freedom and individualism. There is ecological tourism, countryside tourism, drifting, exclusive tourism (with its lack of crowds and individual treatment by the service staff)... and also so-called "backpacking". The present chapter focuses on this latter type of tourism, which is something of a new model. It is quite symptomatic that centres of exclusive tourism designed to remind tourists of the simplicity of backpacking are rapidly developing, for example the most expensive resorts in the Maldives such as Soneva Gili and Soneva Fushi (with a shower in the garden, no air conditioning, a covered television set, and walking barefoot as the norm...).

Definition and methods

Backpacking has aroused the interest of researchers into tourism, sociologists, economists, and psychologists, perhaps more than any other type of tourism. Questions raised go far beyond the methodology of one scientific field: questions about motivation, about whether backpacking is tourism or just an escape (if so, from what: civilization? routine? the

European winter?); backpackers are called contemporary nomads, so are they people without roots? without attachment to one specific culture? without a home? The question arises as to whether or to what extent backpacking fits into a scheme of tourist movement, and to what extent it is a form of migration.

There is no clear definition of backpacking, and there are contradictions between different interpretations. Are backpackers young people? Are they well educated? Do they act consciously? Are they looking merely for cheap entertainment? Are backpackers people with backpacks? Participants of this type of tourism already know the latter is not necessarily the case, for every so often people with elegant suitcases appear on Khao San Road in Bangkok, the Mecca of backpackers. Elderly people, parents with children, as well as affluent people are appearing there more and more frequently.

The existence of backpacking is confirmed by the vocabulary used in almost all tourist guides, not only in those which dominate on the individual tourist market. The notion of "backpackers" does not really seem to need further explanation, for it is automatically associated with a certain category of tourist. People talk of hotels for backpackers, means of transport for backpackers, internet portals for backpackers, etc. A similar terminology describing this type of tourism is used by travel agents in destination countries: travel agencies organize transport for backpackers, trips for backpackers, etc. The idea was even taken up by the "Backpackers Research Group", one of nine Special Interest Groups (SIGs) within ATLAS (Association for Tourism and Leisure Education).

The aim of this chapter is to characterize backpacking tourists, and to set out some basic guidelines for the delineation of their activities and preoccupations. Focusing on the division of backpackers into particular kinds, and on the most popular regions for backpacking tourism, our sources are field studies carried out in Asia and in Central America in the years 1998-2005 (Thailand 1998, 2000, 2001, 2002, 2003, 2004, 2005; Indonesia 1999; Belize 2000; Guatemala 2000; Vietnam 2002; Cambodia 2002, 2005; Laos 2004, 2005; Myanmar 2005; the Philippines 2004; Hong Kong 2004). Methods and research tools from the American School of Cultural Anthropology were used (Finn, Elliott-White & Walton 2000; Sztumski 1984; Wodz & Czekaj 1992). These methods are widely used for research on cultural identity in Asia and Africa. While sociological tools (questionnaires, statistical analysis) provide quantitative data, the Chicago School Tools are most effective in research on taboo issues and behaviour which the researched group of people is not necessarily aware of. The following tools in particular were used: direct participant observation, indirect participant observation, open questionnaire interviews, and open anonymous individual interviews (Hammersley & Atkinson 1995; Mason 2000; Spradley 1980).

In a first phase we could not really talk about conducting research according to a plan, with the questionnaire prepared in advance. It was more a case of spontaneous observation, conversations with dozens of people "on the road". The first trip was—as in the case of most backpackers—a trip to Thailand, then Malaysia and Singapore. Later travel in Asia was on a regular basis (two or three times a year). The aims of those trips were of a scientific, recreational and business character, allowing observation of a wide range of types of tourism on this continent.

Apart from active participant and non-participant observation, which had been done for over eight years in the most important regions of Asia, several hundred interviews with backpackers of different levels of education and income from various countries have been conducted. The survey group was made as diverse as possible. The research was rather of confidential than of an overt character. A non-categorized open questionnaire was used. The conclusions drawn from the survey are of qualitative as opposed to quantitative character; they do not constitute "discoveries" of a scientific nature. Similarly, the terminology and divisions applied are only suggestions. The reason is the huge diversity of participants in backpacking, with no possibility of examining a "representative" survey group. For example, if we are conducting a survey among people taking part in a cruise in Halong Bay in Vietnam, the characteristics of people who paid $50 for the cruise would be different from those of people who paid only $5 (remaining among the crowd on the ship), although both groups are backpackers.

During the research the interviewees were asked about the length and frequency of their travels, the places they visited, the level and the objects of their expenditure, the reasons for choosing this type of travelling, other types of tourism they have participated in, their nationality, education, job position, family situation.

Turning hippie

Backpacking, or travelling "with only a backpack", has nothing to do with a mountain walk from one hostel to another or, even less, with lack of money. Backpackers are often affluent people who hold important jobs: company executives, doctors or computer scientists. Once a year they take off their suits, have their body decorated with a washable tattoo and... set off to have a rest, the way they want and wherever they want. They turn a bit "hippie". They do not feel at ease in an organized group. Among backpacking zealots we can also find students, people who have just graduated, and in recent years also pensioners. What attracts them is the freedom, of choice of destination and the way they organize their trip. They have one thing in common—they are all individualists, and as the level of individualism in the world is rising, backpacking is becoming something more than a fashion, it is becoming a way of life (Dluzewska 2005).

The nationalities which dominate in backpacking are the English, Dutch, Swedish, Germans and French. There are also more and more Americans and Australians. People from the Czech Republic and Poland have been showing up recently (WTO 1999a, 1999b, 2002). The greater the individualism in a given society, the stronger the interest in this type of tourism (Sztumski & Harciarek 2001). Of course, a certain financial minimum to buy a ticket—usually to a faraway place—and the courage to undertake a trip to countries considered "wild", are both needed, and also an awareness of one's value on the labour market. Economic stability is of greater importance than the income level. From the psychological point of view backpackers are the absolute antithesis of people going for vacation, for a week at most, with their laptop and a mobile phone so as to have everything under control. Backpackers have no fear that during their absence someone is going to oust them from their job.

The scenarios of the trips are quite similar. Tourists reach the destination (usually in Asia) by plane. Backpackers stay in the "right" district, where there is a wide variety of small hotels, restaurants, travel agencies, internet cafés, etc. The hotels are usually rather small and not classified, which guarantees to backpackers that there will be no organized tourist groups. But as there are individual tourists there, sometimes the place is very loud and crowded. In spite of "cockroach stories", which are a fashion in this society, not all hotels are dirty and of low standard. There is a choice. There are hotel rooms with air conditioning, a television set, a nice clean bathroom; there are also "places to stay overnight"—rooms without a bathroom and no bedding (you have to bring your own). Prices vary from $5 to $50 a day, never more in the backpacker districts.

The region chosen most frequently by backpackers is southern Asia. The most trendy places for the time being are Laos (although the borders were opened for tourists only a few years ago), Cambodia, Vietnam and Burma (Myanmar). Malaysia, Singapore, some Indonesian Islands, the Philippines, Nepal, India and—of course—Thailand are also quite popular. Bangkok has always been and remains a real centre of backpacking. It is the place where tourists arrange tickets and visas and exchange information. The vicinity of Khao San Road is most important. The street itself expanded to such an extent that not everything could fit there. Khao San Road in Bangkok is maybe the only place in the world where you can arrange a visa to the most secluded and illicit corners of the planet within 24 hours and buy flight tickets for nearly every airline in travel agencies which, in terms of size, resemble telephone boxes. Prices are suspiciously low. A similar suspicion can be experienced as far as special offers are concerned (a trip to Chiang Mai, over seven hundred kilometres away, in an air-conditioned bus, for the equivalent of three euros). Nevertheless the system operates successfully (Dluzewska 2003). Three main factors are crucial in the popularity of Asia among backpackers: uncomplicated organization, low prices and the feeling of security. Tourists are not on their own, everything happens quickly, easily and efficiently. A trip will cost under $100 a day.

In second place after Asia come Central and South America. Tourism for individualists is still possible there, even though it is slightly more expensive and difficult. More experienced and adventurous travellers favour other destinations worldwide. Morocco with its Atlas mountains and the desert areas of the southern part is attracting a growing number of backpackers; the same applies to Mongolia, Uzbekistan, Kazakhstan or Iran. Organizing a trip to such places demands a greater investment and sometimes a lot of persistence. The map of secure countries changes from year to year.

It is much more difficult to do backpacking in Europe, simply because of the prices. A short stay in the cheapest hotel in Italy or Belgium, not block-booked by agencies, is incomparably more expensive than in a good hotel in Asia. Staying overnight in youth hostels does not fulfil the requirement of individualism. Young people with packsacks travel around Europe, but this is not backpacking. Backpacking in Canada and the USA is even less popular, for cultural reasons and due to complications concerning visas, even though prices are relatively low. For backpackers Africa is most difficult and most expensive, and apart from a few enclaves (like Lamu Island in Kenya, or Zanzibar Island in Tanzania) backpacking does not occur on that continent. A huge obstacle is the high level of common crimes (theft, robbery), lack of transport for individual tourists, and high prices in the case of individual tourism.

Three main groups of backpackers

A first group would consist of people on vacation for two to six weeks. They travel from one to three times per year depending on free time from their work as well as on their earnings and the prices of long-distance tickets. Representatives of this group are usually well educated and relatively well off, and often hold managerial positions. They are typical individualists. "I cannot imagine a vacation with a group of people!" says Marc, a forty-five-year-old president of a consulting company from Stockholm. "I have to work with people every day. I have to smile even if I don't feel like it, and have lunch with people whom I am supposed to have lunch with. At a certain point I have had enough of it. I have to let off steam. [...] When I travel alone there is no threat of loneliness. I can go trekking for a few days and sit next to somebody. But I am not condemned to somebody's presence. No one tells me what I am to do during my holiday!" (Van Vieng, Laos, November 2004). Marc had already been to the Philippines, Thailand and Mongolia. He wanted to visit Burma (Myanmar) the following year.

The second group consists of people travelling for two to twelve months, a form of temporary nomadism. They visit several countries during a single trip and when funds run out, they earn money (usually in Singapore, Hong Kong or Bangkok) and start travelling again. After a year they usually return home and begin again normal lives and jobs... until the next change of work: "I have worked as a manager in a big company for three years. I haven't been getting on well with others. [...] I am tired. I have to rest first. Why should I start a new job now, I am not going to ask my new employer for a holiday for a start, am I? I'm going to travel around a few months and I'm going to look for a new job when I have some more strength," says Tom (Siem Reap, Cambodia, February, 2004), a thirty-year-old New Zealander. For him a gig in Singapore is no good, it would be a waste of energy. In this group we also find people who have a lot of free time: people who have just graduated, people who have just quit their jobs and have not yet taken a new one, owners of companies, pensioners (these latter do not run out of funds).

The third group consists of eternal travellers, what we might call permanent nomads. They have been away from home up to a dozen or so years, yet they never call it emigration. When asked about the reasons for such a long journey they rarely answer the way Marie-Jeanne—a retired teacher from Lyon—did, that "in France I feel old, lonely, I am bored and in Asia I feel the adventure all the time." Marie-Jeanne is aware that travel in her native country is the exception not the rule, and her stay in Asia is not a mere holiday. In most cases people classed in the third group act as if nothing special was happening, nothing out of the ordinary. Everything stays within certain limits: they have not managed to see some important site yet, so as soon as they have seen it, they will finish their journey...

And so they postpone their return for the next few years.

The so-called "pre-term pensioners" (e.g. disheartened stockbrokers), who could, from the financial point of view, allow themselves to travel for a few years, have been classified in this group as well. Financial means are usually not an issue. Quite a high percentage of the group constitute the "escapists". These people are often very well-educated, they quickly climbed the professional ladder, they are affluent, yet they have problems with assimilation in their own social environment. This can be a result of a job loss (it is a disgrace to start anew from a lower level, it is better to withdraw, but in such a way that nobody can pity them), professional burnout, or the lack of ability to come into intimate relations with others in a normal way in their native country. We mention this in passing, as it is a subject for research by social psychologists.

Types of leisure and recreation

As far as programmes are concerned, active recreation is also very important. Places which allow several types of recreation activity are of great interest to backpackers. The mountain village of Van Vieng in Laos attracts enthusiasts of cave exploration, trekking in rice fields, cross-country biking, canoeing, etc. Yet it would not be attractive enough were it not for the well-developed entertainment sector (restaurants, bars, clubs with appropriate music). As for the different recreation activities, backpackers have developed a terminology of their own. Terms applied to walking activities, for instance, differ slightly from common usage:

– Trekking is usually understood as a mountain ramble of low difficulty, strictly connected with ethnic tourism: meals and overnight stays in local villages, in local people's houses. Trekking lasts for two to five days. The walk itself lasts for about five to seven hours a day. The most important part of the programme is the possibility of participating actively in the life of a village. The most popular trekking routes are the Laotian mountain tribes trail, the Northern Vietnam mountain tribes trail, the Northern Thai ethnic minorities trail, the mountain rice terraces trail in the Philippines. The notion of a "trail" is understood as "the area of deployment". The respective groups follow different routes, sleep in different villages (which are often the native villages of the guides). Trekking is—besides water sports—the most popular kind of leisure activity among backpackers.

– Hiking is a mountain ramble of varying difficulty without the necessity of coming into contact with the indigenous population. It lasts from a dozen or so hours (e.g. climbing volcanoes) to a dozen or so days (e.g. in the Himalayas). The most popular trails in this group are Indonesian and Philippinian volcanoes, and the easier Himalayan trails like the Annapurna-Nepal trail.

– Climbing is defined as a relatively high level of difficulty. It lasts from a dozen or so hours (e.g. climbing rocks) to a dozen or so days (e.g. in the Himalayas). It demands professional equipment and professional organization (Nepal, Vietnam, etc.).

Water sports such as snorkelling, diving or rafting, cave exploration, biking, all of them popular with backpackers, have also acquired new meanings according to costs or difficulty level. But active recreation is also characterized by its spontaneity and a search for new activities. Some kinds surprise even backpackers themselves. The recently popular river run-off on... tubes (also at night) or liana-jumps is an example. Every year people come up with new ideas.

"Fully Independent Travellers"

Whether they are looking for a solitary and anonymous escape from work, whether they are experiencing temporary or permanent nomadism, backpackers are hard to categorize. Sometimes a tourist, sometimes a traveller, the backpacker is recognizable by a persistent concern for escapism and independence, a persistent need for recreation and entertainment. But recreation and entertainment do not necessarily mean carelessness or indifference. Since backpacking is a type of tourism in which the participants do not have many demands, it does not cause many social and religious dysfunctions. Moreover, backpackers know which shops they are supposed to avoid in order not to support the regime, which hotels they should avoid, and how to behave in temples so as not to offend the faithful. The profits go directly to the natives, money does not go to big corporations. Apart from the feeling of individualism, participation in backpacking provides an opportunity to contribute to the development of poor countries. It is a form of responsible social assistance. Backpacking is gaining more popularity every year, attracting new social groups, especially elderly people and affluent people.

A preliminary analysis shows constant changes within this type of tourism. Due to these changes, participants are often called FITs (fully independent travellers), which to a certain extent characterizes the spirit of this type of mobility.

Bibliography and References

BUTLER R. & HINCH T. (1996) *Tourism and Indigenous Peoples*, London: International Thompson Publishing.

COHEN E. (1973) "Nomads from affluence: notes on the phenomenon of drifter-tourism," *International Journal of Comparative Sociology* 14 (1-2), pp. 89-103.

—. (1984) "The sociology of tourism: approaches, issues and findings," *Annual Review of Sociology* 10, pp. 373-392.

CURRIE R.R. (1997) "A pleasure-tourism behaviours framework," *Annals of Tourism Research*, 1997 (4), pp. 884-897.

DLUZEWSKA A. (2006) "Trendy rozwoju turystyki aktywnej w ramach turystyki ekskluzynej," ("Tendencies of active tourism development compared with exclusive tourism,"), *Rocznik Naukowy,* 2006(4), pp. 136-144.

—. (2005) "Rekreacja fizyczna w ramach turystyki typu back packing" ("Physical recreation into back-packing tourism"), pp. 57-66 in Kubinska Z. & Bergier B. (eds.), *Rekreacja ruchowa w teorii I praktyce* (*Physical Recreation in Theory and Practice)*, Biala Podlaska: PWSZ.

—. (2004) "Backpackers czyli ludzie z plecakiem," ("Back packers—people with back packs") *Biznes i Turystyka*, 2004(5), pp. 26-32.

—. (2003) "Przez Bangkok," ("Passing through Bangkok"), *Biznes i Turystyka*, 2003(4) , pp. 30-37.

FINN M., ELLIOTT-WHITE M. & WALTON M. (2000) *Tourism and Leisure Research Methods: Data Collection, Analysis, and Interpretation*, London: Longman.

GURSOY D. & RUTHERFORD D. (2004) "Host attitudes toward tourism. An improved structural model," *Annals of Tourism Research* 31 (3), pp. 495-516.

HAMMERSLEY M. & ATKINSON P. (1995) *Ethnography. Principles in Practice*, London: Routledge.

RICHARDS G. & WILSON J. (eds.) (2004) *The Global Nomad Backpacker in Theory and Practice*, Clevedon: Channel View Publications.

RILEY P.J. (1988) "Road Culture of International Long-Term Budget Travellers," *Annals of Tourism Research*, 15 (2), pp. 313-328.

SZTUMSKI J. (1984). *Wstep do metod i technik badan spolecznych*, (*Introduction to the methods and tools of social research and analysis*) Warsaw: PWN.

SZTUMSKI J. & HARCIAREK M. (eds.) (2001) *Stres w biznesie;*

Wydaw, (*Stress in business*) Czestochowa: WZPCz.

WTO (2002) *Youth Outbound Travel of the Germans, the British and the French*, Madrid: World Tourism Organization.

WTO (1999a) *East Asia and the Pacific 1989-1998: Tourism Market Trends. Thirty-third meeting, Macau, 11 May 1999 / WTO Commission for East Asia and the Pacific*, Madrid: World Tourism Organization.

WTO (1999b) *South Asia 1989-1998: Tourism Market Trends. Thirty-seventh meeting, Macau, 11 May 1999 / WTO Commission for South Asia*, Madrid: World Tourism Organization.

WODZ K. & CZEKAJ K. (1992) *Szkola chicagowska w socjologii: tradycja mysli spolecznej i wymogi wspolczesnej socjologii empirycznej/ materialy pokonferencyjne*, (*The Chicago School in Sociology: Tradition of social theory and exigencies of contemporary empirical sociology*) Katowice: Slaski University.

CHAPTER FIFTEEN

ABOARD OR ABROAD? WANDERING FILIPINO SEAFARERS

CATHERINE BERGER

Discrepancies in wages and living standards in different parts of the world are important factors in the increase in the world-wide circulation of goods and services that is part of economic globalization. Furthermore, the fact that merchant navies rely on seafarers from low-income countries is one reason why the costs of maritime transport, the main carrier of international trade, remain low. These sailors become a special kind of migrant worker since they leave their home and their country for several months at a time but do not settle anywhere. Today, the Philippines are the country that provides the largest number of seafarers in the world, well ahead of Russians, Ukrainians and the Chinese. Filipino seafarers are to be found on all the world's oceans, on ships of all types and of all nationalities, but most of them occupy low positions. Seafaring conditions today mean that they spend nearly all their time at sea, hardly ever setting foot ashore and, when they do, it is at best for a few hours only. The ship is therefore the only place where they work and live for months on end, but they do have an experience of otherness in that they find themselves on board with crew members and officers of other nationalities. So this chapter attempts to describe some of the characteristics of "paradoxical" transnational migration of Filipino seafarers, with an emphasis on the changes in status and way of life that it brings about. Data collected through in-depth interviews of seafarers met both in France and in the Philippines will help illustrate a complex and moving situation which often alternates between sacrifice and opulence, and which compels the seafarer, his family, his local community and even his country to continuous readjustments of their identity.

Today, the Philippines are one of the leading countries in terms of emigration. The export of temporary labour is indeed an industry in its own right, since the remittances sent by the migrants to their families account for 9% of GNP. This represents a real boon for the country's economy as it brings in foreign currency, greatly improves the trade balance, supports some twenty million nationals and boosts consumption. The absence of these migrants also alleviates demographic and social pressures since, with a population of eighty-nine million and a soaring demography, the Philippines suffer from high rates of unemployment and, especially, underemployment. The country is also heavily indebted and corruption is rampant. A large part of the population lives in severe poverty. It is generally admitted that nearly eight million Filipinos, nearly one in ten, are now abroad. They can be found in over one hundred and fifty countries, mainly in the Middle East (Kuwait, Saudi Arabia, the Emirates...), in Asia (Japan, Taiwan, Hong Kong, Singapore...), in North America and all over Europe. These legal and illegal migrants follow very diverse paths, including permanent settlement with their families and even naturalization in the host country, as in the US. But for the Filipino authorities, the best migrants are the temporary "Overseas Filipino Workers" or "OFWs", who leave the country with a work contract—in theory at least—and send home most of their wages. This migratory trend is not new, and was officially encouraged by President Marcos in 1974 when Middle-East states, made wealthy by petrodollars, were in need of workers, first in the construction sector, then in services. All those who came after him followed in his footsteps and, progressively, different bodies such as the POEA (Philippine Overseas Employment Administration) and OWWA (Overseas Workers Welfare Administration) have been created to manage, organize or even protect those workers who experience situations which are widely recognized as potentially very distressing. There are scores of cases of unpaid salaries, prostitution, forced labour, rapes, sexual harassment and all kinds of brutal behaviour. The country's authorities seem to be caught between a fear of angering foreign employers, and pressure from public opinion, which is more and more sensitive to cases of ill-treatment that might discourage prospective migrants. They are more eager to express their gratitude through publicly honouring migrants as "modern national heroes".

Seafarers make up only a small fraction of these OFWs but it is a fraction that matters financially because, housed and fed on the ship and usually with an official contract, they remit relatively more than other migrants. 80% of their wages is directly sent to their families. It is estimated that there are around two hundred thousand Filipinos at sea at any given time but, as there are far more seafarers than employment opportunities, this figure should be more than doubled. Statistics for 2002 issued by the SIRC (Seafarers' International Research Centre, from Cardiff

University) show that more than a quarter of the world's seafarers are Filipinos. There are big discrepancies in their living and working conditions since, in the merchant navy, there are big variations according to position on board, type of ship, the company, the flag and many other elements. Today, ships are more and more sophisticated and the demand for highly skilled personnel is increasing. There is a shortage of officers but too many ratings. Most Filipinos are in a subordinate position, whether on deck or in the engine room. Only twenty percent of them are petty officers and ten percent senior officers. This large proportion of seafarers at low-level positions, larger than what is found for seafarers not only from western maritime countries but also from India or even China, means that most Filipinos get ill-paid jobs for which competition is the harshest. They sail mainly on ships under flags of convenience or second register and with multinational crews. On these ships which account today for sixty percent of the world's merchant fleet, the whole or part of the crew is recruited from anywhere in the world and employed according to their local wage levels and working conditions.

Away from home and family

If so many young Filipinos keep turning to seafaring in spite of the limited job prospects and the harsh working and living conditions, it is because "seabased migration"—the administration distinguishes between "landbased" and "seabased" migrants—is seen as the only solution in many poor families who are ready to sacrifice everything to have one son trained in the maritime sector. Compared to local wages, a seafarer's pay is very attractive. A skilled rating (AB or Able Seaman) who makes between 600 and 1,500 dollars a month is much better paid than a specialist medical doctor, and his salary is huge compared to those in the menial jobs which most Filipinos have. But before earning this kind of money, the expenses are considerable: in order to sail, seafarers have to spend several years in a maritime academy, sit for exams, spend a year at sea as cadets and take regular compulsory upgrading courses throughout their careers. Seafarers usually come from poor families who have to sell some land or other properties, take a mortgage on their house, renounce studies or marriage for other children, or contract debts in order to be able to pay the tuition fees, get through the intricate red tape and the indispensable "back-up" that will eventually lead, for those who are lucky and sometimes after several months waiting or doing unpaid work as "utility boys", to the first job at sea that is necessary to complete the qualification. As soon as they make money, the young sailors are expected to repay their debt, often by helping another relative or the local community. The weight of this "debt of gratitude" can prove very hard to bear for the seafarer or for his close family since they are now considered as affluent and are sometimes constantly pestered for help. The young man is thus condemned to succeed and he may find himself in dire straights if he cannot complete his course of studies or secure a contract—both situations which are only too common since seafarers are too numerous and the training sometimes not up to standard.

Migrating first means leaving behind a home, a family, a local community, a country. Seafarers leave for a period of nine months, often more, and as a rule they have not been prepared to cope with this aspect of life at sea. There is of course a seafaring tradition in the Philippines, but the dramatic growth of the seafaring profession dates back only to the 1980s, and in most families—usually of rural origin—there are still no role models to help seafarers and their families adapt to this separation. Many sailors suffer from the feeling that life is going on without them. They are frequently absent at important moments in life: a birth, when someone is sick or dies, a birthday, an important date in the school life of a child, local and national events. It's a big frustration to be away and to feel powerless when there is a problem.

> One of my mates learnt on board that his father had died. He couldn't go home to bury him. He had to save the money for the funeral. (Ariel, April 2006)

Some speak of a life "away from the world", always postponed and which they feel in the end escapes them. There are few opportunities to find oneself physically alone in the Philippines and, during their first trip at sea, the young cadets sleep or work on their own for the first time in their lives. Work-related stress, the fear of making mistakes, adjustments to a very different type of life and a feeling of estrangement all combine to make the first years at sea terribly hard.

> My first year on board was the biggest battle of my whole life [...] I often had the feeling I was the loneliest and most powerless person in the world. [...] I only had one idea in mind. I had to go back home, but it would have been too expensive... (Paul, July 2001)

Life at sea can be extremely lonely, in spite of the small number of crew-members—around twenty, sometimes less—and the permanent promiscuity, or perhaps because of these features. Seafarers tend to remain distant from each other as far as possible, if only to avoid sources of conflict which would soon make life hell in such a confined space. Hierarchical divisions limit contacts between officers and crew to work situations, and this reduces even more the number of people to interact with. Working hours can be long—up to ten or twelve a day for ratings—and men are exhausted after a day's work. Social life on board can amount to very little, and seafarers complain about the monotony of their life at sea and the terrible feeling of boredom it brings about. Work in shifts and language barriers make it difficult to share leisure activities such as watching videos. Today, more and more ships are "dry"—no alcohol is allowed on board. This actually reduces safety hazards (which are very real) but it does considerably reduce conviviality. The seafarers who manage to cope best with this recluse life are those who can find interest in the present situation, like this young junior officer from the Cebu area:

> As soon as I have an opportunity, I try to learn something new. I am interested in the stars. I ask questions about the machines. I try to avoid thinking too much about the rest... (Brian, April 2006)

The development of a culture on board

The status of Filipino seafarers as migrants is paradoxical since they leave their country but do not settle in any other. And it is not possible to talk of them discovering the countries where their ship docks, because today calls in port are kept to the minimum duration required for technical and commercial operations. Ships call only for a few hours, and as there are still many tasks to perform on board crew members cannot get ashore, or perhaps they just spend a short time in a terminal remote from everything. Although a career at sea still conjures up images of exotic countries and adventure, reality is very different. Seafarers are no longer travellers: how can we talk of travel if we do not stop anywhere? The ship is the only "territory" where the seafarers spend a long time when they are at sea, and when you meet sailors during a call ashore, they always introduce themselves by announcing the name of their vessel. The ship corresponds, in fact, to the definition of the "total institution" given by Erwing Goffman (1961): an enclosed space where activities which are normally separated are all carried out—work, leisure and home, all in one place. On a ship space is very scarce, the living area is extremely limited, and each member of the crew restricts his movements to places where he has a job to do. Social space is organized along hierarchical lines which distinguish clearly between officers and crew and also separate those who work on deck from those who are in the engine room. In multinational crews, the nationality of the seafarers modifies or reinforces professional and hierarchical distinctions. In theory, potential combinations of nationalities are infinite. Some are actually far more frequent than others, especially when there are officers from rich countries such as Japan, Norway, Germany and crew members from poor countries such as the Philippines, Indonesia or Romania. Each ship thus becomes, for a limited time, a sort of country where emigrants have gathered and where a specific "culture" develops. Its nature depends on all the seafarers who compose the crew, the personality of the Master and his first officers, and the atmosphere which prevails on board. The attention paid by the shipping company to the working and living conditions is obviously of paramount importance, but so are the commanding style of the officers, the opportunities offered for organizing social life, and the respect for different diets and religious practices.

> We are only three Filipinos in the engine room, and we have problems with the cook. The crew members protest about the food and they want to get rid of him. He is an Indian and he keeps cooking the same food that we don't like. (Jayson, August 2001)

Most Filipinos don't seem to be hostile to the idea of working with foreigners, who are at first seen as nationals of another country but very quickly become individualized. Many seafarers say they enjoy discovering different traditions and ways of life and for some, that stimulates their curiosity. Seafarers enjoy having parties on board for birthdays or special events like Christmas but the opportunities are not frequent. Life on board necessarily erases the cultural practices of one national group or another, and retains only a few consensual events. Some specific forms of masculine sociability can be found such as the "barcadas", groups of buddies who go ashore to drink. These sometimes express the cohesion of sub-groups which can include various nationalities. As far as values are concerned, a spirit of tolerance usually prevails at sea, thus making it possible for this very heterogeneous community to function. This is very different from the process of acculturation which can take place when migrants spend a long time in a single country or often return there. The human environment of the ship changes at each port of call, as some seafarers disembark at the end of their contract while others join the ship to replace them. The maritime phrase "friendship ends at the gangway" clearly illustrates the fact that, even if relationships on board are good, they will not outlive the time spent together on board.

Language, style of command and a variety of prejudices are among the problems which arise regularly among international crews. Safety and mere common sense would seem to imply that there will always be a language shared by all the members of a crew on board, but this is not always the case. International regulations require a basic level of maritime English, but in fact the choice of language used is a pragmatic matter, depending on the various nationalities on board. English is actually the most frequent language and, in this respect, Filipinos have an advantage since English is still common in many contexts in the Philippines. Yet, many Filipinos are far from being bilingual and a lot of young sailors have difficulties understanding and speaking the language. Since they try to hide this fact, they can get into dangerous situations. Communication in English can also be impaired by the variety of national accents and idioms which affect the quality of the language. Apart from work-related communication, seafarers who have a poor command of the language do not take part in conversations and can find themselves excluded from social life. Language can also become an instrument of domination.

> The (Danish) officers always want to show that they are superior to us. [...] They speak their own language to make sure we don't understand what they are saying. (Nino, July 2001)

A ship is above all a work-place, and it is work which structures life on board. Sailors are particularly sensitive to reproaches concerning work, and in this context prejudices about different nationalities exacerbate tensions. Consequently, because of their generally subordinate positions, Filipino seafarers say they find it very painful to be under the command of authoritarian officers, especially if Korean, Japanese or European officers raise their voice to give orders in a way which appears scornful. Moreover, if the multinational origin of seafarers is as a rule no obstacle to bonds of solidarity among them, it makes all collective action very difficult, whether for the defence of rights or wage bargaining. Employers are quite aware of the fact and it hinders trade-union action.

The only time when seafarers arrive anywhere is when they come home. This moment serves as a time marker on board, since seafarers count not the days they have done but rather the days they still have to do, just like prisoners. Yet, coming back home is not always that easy. After being far away for several months, sometimes more than a year, relationships between spouses or between parents and children can prove very difficult to revive. The wives have become used to living without their husbands and the children without their fathers. Seafarers and their families relate to very different universes and there are many accounts indicating that the pleasure of reuniting the household can soon give way to tense situations of mutual irritation and lack of understanding. At sea, there is a strict time schedule and a rigorous discipline, and seafarers find it difficult to adapt to another rhythm at home. They are accused of wanting to regulate everything and everyone to their timetable. It takes time to readapt, but money is soon spent and those who are not employed on a permanent basis have to go back to Manila to look for a new contract after only a few weeks. Because of such a disturbing rhythm, seafarers sometimes appear as incapable of living in the present. No sooner have they got home than they are already thinking about going back to sea and, as soon as they're back on board, they are anxious to get back home. For some of them, this restlessness may become a chronic instability which expresses itself through compulsive attitudes towards alcohol, tobacco, medicine, sex, gambling or through an urge to accumulate consumer goods. Many seafarers suffer from stress and depression.

Adjusting to transnational maritime migration

Isolation at sea and the absence of a country of immigration make the experience of "seabased" migrants noticeably different from the life of "landbased" ones. In the communities of expatriate Filipinos there are specific forms of social practices organized to maintain contact with the country of origin: informal but regular gatherings, associations and organizations for the defence of rights, societies and groups for cultural and religious activities and sport. These networks make the distance from the home country less painful and also give more visibility to these migrants: Sunday gatherings of Filipino maids in Hong-Kong, NGOs like "Babaylan" which denounces the ill-treatment suffered by Filipinas, etc. When seafarers are at sea of course they cannot participate in such activities, but they have one advantage over other nationalities, that of numbers. They can organize parties or celebrations on board, such as a Sunday barbecue or a musical evening with a guitar or a karaoke… During calls in a port, they sometimes join another Filipino crew to spend an evening together. On land, there are different networks of mutual aid for seafarers. They are often connected to Christian churches or to international or national trade unions.

At an individual level, today's migrants are great users of new communication technologies such as satellite phones and the internet. At sea, technical problems may arise. Using the internet and cell phones is still expensive and it is usually restricted to technical and emergency calls. Seafarers used to receive letters which were delivered by the company at the different ports of call. Getting letters was a very important ritual. Today, few seafarers still send letters but those who knew that time miss the news on paper that could be read again and again.

> Whenever I received a letter, I would sleep very well that night. (Ariel, April 2000)

Consequently, most seafarers have to wait for a chance to get ashore and rush to telephones to speak to members of their family at home, even if they wake them up in the middle of the night. The cost of calls puts a limit on the length of conversations and they often feel frustration because such moments go so fast and because communication can be awkward. A characteristic shared by seafarers all the world over is to avoid speaking about what goes on on board, especially when there are difficult or dangerous episodes. The wives, for their part, also tend to hide the problems they have to face, so as not to alarm their husbands.

> I told my wife to avoid announcing bad news on the telephone. (Pinoy, April 2006)

Many dream of being a seafarer but the reality of such a life can be very ambivalent, not just for the seafarer himself but for his family as well. The wives who live in a traditional environment suddenly discover unusual circumstances. They must run the household, exert authority over the children, in short, play a masculine role that the society which surrounds them is not always ready to accept. The money earned by the husbands changes the social status of the families. They can afford to have domestic help, they can send their children to better schools, move to a better house. There are streets or districts inhabited by seafarers' families, which helps the women to overcome the isolation brought about by all these changes. When possible, some wives will do some work which is compatible with their family responsibilities: running a nursery school, driving schoolchildren to school, starting a little shop at home, etc. Women usually enjoy having an occupation but, here again, they acquire an independence which is not always well regarded, even by the husband. Relationships within the family suffer from the alternating departures and homecomings, the very long periods of absence, the changing roles of the two partners. Each of them is unaware of the other's way of life and the difficulties he or she has to face. Tensions about the children's education, money, and fidelity get worse because of the long separation. The children do not see their father very much. Some hardly recognize him when he comes back and it is difficult for them to accept his authority. Teenagers sometimes feel completely stifled by their father as they keep being told about the sacrifices he is making for them. Seafarers may also have difficulties connecting with children who have changed since they left. Relationships within the family are deeply disturbed by this way of life, and many families cannot cope. Numerous studies now highlight the impact of migration on the divorce rate, the cases of desertion or the delinquent behaviour of some children.

The impact and contradictions of maritime migration

The migration of Filipino seafarers has an impact on many sectors of the economy. There is a profusion of navy schools and academies, mostly private companies. Some are good quality schools but many are just profit-seeking businesses which take advantage of the credulity of poor families by making them pay a lot for substandard training. Job agencies are also flourishing and some are very corrupt in spite of legislation to regulate them. A lot of young people are exploited by unscrupulous recruiters who make them work for free or demand large sums of money to find their first ship. The migrant has also become an icon in Filipino society. There are now so many of them that they are the subject of many articles in newspapers or reports on television. A newspaper with national circulation such as the *Philippine Daily Inquirer* publishes a double page on migrants in its Sunday issue, under the title "Global Pinoy". Migrants life stories like the recent *Maid in Singapore* by Crisanta Sampang are very popular. On the other hand, like everywhere else in the world, the condition of seafarers, who are invisible, is widely misunderstood. They are noticed when there is an accident at sea, or when a national Seafarers' Day is organized every year, but little is known about their everyday lives.

In conclusion, the migration of seafarers, like other contract workers, seems very contradictory for the seafarers themselves and for Filipino society. The seafarers have to adapt to a way of life which is extremely disturbing and to repeated changes of status. Most adapt fairly well to a collective life in a multinational environment, as long as their working and living conditions are acceptable and they feel they are respected. At the individual level, seafarers who succeed undoubtedly bring a certain affluence to their families, but the changes in lifestyle can endanger the family structure. One might expect that seafarers who prove tolerant in the multicultural context of the ship, would also be more open-minded about traditional values at home, and especially in their couple. But it seems that this is far from being the case and that, on the contrary, many seafarers cling to very conservative values.

As for the country, the money brought by the migrants seems to bring benefits in the short term, but it doesn't solve any of the fundamental problems. Structural reforms are slow to come, corruption is still rampant, and only a fraction of the population benefits from the remittances. The figure of the seafarer, as with other migrants, is still very ambivalent, marked by success but also by deep suffering. It is above all his sacrifices which are praised. Many young seafarers, often the eldest children in their family, claim they are giving their lives for the well being or the mere survival of their family. The idea of sacrifice, with its obvious religious connotations, crops up over and over again in the media or in official discourse on migration. It serves well those who want to maintain a market based on unequal working conditions. Seafaring could actually have less destructive consequences if sailors spent shorter periods at sea and were employed with long-term contracts, which is in fact the case when companies employ western sailors.

Bibliography and References

BERGER Catherine (2004) "Les marins philippins, nouveaux héros de la mondialisation," pp. 143-160 in *Nouvelles mobilités, nouveaux voyageurs, Interculturel Francophonies*, Alliance Française de Lecce n°5, June-July.

—. "Filipinos as Transnational Migrants", special issue of *Philippine Sociological Review*, volume 44, 1-4, 1996.

GOFFMAN Erwing (1961) *Asylums: Essays on the Social Situation of Mental Patients and Other Inmates*, New York: Doubleday.

KAHVECI Erol, LANE Tony & SAMPSON Helen (eds.) (2002) *Transnational Seafarer Communities*, Cardiff: SIRC.

SAMPSON Helen (2003) "Transnational drifters or hyperspace dwellers: an exploration of the lives of Filipino sailors aboard and ashore," *Ethnic and Racial Studies*, 26(2), pp. 253-277.

TARRIUS Alain (2002) *La Mondialisation par le bas. Les nouveaux nomades de l'économie souterraine*, Paris: Balland.

URRY John (2000) *Sociology Beyond Societies: Mobilities for the Twenty-First Century*, London: Routledge.

Most quotations come from face to face interviews with Filipino seafarers conducted in the Cebu area (Philippines) in 2001 and 2006. More informal interviews were conducted during two periods of participant observation (2000 and 2001) in the Seafarers' Centre located in Port de Bouc near Fos-sur-Mer. The author also used a few passages from letters written by Filipino seafarers to the chaplain of the Cebu Seafarers' Centre. These letters have been published regularly since 1992 in the local newsletter of the centre. Particular thanks are due to the chaplain of the Cebu Seafarers' Center, who was one of the author's main informants.

CHAPTER SIXTEEN

POSTMODERN TRAVELS THROUGH STANDARDIZED UTOPIAS: THE CASE OF THEME PARKS

SIMONA SANGIORGI

Theme parks, and especially Disney theme parks, have been explored by many scholars from different fields. The investigation of their complex and multifaceted character offers scholars an insight into the identity of Western societies. The development of the first *amusement* parks is generally considered to be an outgrowth of the profound changes following the industrial revolution, which transformed cities, as well as people's perception and organization of work time and leisure time. Agricultural workers, who had been subjected to variable, nature-bound seasonal rhythms and landscapes, moved to the cities and had to adapt to completely new temporal and environmental conditions. Industrial workers followed a precise routine and schedule, according to their jobs in the manufacturing plants, which implied a complete transformation of theirs and their families' lives. Alain Corbin (1996) argues that the very conception of work and leisure became polarized at this time: a time for work and a time for play, free from pressure and constraints. This new concept of free time, to recuperate for a new working week, gradually acquired a positive and active role in the construction of identity. Free time was for personal enrichment, satisfaction, time dedicated to the search for happiness and pleasure. In other words, it developed into an alternative personal time, to be created and enjoyed while forgetting about "ordinary" time (Rojek 1993; Breedveld 1996). It was not by chance that among the several forms of leisure activity emerging at that time, permanent amusement parks acquired a significant role and started to spread in the major European cities, with their mechanical attractions, lights and simulations that offered their visitors a temporary, illusory escape from the alienating work environment and daily routine (Coltro

1992).

These parks had their origin in the travelling amusement shows, like the traditional European circuses or fairgrounds. They departed from the itinerant and temporary character and presented new elements. They featured the first examples of artificial park settings, with Oriental-style buildings or exotic flower gardens, together with new shows, games, and attractions such as fireworks, acrobats and primitive models of mechanical rides, like the first merry-go-rounds and scenic railways (Pretini 1984; Coltro 1992). The most famous among them were the Danish Bakken and Tivoli, the French Bois de Boulogne and the British Blackpool. These models soon reached America where they were further developed. The most elaborate of these was the world famous Coney Island Park in New York, which opened in 1895. As Pretini (1984) observes, the evolution of the amusement parks, which introduced complex technologies in order to build faster and more vertiginous attractions, was interrupted by the two World Wars. In the late forties Walt Disney's amazingly successful project provided further inspiration.

From amusement park to theme park

Walt Disney was inspired by an idea that went beyond simple amusement. He was constantly in search of innovative ways of entertaining people and creating new sources of income. He envisaged an alternative approach to this kind of family entertainment. According to Bryman (1995), Disney started thinking of a place where his cartoon characters, which he had created back in the thirties, would be protagonists and the attractions could offer a tribute to America's past, whilst also providing a vision of its future. He thought of an appealing place that could captivate both children and adults by offering an all-encompassing environment conveying the feeling of a "real" experience in the happy world of fantasy and a "real" escape from everyday life. His strategy was to engage adults in the experience so that they would be less cautious about spending money on non-essential purchases and they would therefore be more likely to consume, buying merchandise, drinks and food which are in many ways the key to the profitability of an amusement park (Bryman 1995, Wasko 2001).

These principles gave life to Disneyland, which opened to the public on 17 July 1955. The park's layout immediately revealed how its interpretation of the notion of amusement clearly differed from that which had been developed by traditional amusement parks. Disneyland was not just another conventional park featuring a random collection of roller coasters, merry-go-rounds and Ferris wheels, in a casual, carnival atmosphere. For the first time it claimed for itself a new identity and status as an alternative place or, better, a "land", physically and ideally separated and independent from the urban environments and everyday reality. Its several attractions were (and still are) immersed in artificially constructed narrative flows, which appeared in the form of proper distinct "regions", each of which was given a name and was designed and built according to a selected theme. "Main Street USA", for instance, reproduced America's typical town of the thirties; "Adventureland" evoked exotic adventures; "Tomorrowland" depicted the future world; "Fantasyland" recreated childhood fairy tales; "Frontierland" celebrated the frontier life of the nineteenth-century American West, and "Mickey's Toontown" presented the world of the Disney cartoon characters. This radical new model of amusement park, conceived as a collection of fantastic, exotic and idealized worlds, reproduced in detail by a synergy of architecture, landscaping, costuming, music, live entertainment, attractions, merchandise, food and beverage, marked the beginning of the modern idea of the so-called theme-park era.

In the wake of Disneyland's huge success, other theme parks, including the bigger Walt Disney World Resort in Florida, opened throughout the Unites States during the 1960s and 1970s. They gradually eclipsed many of the old traditional amusement parks built on the Coney Island model, which had by that time already been threatened by increasing urban decay (Sorkin, 1992). It took another decade before the theme-park phenomenon would spread in Europe, but today it constitutes one of the most profitable tourism resources on the global level, making over a billion dollars a year (Minardi 1998).

The theme-park travel experience

Theme parks are usually built around either a single concept, or various specific concepts or themes derived from the worlds of fantasy, fairy tales, cinema, history, nature, myths or legends and shared by the public. Park areas suggesting, for instance, the adventures of Indiana Jones, pirate raids, medieval tournaments, or magical encounters are quite common manifestations of such themes, which are in evidence throughout the themed space, from attractions to shops and restaurants (Minardi 1998). Theming requires a series of strategies and technologies aimed at "making believe" that everything that is unreal is "real". Attractions, in particular, with their special effects, robots and holograms, are supposed to offer a type of experience that is coherent with the theme developed:

boat rides, for instance, may appear in those areas reproducing pirates' adventures or jungle-related themes; roller coasters are often presented in the form of goldmine carts and installed in Old West-like settings; and 3D movies are frequently employed to simulate flights or spaceship missions within the future-inspired environments. Moreover, as Augé notes in his book *L'impossible voyage. Le tourisme et ses images* (1997), themed architecture and design are usually associated with fauna, flora, scents, sounds and music evoking typical or idealized features of the theme established. This theme is also extended to merchandise, costumes and even the names of food and beverage items, so that nothing within a particular "themed" area remains untouched, or left outside that theme, which is implicitly extended, likewise, to visitors immersed in the theme. Disneyland represented the first realization of these principles, which rapidly spread and developed, until they reached the very heart of most contemporary theme parks' philosophy and led to deep changes in the visitors' amusement experience.

The purchase of the admission ticket at the park entrance, and then the entry into the park, seems to mark a sort of first crucial "border crossing", a passage from the chaotic world of work, traffic jams and conflicts to an enclosed, protected, safe area promising fun, joy, magical adventures and dreamlike memories. Eco, in his essay *Travels in hyperreality* (1986), provides a particularly interesting description of this moment on the basis of his personal experience. He had been on a tour of America during the seventies to observe the numerous imitations and replicas of monuments, statues, paintings and other works of art from the "Old World" that are on display in several national museums and tourist attractions, in order to investigate possible cultural values and implications at the origin of this phenomenon. He also visited some theme parks during the tour. According to Eco, the entry into the park is the moment when the whole theme park, with its timeless landscapes and streets, its reconstructions of buildings, castles and fantastic settings, appears to the public in all its sensational and multifaceted form and exposes their senses to an overwhelming flood of stimuli. It may be argued that the intense power of this impact, also noted by Augé (1997), determines the first stark contrast between the outside world and the atmosphere inside the park, and paves the way for the park's illusionistic experience. In but a few steps, visitors already find themselves completely surrounded by strategic elements aimed at displacing them into an apparently authentic, but alternative reality. Firstly, the realistic reconstruction noticed by Eco, which today is a typical feature of most theme parks, immediately catches the eye and fascinates the visitor with its amazing attention to detail. Theme buildings, for instance, which may contain shops, restaurants or attractions, are not mere reproductions of architectural styles evoking a given fairy tale, country, or historical period in their exterior form. Their furnishing and materials, their inhabitants, and even details indicating decay such as flaws, dust or cobwebs, as in the so-called haunted mansions, add a touch of authenticity and reinforce the theme's coherence. Secondly, the absence of things that might interfere with the illusion and in some way remind the public of a behind-the-scenes world creates a further level of simulation: power supplies, equipment, plumbing, pipelines, electrical lines are often concealed or disguised; garbage is usually quickly removed; backstage rooms are hidden behind scenographic doors or hedges. Thirdly, the clean, colourful, toy-like scenario filled with parades, celebrations, fireworks, movie or cartoon characters, not only encourages optimism and averts negative thoughts, but, as Bryman (1995) shows, conveys a general sense of harmony and safety that elevates the park to a sort of "utopian" fantasy world.

The core of a theme-park experience, however, is represented by the condensed ensemble of perceptions and sensations provided by the several types of attractions offered. Corbin (1996) focuses on roller coasters, and on the visitors' fascination with them. These so-called "thrill rides", with their high speed acceleration, breathtaking twists, loops, turns, and sudden falls, seem to give extraordinary powers to the riders who might feel as if they are defying the laws of gravity and physics, while also exciting their senses to such an extent that they feel enthusiastically giddy and lose their sense of time and space. Visitors may even feel the sensation of flying while their bodies are thrown into the air in a series of movements made possible by increasingly complex technologies. They are offered the opportunity to be thrilled by the challenge of surviving such strong emotions, being aware, at the same time, that everything occurs in safety. They are able to experience a sedentary transgression that allows them to take what seem to be daring actions within a controlled system of safety measures. For the less intrepid "travellers" there are the boat rides, which are presented in the form of journeys through the jungle or prehistoric settings, or rides offering travels through the past and future or through the world of fairy tales, providing less frenetic but equally intense experiences. Here, as Eco noted during his visit to a theme park, viewers are encouraged to play with time while physically immersed in completely artificial environments, where rivers, castles, animals and human figures, despite their being fake, appear to have come to life and been made believable by a whole synergy of technologies and details reconstructing scenes set in a specific time and place. Animals and humans in particular are represented by robots who speak, move, fight, or dance with lifelike expressions and features and who, following a precise programme to synchronize words and sounds with their movements, repeat their part ride after ride, day after day.

From Sorensen (1989) and Young (2002), it may be inferred that boats or wagons passing through these scenographies, recreating episodes of classical fairy tales, celebrating history and progress and synthesizing European, American or exotic landscapes, serve as playful time machines (Sorensen 1989: 66). They give the riders the illusion of participating in fantastic journeys, where time and space are arbitrarily expanded, restricted, and manipulated by human imagination. The role of nature in this respect deserves further consideration. Attractions often present scenes with animatronic animals and plants whose behaviour and appearance are clearly anthropomorphized. Smiling flowers, bunnies waving their paws, and singing bears are just a few examples. Northrop Frye, in his book *The Educated Imagination* (1964), provides interesting observations which may suggest an interpretation of this practice. In his analysis, focused on the relevance of literature to life, he argues that human beings, when creating fictional works, tend to transfer to nature some typically human values and behaviour even though such elements are foreign to nature, in order to construct controllable places over which imagination may have power. This line of reasoning may apply to the case of theme parks, where a manipulated and humanized nature, often represented as living in harmony with people, enhances the impression of experiencing a utopia-like world where everybody is friendly, safe and happy. Finally simulations provided by 3D movie theatres produce a further range of sensory perceptions which are worth examining for the purpose of collecting enough elements that may help in exploring at least part of the great variety of "travels" characterizing the theme-park experience. 3D shows are not simply spectacular movies projected on a giant screen for seated viewers. Here, as most scholars point out, viewers become protagonists. They are directly involved in the story in that they are given the impression of "really" leaving reality and of "really" finding themselves inside a movie through a series of visual, auditory, olfactory and even tactile stimuli. Technology—once again—studies, generates, constructs and controls this illusion. Computer-generated images, seen through special glasses, create scenes and characters who virtually surround, and occasionally run towards or attack the audience, while high-quality sounds fill different sides of the theatre according to the action performed and special effects based on water, air, aromas, or movements of the seats, simulate sea waves, wind, spring scents, or earthquakes. The fulfilment of the wildest adventure dreams then becomes possible in an ephemeral, thirty-minute virtual show where, in line with Eco's thought, flights, sea journeys or teletransport are made believable in a dimension that transcends the limits of reality and therefore appears far more appealing.

Shaping an ideal reality

In the light of these observations, though based on a general analysis of only a few attractions and their related mental and sensory perceptions, some key elements defining the theme-park experiences and "travels" emerge quite clearly. The "cinematic approach" is one of the most compelling. Finch (1973), in his research on the Disney parks, suggested that several essentially cinematic techniques were employed to emphasize the narrative elements and the visitor's experience of them. These techniques seem to apply today as well, not only to the Disney parks, but also to the numerous theme parks imitating the Disney model. Plunged into a sort of three-dimensional cinematic event, free from potentially disturbing factors, visitors may in fact feel that they are being carried through, and are actually inside, stories and scenes. Many of the rides are actually structured in such a way that they give the visitors the impression of being at the cinema. Guests do not go backstage, are made to sit in a dark place, on chairs or on moving vehicles, and gaze at images or robots. It can therefore be argued, drawing on Eco's conclusions, that park visitors, surrounded by an all-encompassing environment that does not stimulate them from an intellectual point of view, play a role that is as passive as that of a movie viewer.

Besides making the visitors sedentary, theme-park adventures are completely controlled. Park personnel, for instance, enforce safety measures, making sure that everybody is seated properly in the vehicles, and that they follow the indicated paths correctly. The park maintains the environment's integrity as well, as many commentators agree, from its flowers to its rivers, from its sounds to its landscaping. Though artificial, the grounds look authentic and ensure thematic coherence. Most importantly, even the dimensions of space, time and reality are controlled. As a matter of fact, they are intentionally altered and manipulated by the attractions' various simulations, which are aimed at creating the illusion of travelling through time, fantasy and remote places. Both Eco (1986) and Augé (1997) see, in this form of control, the manifestation of one of the deepest human desires—that of exerting power over the world's natural laws, which here results in the attempt to shape an ideal reality.

This reality, where it is possible to pretend that everybody is free to transcend the limits of distance, time and physics, is imagined and obeys exclusively the human will. As both Eco and Augé argue, it allows a momentary escape from the actual world and from the difficult truths of the self and of society, because it incarnates a better alternative and guarantees a variety of exciting experiences, a wide range of intense emotions, a safe thrill of danger, and even positive nostalgia conveyed by idealized representations of history. Such a promising scenario, however, is so appealing and preferable that visitors forget it is artificial, and, at the same time, it stimulates the individuals' desire for illusion. Such a tendency, already quite widespread in television or advertising, may produce a potential confusion between what one understands as the virtual and the real, which, according to Baudrillard (1983), overwhelms human imagination and may induce false ideas about values which are worth striving for in everyday life.

Imagination is also challenged by the density and fullness of theme-park travels, often seen as a metaphor of postmodernity because of their patchwork-like character. The rides, for instance, that combine historical reconstructions with the fantasy of fairy tales and visions of the future, and finally celebrate the whole in spectacular special effects and vertiginous evolutions, overload the senses and disorient critical discernment. The abundance of images inside and outside the rides produces a similar effect. Every space is filled with offers, images, activities and entertainment. Visitors consume one experience after another, pushed by the invisible forces of consumerism (Eco 1986; Augé 1997; Bauman 2000), and risk acquiring a "spiritual obesity". This abundance, this ambiguity between the fake and the real, this manipulation of the notions of time and space are synthesized by the term *iperrealtà*, coined by Eco (1977) and are constitutive aspects of Augé's *surmodernité* (1992) and Bauman's "liquid modernity" (2000), two terms that define the contemporary era. Elements characterizing the theme-park experience—no doubt entertaining but without any claim of educational value—are assigned a central role in the present society as well, and on the basis of the previous observations and of Bauman's theory (2000), the western world in particular seems to be moving towards a spectacularization of the human experience.

One other noteworthy feature emerging from the present analysis of the theme-park adventures is an explicit lack of "sociality". It is interesting to see how the same concept of the solitary crowd occurs in the several sources consulted as far as the enjoyment of the park is concerned. Augé (1997), for instance, depicts scenes where visitors, amid themed spaces, look like both actors and their own spectators, engaged in the full appreciation of attractions without any interaction with others. Bauman (2000: 200) goes a step further in his description of the "cloakroom" or "carnival communities", representing temporary aggregations of people in places, such as theme parks, where individuals, after having left their "coats" outside—their identities—look for moments of distraction and relief from everyday schedules and schemes, with the desire of avoiding or being ignored by others. This wished-for absence or voluntary reduction of human contacts, in a place meant to produce happiness and to facilitate the avoidance of negative thoughts, may lead to the conclusion that the Other is a disturbing factor, or that this perceived disturbance gets translated into a sense of fear towards what is unknown or different.

Finally, the ride experience, as previously noted, has a significant impact on the sense of freedom perceived by the public. The amazing simulations, the wonders of technology, seem in fact to deliver extraordinary powers to the individuals, who suddenly feel free from the world's laws and abandon themselves to the illusion of overcoming the limits imposed by life and, according to Augé (1997), feel that they achieve a form of pure freedom produced by imagination without the support of reason. But this is a momentary state of mind, as many commentators agree, that makes most visitors unaware that everything occurs under completely controlled and standardized conditions. Eco (1986), in particular, shows how theme-park experiences are created by machines featuring predetermined movements, which stay the same, ride after ride, and how such experiences are governed by a series of control measures, aimed at ensuring the same safety and quality standards to all users. As a result, the perceived freedom reveals itself as another level of simulation, defined by given artificial means and which actually prevent any individual initiative by channelling imagination towards a specific set of sensations and images, offered to each and every visitor in the same way.

It is by virtue of these aspects that Augé (1992) classifies theme parks with "non-places", described as typical products of the contemporary era, consisting in transitional places and spaces where individuals look for anonymity and recognizable standards. He also adds that a given non-place is better defined in its modes of use by the words and texts it produces. In order to achieve a deeper understanding of the theme parks' modes of use, and particularly of those connected to the notion of travel, it may therefore be useful to have a look at their texts. In the commercials or promotional materials of the parks, the idea of travel seems to rank as one of the main purposes of the park experience: phrases such as "Travel further into a jungle [...]", "Transport yourself back to medieval times

[...]" or "Travel back in time [...]", and other similar ones, occur in fact very frequently in the park presentations. It is clear that the word "travel" appearing in this context, in the light of the previous analyses, becomes itself part of the simulation, and, in line with Baudrillard's theory (1983), it may be seen as a simulacrum. What now needs to be explored is the concept of travel in its traditional form, with the whole universe of meanings it evokes, so that the value of the signified may emerge in its main aspects, despite the possible ambiguous use of the signifier.

Non-fiction travels

The etymology of the word "travel", according to the *Oxford English Dictionary* (1989) is curious. While we are accustomed to the idea of travel as the action of journeying, particularly through foreign parts, its origins seem to come from the word "travail", an English term meaning "torment" or "distress", also referring to the labour of childbirth. The English word, in turn, seems to be derived from the French verb *travailler*, "to work". This etymology enables one to argue three main points. Firstly the notion of travel can be linked to painful effort and hard work, probably because, as some researchers maintain, it initially referred to distances travelled for commercial or political purposes; secondly that the link between "travail" and child-birth certainly implies the crossing of a border, leaving the safe and secure and going to the unknown; and thirdly that, in its contemporary use, "travel" does not necessarily coincide with pleasurable activities.

The notion of travel proposed here is that described by Magris (2005) and Augé (1997), according to whom travellers are those people who avoid ready-to-consume products, such as all-inclusive resorts and vacation clubs which often transform nature into holiday oases isolated from the social and cultural reality of the surrounding territory. They prefer to choose their experiences freely, and to commit themselves to shape them actively, by going to places, searching for sights, and sharpening their senses in order to achieve a full appreciation and sensory enjoyment of what they live. They are ready to wait and to strive for satisfaction, which may not only derive from amazing views or exciting explorations, but also from the feeling of having entered into contact with traces of nature, history and culture that allow introspective deconstructions and deeper interpretations of the self and of the world (Magris 2005). Travelling, according to Magris, does not consist then of a mere collection of visits and images of enchanting castles, woods, sculptures or rivers. It is instead an enriching interiorization of manifestations produced by nature and by human creeds, actions and traditions, which may disorient the individual perception of one's own and of the other's identity, but at the same time enhances the value of diversity and stimulates curiosity towards what lies beyond given political, geographical, social or cultural borders.

Borders, of any type, and especially their crossing, may be seen as the actual essence of travel. As Magris (2005) points out, there is no travel if no border is crossed. Ryden (1993) conceives of borders as abstract lines, that separate one life and place from another, and suggests that their crossing implies a transition between realms of experiences and states of being. A transition, therefore, that is not limited to the passage from one language, one nation, one tradition, to a different one, but that instead has a more complex and wider meaning (in that it affects people), requires open minds and encourages the encounter and the discovery of the unknown in its manifold strata. This, according to Augé (1997) and Magris (2005), represents both the challenge and the very pleasure of travelling, of traditional travelling, in which different people and psychologies confront one another, communicate with one another, and relish the world in its diversity by adding meaning to their identities.

The world itself, though, may also become an obstacle to the travel experience. Being governed by physical laws, or other people's desires, or chance, travel may in fact reveal disappointing elements, arouse anxiety, a sense of powerlessness, and subject the traveller to risks and dangers. As a result, travellers must often be ready to face not only unexpected events or sudden changes in their programmes, but, as many researchers observe, also deeper questions about reality and its whole complex, precarious structure, with its conflicting moral values and social injustice. In other words, explorations of non-artificially constructed worlds are likely to foster meditation, reformulation of expectations, and a more critical approach to the self and to society at large.

Despite such potential negative aspects, the unpredictable nature of reality offers chances for salvation as well. Augé and Magris describe the power of authenticity delivered by historic sites and nature in their various forms. Highly emotional moments may suddenly emerge out of spontaneous mental associations, evoked by tangible fragments of history acting as witnesses of the human development in their interaction with the surrounding environments. Moreover, landscapes, colours, scents and sounds may sometimes appear and manifest themselves with such unexpected intensity and fascination, that the individual relationship to nature seems to win back its purity and to eventually make sense. Here lies the adventure's climax, the fulfilment of both intellectual and sensory desires for harmony and the most precious source to quench imagination's thirst for stimuli.

Two poles

Our focus on the categories of fiction/non-fiction, artificial/real, simulation/authenticity reveals two significant interpretations of the concept of travel. These same categories, however, represent a further problematic issue, which is seen in their definition. Moreover, there is a wide variety of cases between the "absolute fake" (Eco 1986: 8) and the "absolute real", in which simulation and authenticity are so intertwined that they become almost indistinguishable (this is, incidentally, comparable with the notions of the "real" and the "false" in orientalist paintings, as mentioned in chapter 6). The use of such terms as "reference tools", or heuristic devices, has allowed a general identification of two poles which, by their nature, are characterized by different approaches to what one attempts to grasp as the "real".

A final comparison aiming to convince the reader that theme-park travels are mere ersatz experiences, with nothing but negative effects on the value of traditional travels, would at this point be a biased, simplistic, and unnecessary conclusion. The two perspectives described, despite their formal common denominator, are undoubtedly characterized by such different and sometimes opposite approaches, means and objectives, that it would not be appropriate to speak of theme-park attractions as complete substitutes for travel experiences. On the one hand there is the total oblivion of everyday life, achieved through simulations and manipulations creating a better reality where past, present, future and fantasy merge and convey extraordinary feelings of power and enthusiasm. Optimism and safety are in this case the result of a positive trust in technology, which seems to allow transcendence of the limits of society and guarantees the same quality standards and variety of emotions to all visitors. The focus is on the individual, who passively consumes a whole abundant, synthetic utopia providing immediate satisfaction and ready-made dreams, but also anaesthetization of imaginative ideas. On the other hand there is the active search for meanings, sensations and communities, in a dimension where time and space still maintain at least part of their weight. There is the encounter with people and their otherness, with reality and its precariousness, with the self and its powerlessness—a formative experience that is also exposed to failures and disappointments, but that stimulates constructive intellectual filling of society's natural voids and that eventually leaves lasting memories and influences on travellers.

These two models coexist, although not without potentially negative contamination. What really matters, however, is to distinguish the desires and the values they incarnate, in order to suggest possible final evaluations. The first one may be considered the direct expression of the driving forces characterizing Augé's *surmodernité*, because of the typical forms of simulation, excess, and patchwork culture it features. Theme-park experiences seem to actually offer quick answers to the main fears and uncertainties of contemporary society, by leaving the whole world behind, blurring the lines between fact and fiction, and constructing an invented, simulated reality responding to the most capricious desires for power and satisfaction. The second model seems to represent the manifestation of a more silent, less evident but persistent energy, identified by Augé within the kaleidoscopic carnival of impressions seen above—a trace of solidity, running parallel to Bauman's "liquid modernity", which, inspired by principles of common good and authenticity, operates in everyday life instead of promoting alienation from it, and encourages a deeper immersion, in order to understand and improve its problems and appreciate its good qualities.

Theme-park travels are therefore not meant to replace the existing notion of travel, they rather present themselves as an additional meaning, as an appealing possibility that offers an alternative solution to the experience of the world and of the self, one that produces new responses to postmodern desires. In other words, their relation to "real" travels may be interpreted according to the two choices Italo Calvino presents in his novel *Invisible Cities* (1974). The story is based on a dialogue between Marco Polo, a Venetian traveller, and Kubla Khan, Tartar emperor, who feels that the end of his reign is near. Polo entertains the emperor by telling him about the cities he has visited during his travels through the empire; he answers his questions and stimulates his curiosity. At the end of the account, the emperor, resignedly, sees the inevitable failure and fall of his world, slowly sucked into metaphoric hell. And Polo concludes:

> The inferno of the living is not something that will be; if there is one, it is what is already here, the inferno where we live every day, that we form by being together. There are two ways to escape suffering it. The first is easy for many: accept the inferno and become such a part of it that you can no longer see it. The second is risky and demands constant vigilance and apprehension; seek and learn to recognize who and what, in the midst of the inferno, are not inferno, then make them endure, give them space. (Calvino 1974: 165)

Similarly, the escape from today's reality may be possible either through an easy and total immersion into simulation, or through constructive effort and commitment in the search for human and natural values. The crucial point is to be able to discern such choices and their implications within a contemporary era featuring similar dichotomies in numerous other sectors of life—a discernment that should be stimulated and promoted through further research, aiming to develop new frameworks and tools which may allow a more capillary diffusion of critical awareness at all social levels.

Bibliography and References

AUGÉ M. (1992) *Non lieux*, Paris: Seuil.
—. (1997) *L'impossible voyage. Le tourisme et ses images*, Paris: Éditions Payot & Rivages.
BAUDRILLARD J. (1983) *Simulations*, New York: Semiotext(e).
BAUMAN Z. (2000) *Liquid Modernity*, Cambridge: Polity Press.
BREEDVELD K. (1996) "Post-fordist leisure and work," pp. 67-90 in *Loisir et société*, 19(1).
BRYMAN A. (1995) *Disney and his Worlds*, London: Routledge.
CALVINO I. (1974) *Invisible Cities*, New York: Harcourt.
COLTRO D. (1992) "Dalla fiera al luna park," pp. 10-41 in G. Tauber, *Nel mondo dei parchi,* Padua: Facto Edizioni, 1992.
CORBIN A. (ed.) (1996) *L'invenzione del tempo libero 1850-1960*, Bari: Laterza.
ECO U. (1977) *Dalla periferia dell'impero*, Milan: Bompiani.
—. (1986) *Travels in Hyperreality: Essays*, New York: Harcourt.
FRYE N. (1964) *The Educated Imagination*, Bloomington: Indiana University Press.
MAGRIS C. (2005) *L'infinito viaggiare*, Milan: Mondadori.
MINARDI E. & LUSETTI M. (eds.) (1998) *I parchi di divertimento nella società del loisir,* Milan: Franco Angeli.
PRETINI G. (1984) *Dalla fiera al luna park*, Udine: Trapezio Libri.
ROJEK C. (1993) *Ways of Escape. Modern Transformation in Leisure and Travel*, Basingstoke: Macmillan.
RYDEN K.C. (1993) *Mapping the Invisible Landscape: Folklore, Writing and the Sense of Place*, Iowa City: University of Iowa Press.
SORENSEN C. (1989) "Theme parks and time machines," pp. 61-73 in P. Vergo, *The New Museology*, London: Reaktion Books, 1989.
SORKIN M. (ed.) (1992) *Variations on a Theme Park: the New American City and the End of Public Space*, New York: Hill and Wang.
WASKO J. (2001) *Understanding Disney: the Manufacture of Fantasy*,

Cambridge: Polity Press.

YOUNG T. (2002) "Grounding the myth—Theme-park landscapes in an era of commerce and nationalism," pp. 1-10 in T. Young & R. Riley (eds.), *Theme Park Landscapes: Antecedents and Variations*, Washington DC: Dumbarton Oaks Library & Research Center Press, 2002.

AFTERWORDS

Travel Tales

A strapping young fellow, a six-foot, twelve-stone, heavy-boned, muscular figure stood hesitant on a New York quay. He was tall for his age, but shy beyond imagination. He had just alighted from a ship that had crossed from Le Havre. It was two years after the Klondike rush, when the gold-hungry descended from everywhere upon the American continent and somehow made their way to north-western Canada and its Yukon placers. The thrill had not died down yet. If this had been what he had had in mind, it would have been easy to follow the crowd without asking or answering questions. For that was his greatest embarrassment. He did not speak any English at all. He could speak and write beautiful French, he could compose verse in Latin, he could read *The Odyssey* in the original tongue with pleasure, but that was the end of his linguistic talents—a preposterous position for an educated traveller. So that he had no option but to follow the plans that had been laid for him in Paris, and find a ship to Halifax en route for St-Pierre. He did not tarry in New York, nor had anything ever to tell about a place which frightened him, with its cosmopolitan bustle and babble of fast growth and massive migrations. Halifax proved quieter and coarser at the same time, but he soon found his way to St-Pierre and arrived at his destination.

He was the scion of a long line of coopers from a tiny village in Maine in western France, and the first to make it to higher education—social mobility within geographical stability. At twenty-four, after graduation in classics at the Sorbonne and a two-year stint as a conscript in the army, he had been appointed editor, and almost sole journalist, of a local newspaper in the distant French possession of St-Pierre-et-Miquelon. Frictions and ructions were constant between French and British cod-fishers in nearby Newfoundland, but at St-Pierre itself nothing of note ever happened and in a community where everyone knew each another the role of a local newspaper did not strike anybody as essential. There were notices announcing births, marriages and deaths, which required the skill of a compositor, not of a writer. But he embarked upon a modest form of investigative journalism, whereby he felt duty bound, as a Christian, a citizen and a journalist, to expose the utter corruption of the local grandee.

This parochial supremo did not like it, and when he did not like it, he exacted a duel. The young man was of very peaceful temperament, but did not flinch. In a snow-covered field, clad in thick otter and seal coats, they agreed to a pistol decision, at one shot each. The experienced duellist was a poor shot and his bullet thumped into a tree. The young man shot in the air, so afraid was he of wounding a fellow human creature. They shook hands and honour was declared cleared on both sides. But the newspaper proprietors came under pressure to remove the troublesome young man, and in any case, he was beginning to wonder what use he could put his pen to in such a place.

So everybody agreed he should go back to France. Apart from photographs of the duel, the only thing he ever kept of his sojourn in the north-western Atlantic was the warm deck blanket given to him on board ship—black on one side, with golden eyes like the skin of a panther, reverse colours on the other side. His patrons sent him to a small town in south-west France, as editor of a daily sheet. A fighting spirit was expected from the new editor, but the young man did not come back from the wind-stricken barrens of the cold Atlantic isles with the haunting lust of unsatisfied adventure in his eyes. On the contrary, he had had more than he cared for. His dream was of settling down, of living at peace with his fellow-citizens, not of discovering the world. After nearly five years working side by side with a young woman he had recruited as a journalist, he collected sufficient courage to propose to her. Of course, the new bride insisted they spend their honeymoon in travels—they went to Paris, where they saw Sarah Bernhardt on stage, then to sedate and safe Switzerland, no further than Lake Geneva, but with horizons to meet her romantic demand for the spectacular landscape, and to convince him that the rounded and eroded and grassy mountains of Cantal were enough movement for his sanguine nature. Then three children were born, of whom two survived. In August 1914, he had to make his backpack again, and was to spend four years in the horror of the trenches, in the thick mud of north-eastern France, travelling, most of the time, on his belly. He was made an infirmary sergeant, and had to crawl between the lines whenever there was a respite or a truce to collect the dead and the wounded. Death, in his view, meant the final rest, not the last travel, and more and more this was what he longed for. He dreamt very simply of his wife and children and sensed he risked never seeing them again. He was desperately longing for the warmth of homeliness. The only travel he wished for was home-bound.

The armistice reunited them, and he dug his heels deep into the volcano dust of old Auvergne with the firm intention never to move again—except to Brittany for holidays with the children, so that it was not really travelling. More and more he stayed indoors, in the glass structure of the print works which was his office. The news of the world which he read in the national press unsettled him, and his foreboding proved true in September 1939. By May 1940, his son was a prisoner of war in Germany, and would be moved from camp to camp, further and further towards the centre of the country, when the Allies began to close in after 1942. When the war ended, he did not come back immediately. He was on the surgeon's table at the time of the liberation of his camp, and had to convalesce in chaotic Germany, and then, beg his way back on foot, on his own, through half of Germany and half of France, nearly nine hundred miles, holding his belly with his hands.

The young man of the beginning, now in his late sixties, ageing, did not understand the way the world was going. There was another horrid war in the Far East, which shamed him as a Frenchman. His wife wrote and published short stories against emigration, against settling down in remote lands. No sooner was this distant conflict over, than another one began in North Africa. He did not understand why his children, hardly reconciled to peace, were on the move again, to Paris, nor why they found the area of circulation of his former newspaper too small. When he had his second stroke, he could no longer speak, but on every piece of paper he could find, he scrawled with a shaky hand that he did not want his teenage grandson to go to fight the ugly war in Algeria. He died in April 1962 without knowing that this war was ending.

As you have guessed, he was my grandfather. I did not go to Algeria—except years later as a welcome academic visitor—and wanted to tell this story of unwilling and reluctant travels performed by people who were adventurous only by the force of necessity, and did not come back with tales of adventure but with the memory of miseries they would rather forget than tell about. And here we come to the methodologically difficult part of anything to do with travel tales. Not only do these tales tell us more of the viewer than of the viewed—the theme has been rehashed countless times—but they tell a story that is adapted to the time of telling, more than the time being told; adapted to the likely audience, rather than to the characters described; and especially adapted to the way the teller himself or herself wishes to be seen and understood. The story of my grand-father above is not his story, it is mine, it is the way I have reconstructed his life, through his silences, through the tales of his wife, through the letters found long after his death.

I hope this also strikes the reader as the evidence of ordinariness, of the most likely fate of the common man. It must always be remembered that most travellers in history have been at best reluctant ones, urged by hunger or fear, hunted or pushed out, ordered about. Of course, the most unfortunate of such travellers were the African slaves at the height of the Guinea trade. But "economic" migrants since the agricultural and industrial revolutions of the eighteenth century were in most cases just as unwilling to go. The Scottish clearances drove thousands into forced emigration—they were physically forced on board ships—and so did the Irish famine for millions and with the same methods. When in England some Poor Law guardians offered the alternative of subsidized emigration or an end to any relief, was there any freedom of choice for the paupers concerned? When in France some rebellious characters were offered either jail or the colonial armies, was there a real choice? Then they either hated it all the way, and had nothing to say, or they made the best of it, and told tall tales.

For sedentary folks are fond of travel tales. The 1960s at last absorbed the peculiar atmosphere initiated in the late 1950s by Jack Kerouac's road stories. Road movies came into being, backpacking a way of life. In the wake of this, Jack London was rediscovered, Walt Wiltman exalted higher still, and American folksongs of railroading and trailing and westering rediscovered—remixed, rearranged, remastered. New forms of tourism developed, emphasizing the ethnographic discovery of living people rather than dead remains in museums, and were criticized as a new aspect of voyeurism. Travel became faster and cheaper, communications reached out to parts of the world that, before that, could not be attained by ordinary people with ordinary means. New tourists and old-fashioned migrants jostled side by side in the same means of conveyance—hence the emotion of airline passengers witnessing the forced repatriation of illegal immigrants. The ideology of a flexible labour market has transformed many young travellers into unattached electrons, prepared to aggregate themselves to something new as opportunities arise, through chance encounters even in leisure travel. Yet this constant invitation to become rolling stones and to hit the road, this facility now open to millions round the world, is in fact realized only exceptionally. Most people do not want, do not try such things. Most people do not travel, if they can avoid it. Or travel in such a way that it looks like home on wheels.

If the location of production is no longer governed by access to raw materials or to a market—transport is everywhere possible at lower costs than before and quicker than ever—but by the social, legal and political conditions of the chosen site, industrialists can displace their production wherever they wish. The globalization of certain work practices makes this easier. To make it acceptable to the workforce here and there, glamorizing the traveller, combining leisure and work, can be a nice communication trick. But how new is this? The study of the nineteenth century shows that technological transfers as well as industrial spying implied the cross-border mobility of skilled-workers—for it is the skilled ones who moved most freely, according to opportunities. When such mobility as existed in any case was conflated with the mobility forced upon some by political exile, it simply meant that technological transfer walked side by side with political hybridization. And glamorization worked through boys' literature, from Captain Marryat though Ballantyne and Verne to Henty and Pemberton. According to the period, particular areas serve as the focus and locus of cultural transfers, become the epitome of cross-fertilization. The Franco-British case is one such area, attaining prominence several times in history since 1066 and all that. Capri may have been such a place in the 1920s for a select set, or Marrakesh today, or mid-Asia for backpackers, when they do not treat it as a theme park.

As for large migratory movements, it is necessary to study the history of networks and networking, and also of returns—the largely untold stories of those who migrated, but came back soon. Chinese communities in Liverpool and Manchester are typical of networks that extend over several generations and continents. For many migrants, the idea of completely severing any link with their past residence is quite simply preposterous. Why should they do anything of the sort? Why should they impoverish themselves so deliberately? Keeping the links alive makes sense also in the perspective of survival, it is a life-line kept in good order and that can work both ways, for further emigrations, or for a return home.

Gender boundaries are shifting too in the world of travel. If the family model of migration, whereby men go first, and wives and children follow, is still largely dominant, its position is being slowly eroded. Independent travel may be becoming as much a female as a male phenomenon, including the adventurous sort of travelling. Perhaps this instability of roles has as much to do with the push for more flexibility as with the claims of feminism. Both belong to our own time, in which a handful travel for pleasure, millions out of necessity, while billions stay put.

François Poirier, Director of CRIDAF
(Research Centre on Intercultural Relations, Paris XIII University)
http://www.univ-paris13.fr/CRIDAF.htm

De Ciconiis, About Storks

When my brother and I were children, our grandfather would tell us how "African people" believed storks were in fact people who had been transformed into birds with the aim of travelling and discovering the world, and this was why storks were respected and especially cared for there. This legend, I later discovered, is part of Berber folklore and has little to do with the tales of fairies, werewolves and the host of more or less well-disposed talking animals he would have heard during the *velhadas* of his own childhood—the evenings country people used to spend at each other's houses in his native Limousin. We children relished the idea of storkpeople and were proud our grandfather knew something about "Africa", but we never wondered how or where he had come across a pretty story that had obviously captured his imagination enough for him to want to pass it on to his grandchildren.

Today's storks—tourists, economic migrants, political refugees—are not always welcome, as they are felt to disturb local environments, disrupt local ways of life and upset traditional values. We hear much passionate talk about the threat to our "roots". Some would have us believe that Man, like the vegetable, is a product of the land, of some timeless coordinates whose characteristics determine his idiosyncrasy and nature. But Man has feet, and he will walk, and since the time of *Homo erectus*, he has visited all four corners of the earth, driven by his innate instinct and his longing for surroundings suitable for the satisfaction of his elementary needs, in search of more abundant food, more benign climates, or places where he can seek shelter from inclement weather and the brutality of his fellow men.

Nothing much has changed under the sun. In this age of mass communication, with satellite dishes throwing up images of a world of ostentatious wealth that appears to be within reach, masses of men, women and children are lured into embarking upon death-defying voyages across wildernesses and seas, in flight from deprivation, oppression and brutality in countries somewhat deceptively known as "developing". They dream of an impossible visa and risk their lives to reach forbidden shores or cross forbidden borders, and the very same satellite pictures almost daily show us shipwreckees rescued off the Spanish, Italian, or Maltese coasts, while other less fortunate boatpeople drown. It is one of the main paradoxes of today's migratory movements that luring images, goods and capital can travel freely, while people may not. Wealthy host countries are on the defensive, fearing that they will be "swamped" by "swarming" invaders whose disturbing otherness will erode community structures, and so they build up walls around themselves. Exclusion and marginalization, or blinkered assimilationism, are a breeding ground for violence and a backwards leap to myth, however, when hosts and migrants alike try their hardest to develop fixed identities, perennial essences, binding ethnocentrisms. We ought to have some notion that "immutable" and "eternal" traditions, supposedly exuding the essence of particular geographical areas since the dawn of time, are illusory transient constructs (the antithesis of timeless essences and fixed identities), that culture is the sum of the influences that we have received throughout History, and that movements and migrations, including of conquest, invariably result in the eventual sharing and mutual transmission of at least some degree of knowledge and skills.

The world is a heterogeneous, evolving place, and will continue to be so to an increasing degree. Circumscribed identities and nationalisms which only look backwards and cultivate their exclusiveness, are turning their backs on the unstoppable movement of peoples, languages, customs and artistic expressions. Yet another paradox is that many of the very states with an assimilationist drive that fear the crystallization of "particularisms" on their soil, also fear the global dilution of their own culture into the dominant American model, which has led some governments to invoke their "cultural exception" to preserve the diversity of both languages and high culture. The cultures of the future will put forth shoots in the culture of the host countries—where migrants will have integrated with a greater or lesser degree of success—and in the cultures migrants have brought with them. Our modern Western cities are thus regularly transformed by the constant emergence of peoples, languages, costumes, customs, culinary practices, in a continuous process of deconstruction and reconstruction. There better than anywhere else, perhaps, because of the accelerated pace, can we apprehend that inescapable pattern.

The likelihood of an unprecedented development of mass tourism in future years may add to the confusion. Tourism already affects over seven hundred million people worldwide, and with the access of the new middle classes of such highly populated countries as China and India, the flows of tourists will increase dramatically and greatly alter the nature of contacts between different cultures. On the other hand, as in other sectors of the globalized economy, there will be an increasingly merciless competition between tourist destinations. Defensive approaches may not be enough when GDP and growth are involved. The expected considerable growth of international mass tourism will not only have to be dealt with in terms of supply and demand, it will also require ever more refined analyses of tourists' motivations and behaviour with, in particular, the establishment of a scrupulous phenomenology of tourists and their relation to the world.

In the past, tourism as the art of accomplishing a *Grand Tour* was reserved for a small class of wealthy educated people with time for leisure. For the rest of society, there was only work, barely compensated for by the Sabbath as a day of rest and prayer. Travelling was something for intrepid adventurers or for unsocial freaks cut adrift from their community. The advent of paid holidays and of the leisure society has meant that people no longer merely aspire to rest physically, but also to "disconnect their brains" from everyday tensions and stress, and to get back to "real living"—i.e. the opposite of the daily drudgery of waged toil. Today's tourists are in search of a pleasant, easy world, free from the anxieties and responsibilities of their daily environment. They like discovering new surroundings and atmospheres, but will only appreciate exoticism within the limits of their own safety and comfort. They want to be no victim of pickpockets, terrorists, tsunamis or natural catastrophes. Nor do they want to be upset, disturbed, pushed around or merely surprised—unless it be pleasantly so.

Discovering new places may not seem complicated: all one has to do is get there. Yet things are not quite so simple when "there" has become in itself a commercial product that has to be marketed to meet the tourist's often contradictory expectations—sophisticated or simplistic, unconscious or poorly formulated. The conception and marketing of the product is all the more delicate as, unlike the toothpaste trade, the tourist trade involves the interaction—encounter and confrontation—of identities, with a whole train of emotional, intellectual, as well as economic, interchanges and dealings. As the definition of "identities" is a question of both self- and external perceptions, commercial transactions between identities generally ultimately mean trading fictions. Those do not necessarily lack authenticity, but their authenticity is often reinvented and staged as a show. The museum city of Vienna, with its centre almost exclusively dedicated to tourists, stages the Vienna of the Habsburg Empire and the artistic dynamics of the end of the nineteenth century. A boredom-stricken, grog-ravaged Aboriginal community in remote Outback Australia may rediscover the production of traditional artefacts when a compound for tourists desperately in want of ethnological genuineness opens in the area. This may work provided the community itself decides what image it wants to sell, but it may be viewed as adulterated culture in the sense that it is produced to match what the customer expects. It is, however, part of the tourist industry's business to mass-package deep-frosted culture ready to be warmed up and served to tourists who have travelled distances to find something "typical": jazz in New Orleans, art in Venice or *châteaux* in the Loire valley. New identities may be invented and old or forgotten ones may be recycled on an industrial scale: a good number of supposedly genuine Paris *bistrots* get their "home-made" food from specialized industrial firms. Some destinations, such as those with a UNESCO "World Heritage" label, have become real trade-marks. Of course, such artificialization and standardization of cultural exchanges may be regretted, but then since the 1930s, the production of cultural goods has been industrial, and there is no reason why tourism should escape that logic.

Another way of looking at things consists in recognizing what a powerful factor of cultural and identity production tourism has been and will continue to be. It may be fake in the eyes of those lucky enough to belong to a miraculously unadulterated culture, but the contaminating effects of the democratization and globalization of tourism can hardly be avoided. Nevertheless, it is not just a matter of adapting supply to demand. If tourism involves the interaction of identities, the customer—i.e. the guest, and not just the host—must have a minimum understanding of the product. Currently in Asia, the inhabitants of the tourist destinations visited by the new tourists from China complain about the latter's rudeness, arrogance and meanness: just because they are privileged enough to be able to get out of their own country, they think they can behave as if they were on conquered territory and treat the residents with condescension, while not even having the excuse of spending any significant amount of money locally. This will probably induce a double-tiered adjustment. The supply will quickly shape itself to the requirements of this particular type of Chinese custom, but if they want to be welcome, the new Chinese tourists will have to be educated—or at least properly briefed—by their tour operators.

The superior culture of the *happy few* who made the trip to Italy with letters of introduction to the aristocratic families of the region was undoubtedly more lofty than the deep-frosted, ready-to-consume culture of touristy Venice. Yet is it not the nostalgia of those grand old days that has been turned into a consumer product to attract tourists in their hundreds of thousands to Saint Mark's Square? This illustrates the luring trick at the heart of the tourist rationale: it consists in justifying our own motivations by reconstructing a mythical past that probably never existed. Authentic though the Eiffel Tower and the Paris of Haussmann may appear to today's tourists, they were creations of nineteenth century industrial France that the Parisians of the time thought objectionable: *they* would have preferred to preserve the Paris of Balzac and Rétif de la Bretonne they were familiar with.

There is in fact no real difference between this and the reinterpretations that found the allegedly immutable and eternal identities certain groups and individuals would like us to believe in. Tourist and political marketing strategies and techniques are very much akin. The tourist industry trades identities for obvious commercial reasons; politicians trade identities with the purpose of avoiding ethnic strife—or for less noble motives.

In the meanwhile, storks continue to travel and discover the world. I was never told the complete story and never knew whether the storks were meant to get back home or become human beings again. Perhaps the spell is best kept unbroken.

Martine Piquet, Director of CICLaS
(Research Centre on Cultural Identities, Paris-Dauphine University)
http://www.dauphine.fr/index.php?id=1048

NOTES ON CONTRIBUTORS

Sylvie Aprile teaches at the University of Tours. She specializes in the political and social history of nineteenth-century France and Europe, and is currently working on political exile, expatriation and migration.
saprile@noos.fr

Christian Auer lectures at Strasbourg Marc Bloch University. His research interests include the Scottish press and the economic, political and social evolution of Highlands society in the nineteenth century. He is working on a postcolonial reading of the Highland clearances, and on issues of gender and national identity.
christian.auer@libertysurf.fr

Constance Bantman is at present working at Imperial College London and Paris XIII University. She is interested in Franco-British relations in the nineteenth and twentieth centuries, and recently completed a PhD on the connections between the French and the British anarchist movements between 1880 and 1914.
cbantman@imperial.ac.uk

Catherine Berger teaches at Paris XIII University and is doing research on maritime worker-priests for the Seafarers International Research Centre of Cardiff University. Her main research interests are maritime missions, Filipino seafarers, multinational crews and multicultural working places, as well as the construction and propagation of representations and stereotypes of foreigners.
cpberger@club-internet.fr

Rachida Saïgh Bousta is professor at Cadi Ayyad University in Marrakesh. Founder of the "École Doctorale Internationale du Tourisme" and Director of the "Bureau d'étude Marrakech action", she has published and done consultancy work on tourism and national heritage, including collaboration with UNESCO.
saigh@iam.net.ma

Michel Bruillon teaches at Nanterre Univeristy and is a former director of the "Institut Universitaire Professionnalisé Métiers des Arts et de la Culture". He teaches British civilization and his research interests include British migration to Europe and the role of libraries in Great Britain.
michel.bruillon@wanadoo.fr

Angèle David-Guillou is a postgraduate student at Paris XIII University. She is writing a doctoral thesis on the beginnings of musicians' unions in France and England, and the changing status of professional musicians from 1870 to 1920.
angeledg@yahoo.fr

Anna Dluzewska is Head of the Tourism Department at the SWPR Alliance for Higher Education in Warsaw. She is working on the influence of religion on tourism dysfunctions, with particular reference to Muslim countries. She has been deputy editor of the business travel magazine *Biznes i Turystyka* since 2001.
a.dluzewska@chello.pl

Charles Forsdick is James Barrow Professor of French at the University of Liverpool. He is author of *Victor Segalen and the Aesthetics of Diversity* (OUP, 2000) and *Travel in Twentieth-Century French and Francophone Cultures* (OUP, 2005), and co-edited *Francophone Postcolonial Studies: A Critical Introduction* (Arnold, 2003). He is currently completing monographs on the representation of Toussaint Louverture and on the Swiss travel writer Ella Maillart, and is co-editing a volume on *Postcolonial Thought in the Francophone World.*
C.Forsdick@liverpool.ac.uk

Christine Geoffroy lectures in English Studies at Paris Dauphine University. In 1999 she won the *Le Monde* Prize for University Research in intercultural communication, which preceded her book *La mésentente cordiale, Voyage au cœur de l'espace interculturel franco-anglais* (Grasset, Paris, 2001). In 2004 she published *Les coulisses de l'Entente cordiale* (Grasset), and has written several articles and chapters on French-British interaction in business and home environments.
cpgeoffroy@wanadoo.fr

Patricia Marcoz is a postgraduate student in French literature at the Sorbonne (Paris IV), where she is preparing a thesis on the French writer Jacques d'Adelswärd-Fersen (1880-1923).
patricia.marcoz@hotmail.fr

Karen O'Reilly is Reader in Sociology at Loughborough University, where she teaches social theory, research methods and the sociology of tourism. Her research is in the fields of migration, tourism and social class, especially contemporary forms of mobility and their implications for sociological issues. Her books include *The British on the Costa del Sol* (Routledge, 2000) and *Ethnographic Methods* (Routledge, 2005).
K.OReilly@lboro.ac.uk

Catherine Puzzo teaches at Toulouse le Mirail University and has published comparative studies of immigration policies and discourse on immigration in France and Britain. She has done research on British immigrants to south-west France and on the reactions of the local media, with a recent article on naturalization ceremonies in the two countries.
c_puzzofr@yahoo.fr

Simona Sangiorgi is a PhD student in Cultural Studies at the University of Bologna at Forlì. Her research activities are focused on theme parks as a possible key for reading postmodern western identities.
sangiorgi@sslmit.unibo.it

Richard Sibley teaches at Paris XIII University. Initially a specialist in French politics, since moving to France in 1975 he has worked on British politics, the history and sociology of sport, and orientalist paintings. He was joint editor of *Le Sport en Grande-Bretagne et aux États-Unis* (Nancy, 1988), and has co-edited several special issues of journals on British sport and British politics. He is currently preparing a book on the Maghreb in orientalist paintings.
richard.sibley@wanadoo.fr

David Smallwood teaches English to economists and finance and management students at Bordeaux Montesquieu University. He assisted in the collection of data for a research project on the migration trajectories of the British community in the South-West of France, and has since researched questions of language and integration among British emigrants to France.
davesm@free.fr

Adèle Thomas is a postgraduate student at Paris XIII University and is currently teaching English at Rennes University. She works on the exchanges, influences, rivalries and mutual perceptions generated by the spread of the French language inside and outside the French colony in England, 1870-1914.
afdthomas@hotmail.com

Joanne Vajda is an architect with a doctorate in history. She is associate professor at the Ecole Nationale Supérieure d'Architecture de Paris La Villette, where she teaches the theory and practice of urban architecture. She is currently working on the representation of urban space in nineteenth and twentieth century European travel guide-books.
joanne.vajda@wanadoo.fr

INDEX

N

O

P

Q

R